a history of
CRICKET

a history of
Cricket

Gordon Ross

Arthur Barker Limited
5 Winsley Street London W1

Copyright © Gordon Ross 1972

All rights reserved. No part of this publication may be reproduced, stored in a retrieval system, or transmitted, in any form or by any means, electronic, mechanical, photocopying, recording or otherwise, without the prior permission of the copyright owner.

ISBN 0 213 99455 0

Printed in Great Britain by
Willmer Brothers Limited, Birkenhead

Contents

1	The Origins	1
2	The County Championship	25
3	Test Cricket	72
4	Grace and Bradman	123
5	Body-Line	134
6	One-Day Cricket and Sponsorship	142
7	The South African Explosion	162
	Appendix	179
	Index	188

Illustrations

between pages 16 and 17
Early heroes; Beldham, Mynn, Lillywhite and Wisden (*MCC*)
First English team in Australia (*MCC*)
D. G. Bradman and W. G. Grace (*Central Press and Reuter*)
1932–3 England team (*MCC*)
1953 England team (*Central Press*)

between pages 64 and 65
Yorkshire County team in 1938
Surrey team in 1955 (*Central Press*)
Hobbs and Sutcliffe (*Central Press*)
Edrich and Compton (*Central Press*)
1934 Australian team touring England (*Sport and General*)
The first season after World War II against India (*Sport and General*)
1949 New Zealand team in England (*Central Press*)
The memorable West Indies side of 1950 (*Sport and General*)

between pages 112 and 113
The first Pakistan team to visit Britain (*Central Press*)
1965 the last South African team that played in Britain (*Sport and General*)
Great Batsmen of their day; Woolley, Boycott, Cowdrey and May (*Reuter, Sport and General, and Central Press*)
Great fast bowlers in action; Larwood, Lindwall, Statham and Hall (*Central Press*)
Great all-rounders; Rhodes, Hammond, Miller and Sobers (*Sport and General, Central Press*)

between pages 136 and 137

Some of the great names; K. S. Ranjitsinhji, Len Hutton, Freddie Trueman and Jim Laker (*MCC and Central Press*)

The Gillette Cup; Sussex in 1963, and Lancashire in 1970 and 1971 (*Sport and General, Central Press*)

between pages 152 and 153

Lord's—the home of cricket—at peace and at war (*Sport and General, Press Association*)

Two great umpires; Frank Chester and Syd Buller (*Sport and General, Bill Smith*)

1 The Origins

The origin of the game of cricket is swirling about in the mists of antiquity, and will ever remain so. There is no precise line of demarcation as there was, for instance, with the game of rugby football, when, in 1823, a certain William Webb Ellis picked up the ball and ran with it during a game of association football at Rugby School. A tablet set in the wall of Rugby Close bears this inscription: 'This stone commemorates the exploit of William Webb Ellis, who, with a fine disregard for the rules of football played in his time, first took the ball in his arms and ran with it, thus originating the distinctive feature of the Rugby game. AD 1823.'

The inception of cricket is far more complicated and obscure, none more than the name itself. Some believe that it is the diminutive of the Anglo-Saxon *cricce*, a staff or crutch. The Bodleian library contains a picture of a monk bowling a ball to another monk, who is about to strike it with a *cricce*. In the field are other monks. There are no wickets, but the batsman stands before a hole, and the art of the game was either to get the ball into the hole, or to catch it. The monks depicted in this picture are thought to have lived in the fourteenth century, and the game was almost certainly called Club-ball or Cricce or Creag. There is also a theory that it might have been identical with a sport of roughly the same period called 'Handyn and Handoute'.

J. J. Jusserand, in his *Les Sports et Jeux d'Exercise dans l'Ancienne France*, quotes a document, dated 1478, in which occurs the sentence '*Le suppliant arriva en un lieu ou on jouait à la boule, près d'une attache ou criquet.*' According to M. Jusserand, the word criquet '*designait un baton planté en terre, qui servait de but dans une des formes du jeu.*' The game alluded to may, therefore, have been club-ball.

Earliest references

One of the earliest references to 'crickett' in this country is to be found in Russell's *History of Guildford*, a document relating to a dispute in 1598 in respect of a plot of land at Guildford. Here is an extract from it:

Anno 40 Eliz., 1598. John Derrick, gent, one of the Queen's Majestie's coroners of the county of Surrey, aged fifty-nine, saith this land before mentioned lett to John Parvish, inn holder, deceased, that he knew it for fifty years or more. It lay waste, and was used and occupied by the inhabitants of Guildford to saw timber in, and for sawpits, and for makinge of frames of timber for the said inhabitants. When he was a scholler in the Free School of Guildford, he and several of his fellows did run and play there at crickett and other plaies. And also that the same was used for the bating of bears in the said towne until the said John Parvish did inclose the said parcell of land.

The very fact that crickett is mentioned specifically and is not included with 'other plaies' suggests that it was sufficiently well known to be taken for granted.

A reference at about the same time appears in Giovanni Florio's dictionary, published in Italy in 1595. The word *sgrillaire* is defined as 'to make a noise as a cricket; to play cricket-a-wicket and be merry'. Oliver Cromwell was described by Sir William Dugdale as having in his young days thrown himself 'into a dissolute and disorderly course', as becoming famous for football, cricket, cudgelling, and wrestling. This would, in all probability, have been about the year 1613.

In 1662 John Davies of Kidwelly, issued his translation of Adam Olearius's work entitled *The Voyages and Travels of the Ambassadors from the Duke of Holstein to the Grand Duke of Muscovy, and the King of Persia*. Olearius began his book in the year 1633, and finished it in 1639. On page 297 is a description of the exercises indulged in by the Persian grandees in 1637, and the statement is made that 'They play there also at a certain game, which the Persians call Kruitskaukan, which is a kind of Mall or Cricket.'

A belief has been handed down through the years that the

Hambledon Club was one of the first cricket clubs, and thus was the cradle of the game in this country. Whilst Hambledon may have been the first club of such considerable strength that it could take on the All-England side, there is a reference to the St Albans Club practically a hundred years before the formation of Hambledon. An account of a great ball given to the ladies of Hertfordshire by the St Albans Club in August 1824, stated that 'At the upper end of the room was a transparency, representing the insignia of the club, first established in the year 1666.'

Whereas, in later years, the game of cricket belonged principally to the aristocracy, a catalogue of games published in 1720, having given a long list of rather more refined sports such as Riding out on Horseback, or Hunting with my Lord Maiors Pack, concludes: 'The more common sort divert themselves at football, wrestling, cudgels, ninepins, shovel-board, cricket, stowball, ringing of bells, quoits, pitching the bar, bull- and bearbating, throwing at cocks, and lying at alehouses.'

Further proof that cricket was very much in existence by the middle of the seventeenth century is provided by Henry Teonge, who wrote that in 1676 a party of sailors from HMS *Assistance, Royal Oak* and *Bristol* went ashore near Antioch and on 6 May played a game of cricket near Aleppo. The mere fact that this game took place at all confirms that it was a game already widely known. No reference is made as to whether or not the officers took part, or whether, even in the Royal Navy, cricket was very much the pursuit of the lower deck.

A somewhat gruesome aspect of cricket is shown as early as 1622, when certain parishioners of Boxgrove, on the edge of the Goodwood estate, were arraigned for playing in the churchyard on a Sunday in May and, moreover, playing in such a violent manner that 'they used to breake the church windows with the ball; and that a little childe had like to have her braynes beaten out with a cricket batte.' The activities of cricketers were, happily, not always as disreputable as this, although, however, violence is seen to have erupted on a number of occasions in the early years (and since!).

What is interesting is how cricket was lifted from being the game of the lower classes and was bracketed with 'lying at alehouses' as a sport, to become a game for the rich and leisured classes. It has been suggested that the period of the Commonwealth under Oliver Cromwell saw a real development in cricket. In those years the nobility of the period withdrew to their country estates and no doubt watched cricket being played on the village greens. When they returned to London after the Restoration what could be more natural than that they should take cricket with them?

Another development to be studied, is the move from single to double wicket, and it may surprise the connoisseur to know that a genuine double-wicket game was played in Scotland about 1700, under the name of 'Cat and Dog'. The following account is given of it:

> Three play at this game, who are provided with clubs. They cut out two holes, each about a foot in diameter, and seven inches in depth. The distance between them is about twenty-six feet. One stands at each hole with a club. These clubs are called dogs. A piece of wood of about four inches long, and one inch in diameter, called a cat, is thrown from one hole towards the other, by a third person. The object is, to prevent the cat from getting into the hole. Every time that it enters the hole, he who has the club at that hole, loses the club and he who threw the cat gets possession both of the club and of the hole, while the former possessor is obliged to take charge of the cat. If the cat be struck, he who strikes it changes place with the person who holds the other club; and as often as these positions are changed, one is counted as one in the game, by the two who hold the clubs, and who are viewed as partners.

Basically, of course, this seems to be merely a double-wicket version of the Club Ball played by the fourteenth-century monks, but it certainly contains enough to identify it with cricket; the principle of the batsman giving up the bat when he is out and the bowler taking his place, and the batsmen running to opposite ends when a run is scored, was clearly a forerunner. Admittedly, the idea of a hole in the ground instead of a wicket may seem incongruous to the contemporary cricketer, but it was not until a single stump was placed at each hole merely to point out the place to bowler and fieldsmen, that the general idea of a wicket was conceived. In 1700, two stumps were used, twenty-four inches apart and twelve inches high, with long bails atop. A middle stump was added by the Hambledon Club in 1775, and the height of the stumps was raised to twenty-two inches. A second bail was added in 1786. In 1814 stumps were made twenty-six inches high and seven inches wide and in 1823 were increased again in height to twenty-seven inches. There was no further change until 1931 when the stumps became twenty-eight inches high and nine inches wide (after experiments in 1929 and 1930).

Cricket made considerable progress during the first half of the eighteenth century largely, one is obliged to add, because of the great attraction it had for the gamblers; large sums of money were staked on cricket matches, and as it is very difficult to find any hard and fast laws of the game, it must be assumed that the laws were laid down for each match by those financially interested. In fact the first so-called inter-county match, between Kent and London in 1719, gave rise to a lawsuit. That match was played at Lamb's Conduit Fields in May, and a few days later the Kent players brought a suit against the London players at Guildhall for the sum of one hundred pounds. The judge (a wise man, but then aren't they all!) knew nothing whatsoever about cricket so simply ordered that the game should be played again – a shrewd judgement, indeed!

The earliest known laws of cricket were framed in 1774, but although there must have been something in existence before this date, they have never come to light. It is generally accepted that articles of agreement had previously been drawn up for some matches; an original document dated 11 July 1727 was proof enough of this. The articles covered two matches played between teams raised by the then Duke of Richmond and a Mr Broderick, but they were designed mainly for the purpose of deciding bets and supplementing laws generally accepted for common use, so it seemed that before 1774 – 'You paid your money and took your choice'; what rules there were (if any) could be bent to suit the occasion (or the purse!).

The 'New Laws'

So it was then a momentous step when a Committee of Noblemen and Gentlemen of Kent met at the Star and Garter, Pall Mall, on 25 February 1774 and produced *'New Articles of the Game of Cricket'*. Those attending this historic meeting were Sir William Draper (in the chair), His Grace the Duke of Dorset, the Right Hon. E. Tankerville, Sir Horace Mann, Sir John Brewer Davis, Philip Dehany, Harry Peckham, Francis Vincent, James Cooke, Charles Coles, Richard James and the Rev. Charles Pawlett. The result of their profound deliberations was to produce new laws of the game of cricket, as follows:

The Ball
must not weigh less than five ounces and a half, nor more than five ounces and three-quarters. It cannot be changed during the game, but with consent of both parties.

The Bat
must not exceed four inches and one quarter in the widest part.

The Stumps
must be twenty-two inches, the bail six inches long; but by a subsequent meeting it is settled for to use three stumps instead of two to each wicket, and the bails not to exceed six inches.

The Bowling-Crease
must be parallel with the stumps, three feet in length, with a return crease.

The Popping-Crease
must be three feet ten inches from the wickets; and the wickets must be opposite to each other, at the distance of twenty-two yards.

The Party Which Goes from Home
shall have the choice of the innings, and the pitching of the wickets, which shall be pitched within thirty yards of a centre fixed by the adversaries.

The Bowler
must deliver the ball with one foot behind the bowling-crease, and within the return crease; and shall bowl four balls before he changes wickets, which he shall do but once in the same innings.

The Striker is Out

if either of the bails is bowled off, or the stump bowled out of the ground. Or if the ball, from a stroke over or under his bat, or upon his hands (but not wrists) is held before it touches the ground, though it can be hugged to the body of the catcher. Or if in striking, both his feet are over the popping-crease, and his wicket is put down, except his bat is grounded within it. Or if he runs out of his ground to hinder a catch. Or if a ball is struck up, and he wilfully strikes it again. Or if the striker touches or takes up the ball before it has lain still, unless at the request of the opposite party. Or if in running a notch, the wicket is struck down by a throw, or with the ball in hand, before his foot, hand or bat is grounded over the popping crease; but if the bail is off, a stump must be struck out of the ground by the ball. Or if the striker puts his leg before the wicket with a design to stop the ball, and actually prevents the ball from hitting his wicket by it.

If the players have crossed each other, he that runs for the wicket that is put down is out; if they have not crossed, he that has left the wicket that is put down, is out.

When the ball has been in the bowler's or wicket-keeper's hands, the strikers need not keep within their ground till the umpire has called 'Play', but if the player goes out of his ground, with an intent to run before the ball is delivered, the bowler may put him out.

If he strikes, or treads down, or falls himself upon his wicket in striking (but not in over-running), it's out. Or, if under pretence of running a notch, or otherwise, either of the strikers prevent a ball from being caught, the striker of the ball is out.

If the ball is struck up, the striker may guard his wicket, either with his bat or his body.

The Wicket-keeper

shall stand at a reasonable distance behind the wicket, and shall not move until the ball is out of the bowler's hands, and shall not, by any noise incommode the striker; and if his hands, knees, foot or head, be over or before the wicket, though the ball hit it, it shall not be out.

The Umpires

shall allow two minutes for each man to come in, and fifteen minutes between each innings; when the umpire shall call 'Play', the party refusing to play shall lose the match.

They are the sole judges of fair and unfair play, and all disputes shall be determined by them.

When a striker is hurt, they are to allow another to come in, and the person hurt shall have his hands in any part of that innings.

They are not to order a player out, unless appealed to by the adversaries. But if the bowler's foot is not behind the bowling crease, and within the return crease, when he delivers the ball, the umpire, unasked, must call, 'No ball'. If the strikers run a short notch, the umpire must call 'No notch'.

BETS

If the notches of one player are laid against another, the bet depends on both innings, unless otherwise specified. If one party beats the other in one innings, the notches in the first innings shall determine the bet. But if the party goes in a second time, then the bet must be determined by the number on the score.

SINGLE WICKET

If the striker moves out of his ground to strike at the ball, he shall be allowed no notch for such stroke, unless he returns to his ground after he has struck the ball.

In retrospect, it is quite remarkable to consider how thorough these gentlemen were at the Star and Garter, Pall Mall, on that February night in 1774. An examination of the laws as they framed them show them to represent virtually the whole fabric of the game nearly two hundred years later. Laws have been tampered with by cricket's administrators year in, year out, for better or for worse, but the basic principles have stood the test of time, and change.

So cricket had at last achieved a status. It was now something which was not purely the prerogative of the ale-house fraternity. The aristocracy and gambling had been the two cardinal factors in its elevation, but the development must be attributed largely to Frederick Louis, Prince of Wales, who was passionately fond of the game and played it for the first time in Kensington Gardens on 8 September 1735. The prince did a tremendous amount to help Surrey (appropriately, Surrey's emblem is the Prince of Wales's feathers) and in many cases the Surrey elevens were selected by him. When Kent played Surrey and London on

Kennington Common on 14 June 1737 a pavilion was erected for his Royal Highness. 'The press was so great that a poor woman, by the crowd bearing upon her, unfortunately had her leg broke, which, being related to His Royal Highness, he was pleased to order her Ten Guineas.' The Prince died suddenly in 1751 in the arms of Desnoyers the celebrated dancing-master, but the end was caused by an internal abcess that had been long forming in consequence of a blow which he received in the side from a cricket ball while playing in Buckinghamshire.

Bowling at that period was under-arm, and 'sneaks' were the accepted practice, for David Harris had still to develop the style of 'length' bowling introduced at Hambledon by Richard Nyren and Tom Walker. Nor had John Small yet 'found out batting' – the doctrine of the straight bat was still unknown – and the bat, curved like a hockey stick, was designed less to defend a wicket (of two stumps only) than to execute sweeping strokes at a ball, which, because of the extreme roughness of the pitch, followed an erratic course along the ground.

Two Surrey players were responsible for major changes in the structure of the game. The first, Edward Stevens, was universally known as 'Lumpy'. Some say this nickname was the result of his once eating a whole apple pie, but historians over the years have put up a number of suggestions for it, the most likely of which is that it arose because of some unorthodoxy in his action. 'Lumpy's' claim to fame is that during a single-wicket match between Five of Hambledon and Five of England on the Artillery Ground in May 1775 John Small Senior went in as last man to get fourteen runs to win and got them; during his triumphant advance towards the target, Lumpy bowled right through Small's wicket three times, and bemoaned the luck of a bowler (Alec Bedser was doing precisely this nearly two hundred years later, and instanced his sentiments by stating that the last bowler to get a Knighthood was Francis Drake!). But Lumpy's protests were deemed to be in a valid cause, and as a result a third stump was added. The other Surrey player to achieve immortality, was one Thomas ('Shock') White. He once appeared at Hambledon – the shrine of it all – and reached the wicket dragging with him a bat as wide as the stumps. One of the fielding side produced a knife and the bat was shaved to more reasonable dimensions. White watched angrily during the operation but being at Hambledon, he felt there was little or nothing he could do about it. In consequence, a law was passed limiting the width to four and a quarter inches.

Dress

The dress for the players at this time was in accordance with contemporary fashion except that cumbersome items, such as wigs, were removed; these were usually replaced by a jockey-cap; the top hat did not come into vogue until half a century later. The players wore full-sleeved shirts, knee-breeches of various hues, stockings and buckled shoes. The disadvantages of the buckle-shoe were stressed by William Beldham ('Silver' Billy, the noblest Roman of them all) who said: 'Just think of the old fashion, Sir, before cricket shoes, when I saw John Wells tear a finger-nail off against his shoe buckle in picking up a ball.'

Hambledon

The exact date of the formation of the Hambledon Club, like the origin of cricket itself, is wreathed in mystery, but it was probably in the 1770s that it reached its full stature as the leading club in the management and promotion of the game. It is just as much a mystery how Hambledon came to achieve this prominent position in the game's affairs, because at about this date the military had not closed the Artillery Ground; White Conduit and other London grounds were available, Kent cricket was in its prime, and innumerable clubs had sprung up in Surrey. Traditionally, the founder was the Rev. Charles ('Squire') Pawlett an old boy of Westminster School, and although it is thought that its formation came about in approximately 1750, it is confirmed by historical data that in 1756 Hambledon was strong enough to play the Dartford Club, and in the same year a match was played on Broad-halfpenny Down. By 1770 Hambledon was established as the leading cricket club in England, supported by the most eminent patrons, accepted as the chief arbiter of the laws, and able to call upon the services of the leading players in Hampshire and in the bordering counties of Surrey and Sussex. Rules were made at Hambledon to be kept; a minute of 1774 provides that members 'continuing a dispute after having been desired by the President to waive the subject of discussion' were to forfeit one dozen of claret! The gentlemen of the Hambledon Club were uniformly dressed in sky-blue coats with black velvet collars and the letters 'CC' (Cricketing Club) engraved on their buttons. Cricket was now surviving on its own merit. The poor, the gamblers, and the aristocracy no longer ensured its survival by their interest alone.

Hambledon participated in the first match known to have been played with three stumps when they met England on Sevenoaks Vine on 18, 19, 20 June 1777. Hambledon scored 403, the first recorded total of over 400 runs. James Alward scored 167, his innings lasting part of each of the three days. He went in at five o'clock on Wednesday afternoon, and was not out until three o'clock on Friday. Hambledon (with 'Lumpy') played Kent (with Bedster and Yalden) on Windmill Downs, Hambledon, in July 1783 and the match ended in a tie, Hambledon scoring 140 and 62, and Kent 111 and 91. It was discovered afterwards, however, that Kent had actually won the match because Pratt, the scorer, whose method – the usual one at the time – was to cut a notch on a stick for every run, and to count every tenth notch longer in order to count the whole more expeditiously, had, by mistake, marked in one place the eleventh notch instead of the tenth. The stick was duly produced; the other scorer's stick was not! The match was a tie!

The Birth of MCC

Hambledon flourished until 1787 when the formation of the Marylebone Cricket Club struck a death blow to the Hambledon Club, many of whose patrons were among the founders of MCC. The authority for controlling the game was shortly to pass from Hambledon to Lord's, for as early as May 1788, the laws were revised by the Club at St Marylebone, and by 1791 members of the Marylebone Club were called in to adjudicate upon an umpiring decision concerning a 'bump' ball in a match in which

Hambledon were playing; this was rather like rubbing salt into the wound. The minutes of the Hambledon Club continue until 1796, but it is believed that the disintegration began round about 1791 when Richard Nyren, its mentor and General Officer Commanding, left Hambledon. Its glory departed. Still, though the land was deserted, the men survived and imparted a knowledge of their craft to gentles and simples far and near.

The establishment of Marylebone Cricket Club was inexorably linked with the name of Thomas Lord – hence the name Lord's; it was for this reason alone and had no connection whatsoever with the peerage. Lord was born at Thirsk in Yorkshire on 23 November 1755 and his father, who was a substantial yeoman of Roman Catholic stock, had his lands sequestrated when he espoused the Stuart cause in the rising of 1745. As a result he subsequently had to work as a labourer on the very farm that was once his own property. The Lord family later moved to Diss in Norfolk, where Thomas Lord was brought up, and it was from here, on reaching manhood, that he migrated to London and found employment at the White Conduit Club as a bowler and general attendant. The White Conduit Club deserves a special place in any chronicle of cricketing affairs. Formed in 1782, it was an offshoot of a West End convivial club called the 'Je-ne-sais-quoi', some of whose members took to frequenting the White Conduit House and playing their matches in the adjoining fields near Islington. In 1786 the members were tiring of this site, and the Earl of Winchelsea – a great Hambledonian – and one, Charles Lennox, later the Fourth Duke of Richmond, offered to Lord their guarantee against loss, if he would start a new private ground. White Conduit played several matches at Marylebone in 1787, but it seems almost certain that at the end of the season the old club was merged into the newly-formed Marylebone Cricket Club.

With the assured guarantee of two such persons of distinction, Lord went swiftly into action and opened his first ground in May 1787 on what is now Dorset Square. The first great match there was played between Middlesex and Essex – a game played for two hundred guineas. It seemed likely that Lord had not been able to charge admission on the ground at Islington, but he erected a fence round his new ground and instituted an entrance fee of sixpence to the public. Lord's quickly became popular and all went well until 1810, when Lord's lease expired, and its value during the twenty-one years of his tenancy had so increased to be well beyond his pocket. But Lord was a man of considerable vision and he had taken steps to find alternative accommodation as early as October 1808, when he rented two fields – the Brick Field and the Great Field, at North Bank, on the St Johns Wood Estate – for a term of eighty years, free of land tax and tithe, at £54 a year. The new ground was ready in 1809, and for two seasons Lord had two grounds on his hands, the St Johns Wood Cricket Club using the new enclosure. The club was ultimately incorporated in MCC.

The new Lord's

The new Lord's became operative on 8 May 1811. The turf was removed from Dorset Square, but the move, for some reason or another, was not popular with many members of MCC, and the club did not play a single match there in either 1811 or 1812 – and only three in 1813, a year in which another move became necessary. Parliament had decreed that the Regents Canal should be cut through the centre of the ground. The Eyre family, on whose estate the second ground was situated, were willing to grant Lord another plot, which enabled MCC to make its headquarters on the site it has occupied ever since. Once again, Lord was involved in transferring the turf from one ground to another. Lord, incidentally, was now a gentleman of importance in the parish of St Marylebone. He had been made a member of the Marylebone Vestry in 1807 and also ran a wine and spirit business. Surprisingly, Lord himself almost put paid to the ground. As a cricket ground it prospered, but Lord was not satisfied with the financial side of affairs and actually obtained permission from the Eyre Estate to use the ground for a building site; plans were drawn up which would limit the playing area to 150 square yards. William Ward, a worthy patron of the game of cricket (he took the chair at the formation of the Surrey Club), came to the rescue. He was a director of the Bank of England and later MP for the

City of London; he bought Lord's interest for £5,000. Thomas Lord thus ceased his interest in the famous ground in 1825. William Ward was a cricketer of no little skill; he hit 278 for MCC against Norfolk in 1820, the highest score on the ground until Percy Holmes of Yorkshire hit 315 not out against Middlesex in 1925. Having broken a record which had stood for over a hundred years, Holmes held the new record for only one year – Jack Hobbs beat it by one run in 1926 for Surrey against Middlesex.

Round-arm bowling

Standing in the field for a very long time while William Ward scored his 278 was a young sixteen-year-old cricketer playing for Norfolk. His name was Fuller Pilch, now a legend in cricket's folklore. Pilch was born at Horningtoft in Norfolk on 17 March 1804. In the course of his career he made ten centuries (an unusually large number in those days), and any assessment made of him must take into account the fact that under-arm bowling was being replaced by round-arm bowling when Pilch was at the height of his career. Round-arm bowling had been a bone of contention for some time, and although it was a certain John Willes who played a leading role in its ultimate adoption in 1835, Tom Walker of Hambledon had been the first exponent way back in Hambledon days. However, when the Hambledon Club had expressed their distaste for it, Walker simply returned to trundling his slow lobs.

John Willes, on the other hand, was bred more from fighting stock and he was not prepared to dispense with his new form of attack, despite the surge of criticism, the abuse, and even threats of personal violence. Feelings grew so high that on one occasion on Peneden Heath the 'ring' was broken in, the stumps uprooted, and the game brought to a 'dead lock'. Willes was unperturbed; he believed in his idea which apparently came to him when his sister, Christine, bowled to him in the barn at Fonford, near Canterbury; because of her crinolines she was not able to bowl strictly under-arm. The fact that Tom Walker had tried this method of bowling some time before rather destroys this delightful little story, but it is still worth a line in any history of cricket.

In 1816 William Ward, Lord Frederick Beauclerk, and Ben Aislabie, persuaded the MCC to sit in judgement on round-arm bowling. Lord Frederick was the fourth son of the Fifth Duke of St Albans, and became one of the best batsmen of his day. In fact, he is probably the best cricketer of royal blood of all time; he was a descendant of Charles II by Nell Gwynne. In contrast to the cricketing feats performed by Ward and Beauclerk, Aislabie was ungenerously described as a big man who seldom scored a run, and never took a wicket – he just happened to be the Secretary of MCC! The result of all MCC's deliberations was a decree that all bowling must be under-hand, and that any ball delivered with the arm extended horizontally was illegal. Willes was still not to be put down. On 15 July 1822, he was in the Kent team which took the field at Lord's against the 'Marylebone' Club. This was a Lord's which stood in splendid isolation among the fields. It had a Tavern, built some seven years or so earlier, stables, two ponds, and a flock of sheep used, presumably, as a form of grass-cutter. The bookmakers were there in strength. It was six to four on the Marylebone Club. Willes bowled the second over of the day and was no-balled by the umpire, a said Noah Mann. Willes was livid; he grabbed the ball, slung it as far as he possibly could, stalked angrily across the ground, mounted his horse, and was last seen in a cloud of dust riding out of Lord's. In his blaze of anger Willes threatened never to play cricket again, but he did take part in several matches; he was then forty-four. This great character died of typhus, in dreadfully reduced circumstances, on 5 August 1852. He did at least live to see his type of bowling legalized. It became law in 1835.

Growth of county cricket

The 1830s saw the growth of county cricket from what had been more or less scratch matches to games on an organized footing. County clubs were formed, the earliest being Sussex in 1836 (re-formed in 1839 and 1857), Northamptonshire in 1843 (re-formed 1878) and Surrey in 1845. Kent, of course, had been a powerful county for many years, but the actual club was not formed until 1859. Hampshire, Middlesex and Yorkshire all played games during this period, but the county clubs were not formed until a later date. Kent, in those early days, were indeed a mighty foe. Five of their players were immortalized in W. J. Prowse's couplet:

> And with five such mighty cricketers 'twas but natural to win
> As Felix, Wenman, Hillyer, Pilch and Alfred Mynn.

Some early cricketers

By universal consent, Mynn was the greatest match-winning cricketer the game produced before W. G. Grace and was a man of indomitable courage as well as immense skill. In a North *v* South match at Leicester in August 1836 he scored 21 not out and 125 not out, but he was so greatly injured by Redgate's bowling that he was obliged to leave before the match was completed. He reached London safely, but could not proceed into Kent, where he resided. So serious and severe were his injuries that Mr Mynn was obliged to be packed up and laid on the roof of the stage-coach. When he arrived in Kent it was touch and go whether his leg, or indeed, his life, could be saved. Luckily, both were, though it was slow progress.

Another cricketer with Alfred Mynn's courage was William Lillywhite. Once, when playing for England against Kent at Canterbury in 1845, he was so disabled that he had to be carried to the wicket in order to bat. This incident recalled for the elder statesmen the courage of David Harris of Hambledon, who, in his last few years, suffered much from gout. 'A great armchair was therefore always brought into the field, and after the delivery of the ball the hero sat down in his own calm and simple grandeur and reposed. A fine tribute this to his superiority, even amid the tortures of disease.'

But William Lillywhite is not a cricketer to be remembered for his courage alone. He was a remarkable cricketer and a remarkable man. He did not play his first match at Lord's until he was thirty-five years old. No cricketer ever came to Lord's so late in life, commenced playing so old in great matches, and was still bowling splendidly when nearly sixty years of age. He played for

Early heroes

William Beldham

Alfred Mynn

William Lillywhite

John Wisden

First English team to visit Australia 1861–2

Back row: W. Mudie, H. H. Stephenson (Captain), A. Mallam (Manager), T. Hearne. *Middle row:* G. Bennett, W. Caffyn, G. Griffiths, R. Iddison, F. Stephenson. *Front row:* C. Lawrence, W. Mortlock, T. Sewell

Immeasurable influences

D. G. Bradman

W. G. Grace

England teams that won the ashes

1932-33. *Back row:* G. Duckworth, T. B. Mitchell, the Nawab of Pataudi, M. Leyland, H. Larwood, E. Paynter, W. Ferguson (Scorer). *Middle row:* P. F. Warner (Joint Manager), L. E. G. Ames, H. Verity, W. Voce, W. E. Bowes, F. R. Brown, M. W. Tate, R. C. N. Palairet (Joint Manager). *Seated:* H. Sutcliffe, R. E. S. Wyatt, D. R. Jardine (Captain), G. O. Allen, W. R. Hammond

1953. *Standing:* T. E. Bailey, P. B. H. May, T. W. Graveney, J. C. Laker, G. A. R. Lock, J. H. Wardle, F. S. Trueman. *Seated:* W. J. Edrich, A. V. Bedser, L. Hutton, D. C. S. Compton, T. G. Evans

a short time in his own benefit match at Lord's in 1853, when sixty-one, bowling, perhaps, at a later stage of life in a great county match than any other cricketer.

Lillywhite was like a piece of machinery, seldom out of order, and in his old age he wanted only a little oiling, earning for himself the title of 'The Nonpareil Bowler'. It is said that during the whole of his cricketing life he delivered no more than half-a-dozen wides. His delivery was round-arm, rather slow, and was something marvellous for the accuracy of the pitch, besides being, without any doubt, the straightest that has yet appeared with the round delivery. Lillywhite was born at West Hampnett, near Goodwood, in Sussex and was originally a bricklayer by trade. He died very suddenly of cholera and is buried in Highgate Cemetery where a monument erected by subscriptions from members of the Marylebone Club and others stands in his memory. As well as containing glowing tributes to the man himself – 'Few have ministered to more Happy Hours' – it refers to cricket as a sport in which the blessings of youthful strength and spirits may be most innocently enjoyed, to the exercise of the mind, the discipline of the temper, and the general improvement of the man. The monument testifies the respect of the Noblemen and Gentlemen of the Marylebone Cricket Club, and of many private friends, to one who did his duty in that state of life in which it has pleased God to call him. William Lillywhite, 'The Nonpareil Bowler'.

The summer of 1836 saw an important change in the method of scoring, the bowler being credited with every wicket which fell to his bowling whereas previously it had been customary to give only the fielder's name if a catch had been made, the bowler receiving no credit for the actual dismissal. It was in this same summer that William Clarke made his first appearance at Lord's, like Lillywhite, rather late in life – Clarke was then thirty-seven; more remarkable still, he did not appear at Lord's again until 1843 and did not appear for the Players until 1846, but he had started young in collecting his huge bag of wickets with his slow under-arm method. It was in 1846 that he was engaged on the staff at Lord's and started the All England XI which toured the country during the following two seasons.

This venture was not a success, many of the leading players declining to play in an XI organized by Clarke; there seems to have been some personal animosity, but, be that as it may, Clarke must have done reasonably well out of it financially; he began life as a bricklayer but later became a licensed victualler, and in 1838 opened the famous Trent Bridge ground.

In 1846 John Wisden made his first appearance at Lord's. Although he was in the front rank as a bowler for several years, his chief claim to fame lies in the name of *Wisden's Cricketers' Almanack*, the accepted bible of the game. Wisden opened a shop in 1855 in Leicester Square; nine years later, in 1864, the first volume of this now famous Annual was published. Another great player of this period was George Parr; he was the leading batsman of the 1840s and 1850s, took over command of the All England XI after the death of William Clarke, and was captain of the first touring team to go to North America, and the second team to go to Australia. His name lives on into immortality by the existence of George Parr's tree on the Trent Bridge ground at Nottingham, a branch of the tree being placed among the wreaths on his coffin. The early records between 1846 and 1851 show that only two centuries were scored during this period, and Parr got both of them. Bowlers, on the other hand, were making hay while the sun shone. Clarke (954 wickets), Hillyer (769) and Wisden (649) reaped the richest harvest of wickets. Wisden carved a permanent niche for himself in cricket history in 1850. Although a Sussex man, he was playing for the North (he was engaged at Leamington that season) against the South at Lord's, and took all ten wickets in the South's second innings, clean bowling all ten of them.

A unique piece of bowling – again with a bowler taking all ten wickets in an innings – occurred at Oxford in a game between the University and Oxfordshire in 1853. Mr A. Cazenove obtained all ten wickets in Oxfordshire's first innings; a fine performance but not unique in itself; what was unique as well as being a mathematical miracle was that he took five wickets in a four-ball over (the total balls per over until 1889). Just how he did it does not constitute one of those problems so common in cricket which needs profound thought in working out. This answer is simple – the umpire made a mistake! Cazenove's feat is thus unique in history.

For their match against Surrey at the Oval in 1851 Middlesex included in their side William Lillywhite and his two sons, James and John. John Lillywhite was a fine all-round cricketer, a powerful hitter, a splendid field, generally at cover-point. His round-arm bowling, at first of tremendous pace, was subsequently moderated to slow twisters. In 1850 he became coach to Rugby School where he remained for six years; in that same year, in partnership with his father and his brothers, at 10 Prince's Terrace, Caledonian Road, Islington, Lillywhite opened a factory for the making of cricketing articles. The partnership was dissolved in 1856, the year John Lillywhite finished at Rugby, and he then set up in business alone at 5 Seymour Street, Euston Square, 'one of the largest establishments in the kingdom for the sale of all articles for British sports'. In 1861 Lillywhite accepted a coaching position at Harrow, and business being business, also supplied the school with all their cricket apparatus! The name Lillywhite lives on.

The Surrey side, opposing the triumvirate of Lillywhites in 1851, included Julius Caesar (This was no *nom-de-plume* – he was christened such), who seems to have been the mid-nineteenth century character; he was a sturdy cricketer of the best type, and was a past-master of quips and gibes, boisterous and personal at times, but mostly good tempered withal, and taken in good part. Soon to join him in the Surrey side was William Caffyn, one of the best batsmen the period ever produced. He played some huge innings, several over a hundred, and also topped 150 more than once (quite a feat in those days). His style of play was described as being very elegant; his bowling (good in all weathers) was of middle speed with a pretty easy delivery; as a field he was first rate anywhere. Taking him altogether, he was one of the most accomplished cricketers ever seen. Caffyn went out with the second team to Australia in 1863 and stayed behind as coach – one of the leading factors in the advancement of Australian cricket. Caffyn's life, like many of his innings, produced a goodly score; he lived to the ripe old age of ninety-one.

It is difficult over the years to be able to get a clear picture of scoring rates. Just how fast did these players of those early days accumulate their runs? One thing is certain; it was not always at a fast pace; distance does lend enchantment sometimes! E. Willsher, playing against England for Kent and Surrey at Canterbury in 1855, batted four hours for 20; during the last three-quarters of an hour of this innings he failed to score at all. Since the side had gained a first innings lead and he went in first wicket down in their second innings, the reason for this pedestrian performance is hard to discover. Was it that Wisden's bowling was 'something wonderful'?

Overseas pioneers

Eighteen hundred and fifty-nine was a year of truly great moment for cricket. W. P. Pickering of Montreal and E. Wilder of Sussex could not have foreseen how sizeable a foundation stone they were laying when during the summer of 1859 they made arrangements for the first-ever overseas cricket tour. A strong team was collected together under the captaincy of George Parr and sailed from Liverpool for Quebec on 7 September. The team arrived on 22 September and started their programme two days later, defeating XXII of Lower Canada at Montreal by eight wickets. This success was followed by victories over XXII of United States in New York, XXII of Philadelphia, XXII of Hamilton, and XXII of United States and Canada at Rochester. Financially, the trip was a success, the players clearing £90 each, free of all expenses, not to mention the gifts that were bestowed upon them. News of this excursion was not long in reaching Australia. A Melbourne firm, Spiers and Pond, sent a representative to England in the summer of 1861, and Mr Mallam approached H. H. Stephenson of Surrey with a request that he would collect a team and go to Australia with an idea of pioneering cricket of international standard in that country. The terms arranged for the cricketers was £150 each and full expenses; in retrospect, this was handsome reward. £150 in 1861 would have bought a house of quite high quality.

Today, a cricketer would need £10,000 for such a purchase.

It seemed that some of our top cricketers lacked the adventurous spirit and declined to make the long journey, but twelve players did go and shaped cricket's destiny. Their names were: H. H. Stephenson (Captain), G. Bennett, W. Caffyn, G. Griffiths, T. Hearne, R. Iddison, W. Mortlock, W. Mudie, C. Lawrence, T. Sewell, F. Stephenson and G. Wells. Six of the twelve matches played were won, but two were lost – by thirteen wickets against XXII of New South Wales and Victoria at Sydney, and by three wickets against XXII of Castlemaine. The tour opened with a match against XVIII of Victoria at Melbourne on New Year's Day 1862. The crowd is said to have numbered 25,000; the admission charge was half-a-crown, a figure barely exceeded a hundred years later. This raises the question: 'Has county cricket been served up too cheaply in England for generations?' The answer is probably that it has. Spiers and Pond, apparently, made a very handsome profit – and they deserved to for taking the gamble, but why did other companies not follow suit. Why was it a hundred years before another marriage took place between cricket and a commercial company? If cricket had charged more at the gate, and sought sponsorship sooner, would it have eradicated many of the contemporary problems? The question certainly provides food for thought.

In this jet-age, one sympathizes with those early pioneers who travelled to their second match in Australia, a distance of over two hundred miles, in a coach drawn by six greys. All this to play a collection of gentlemen curiously titled 'The Ovens'; who, one might say, were not so hot! They were bowled out for 20 and 53, and when, at the end of the scheduled contest, Griffiths played a single-wicket match against eleven of them, all eleven suffered the extreme indignity of failing to score. To cap it all, when having to bowl Griffiths out for nought in order to tie the match, they sent down two wides! Australian cricket has come a long way since then!

But the all-important seed was sown for English and Australian rivalry. The players brought home such glowing reports of their treatment that no difficulties were found in raising the next side to go in 1863–4.

A change in the laws

At home, in the summer of 1862, an event occurred at the Oval which not only produced a first-class row, but also caused an alteration to be made in the laws of the game. Edgar Willsher (previously mentioned for his slow scoring at Canterbury) was playing for England against Surrey, and the umpire, John Lillywhite (also previously mentioned) no-balled him six times in succession because his hand was above his shoulder. Willsher and his fellow England professionals thought so little of this treatment that they marched off the field *en bloc* and only the two amateurs, Walker and Lyttleton, remained in their places on the field. They were obliged ultimately to return to the pavilion since no more play took place that night, and great speculation began as to what should be done on the morrow. Lillywhite firmly stood his ground and he was right. Willsher's normal delivery did contravene the law, as it stood, of the hand being below the shoulder, but the same was true of many other players, and there seems to have been general agreement among umpires that they would turn a blind eye to it. (Did this not happen a hundred years later in the 'throwing' controversy?) But not so John Lillywhite; there was no personal vendetta between himself and Willsher; they had been good friends – though not immediately after the incident. Ultimately, however, they were reconciled.

Lillywhite, a man of strong principles, just believed that it was his duty to interpret the law precisely as it was laid down – and this he did. For the peace and quiet of this particular match, however, it was decided to replace him on the last day, and the game proceeded, without further incident, to its close. It took the MCC a further two years to re-frame the law which legalized over-arm bowling; Lillywhite was clearly the architect of the change. Although over-arm bowling was not accepted at the 1863 annual general meeting of the MCC, the rising tide of pressure for its adoption was now overwhelming, and it was finally approved on 10 June 1864. Statisticians (and others) generally accept this date as being the 'coming-of-age' of cricket. Was it by mere coincidence that the first issue of *Wisden* was published that summer, and that it also marked the first appearance in important cricket of a young batsman named W. G. Grace? Moreover, in the two years between 1863 and 1865 seven of the now generally accepted first-class counties started their official existence – Essex, Hampshire, Lancashire, Middlesex, Warwickshire, Worcestershire and Yorkshire.

Doubtful decisions

The summer of 1865 produced another major row. This time it was not a personal matter but at county level and, once again, the scene of friction was the Oval. Surrey were playing Nottinghamshire, and in their second innings, when the ninth wicket fell, they needed fourteen runs to win. The last man in, T. Sewell Junior, gallantly obtained them all himself, but a run-out decision given in Sewell's favour so nettled the men of Notts. that this fixture did not take place again for three years. W. Oscroft of Notts. is on record as having said that Sewell was out of his ground by a yard and a half. Was it again a strange quirk of coincidence, or was Heaven taking a hand, when the fixture was finally resumed and W. Oscroft was dismissed first ball in each innings? He was no doubt considerably nettled, once again!

But has there ever been such a strange dismissal in the whole history of cricket as that which took place at Gravesend in 1866 when Sussex were playing Kent? G. Wells hit his wicket down before G. Bennett delivered the ball; in fact the ball was not bowled at all, but as Wells hit his wicket in the act of playing, the umpire, one J. Dean, gave him out. Technically, the umpire was right, as a batsman can be run out before a ball is bowled, if, for instance, the bowler sees that he is out of his ground at the bowler's end, thus gaining an unfair advantage.

During the late 'sixties cricket at all levels was growing markedly in popularity, and the increased number of matches between counties heralded the County Championship and the significant meeting of 1872. The editor of *Wisden*, writing from his offices at 2 New Coventry Street in January 1868, apologized because, in consequence of the great increase in the number of matches played during the past season, he has been reluctantly compelled to limit the Eleven v Twenty-two matches to the 'Results' only. The bowler (whom Alec Bedser has often described as 'The Serf' of cricket) was given much fairer treatment in the 1870 issue of *Wisden*. Hitherto the batsman had monopolized all the attention because only the batting scores of matches were finding a place in this book. That year the compiler tried to do justice to the bowler, by recording, wherever they were obtainable, the bowling summaries to each match, thus bringing the ball and the bowler equally fair prominence and notice with the bat and the batsman. For the bowler, this seemed to be an accolade at last! The year 1870 stands immortalized in the annals of Oxford and Cambridge. This was Cobden's University match. Oxford needed four runs to win with three wickets standing when Mr Cobden bowled his now famously effective last over. From the first ball a single was made (3 to win with 3 wickets to fall). From the second ball Mr Butler was superbly caught out at mid-off. The third ball bowled Mr Belcher, and the fourth ball bowled Mr Stewart. Cobden had done the hat-trick and Cambridge had won by 2 runs. The sudden break up of 'the ring'; the wild rush of thousands across the ground to the pavilion; the waving of hats, sunshades, handkerchiefs, fans, and sticks; the loud shouts for Cobden, Yardley, Dale, Ottaway, Fortescue, Francis and others to come out and be tossed about by their partisans, formed a fitting climax to a match so excitingly contested and a result so astoundedly unexpected. History has not chronicled whether or not the various contestants willingly came out to be tossed about by their partisans. If 1971 provides a genuine guide to human behaviour, then they did not!

But one thing was certain; the popularity of cricket had reached new proportions. It was going from strength to strength; already it was a national heritage. Its future on a strongly competitive basis was as certain as night following day. There would be great striving for the upper stratum – the élite of cricket – the status of a first-class county. The County Championship as an organized competition was in the hatchery.

2 The County Championship

The First Phase 1873-94

The County Cricket Championship is the oldest cricket competition in the world, but its origin is obscure. Historians have not only disagreed as to the year in which it began, but they have even abused each other, so absurdly heated has become their disagreement. It is an argument that no faction can hope to win. The competition was never established specifically in a particular season. *Wisden* did not publish a Championship table for the first time until 1889, relating to the 1888 season, and it was not until the 1911 *Wisden* that a list of County Champions, dating back to 1873, was published for the first time. Why 1873? Because this seems as good a year as any because a meeting had taken place in 1872 to formulate some rules, mainly with a view to preventing a player from appearing for more than one county in the same season; this he had previously been able to do. The meeting took place on 11 December 1872 at 15 Hanover Street, London, and a number of resolutions were passed. A further meeting convened by Surrey for the representatives of the first-class counties took place on 15 April 1873. Various rules governing qualification were prepared. Two months were to pass before the new legislation became law. At a gathering held in the pavilion at the Oval on 9 June 1873 the following rules, which in essence stood for many years, were finally accepted:

1 No cricketer, whether amateur or professional, shall play for more than one county during the same season
2 Every cricketer born in one county and residing in another shall be free to choose at the commencement of each season for which of those counties he will play, and shall, during that season, play for the one county only
3 A cricketer shall be qualified to play for any county in which he is residing and has resided for the previous two years; or a cricketer

may elect to play for the county in which his family home is, so long as it remains open to him as an occasional residence

4 Should any question arise as to the residential qualification, the same shall be left to the decision of the Committee of the Marylebone Cricket Club.

What ought to have been decided at this meeting, but was not, was the method of awarding the Championship. The inference could be that the counties themselves did not even recognize the existence of a Championship. It was left to the Press to issue a merit table at the end of each season, and at some stage or other this unofficial method of deciding the team of the season seems to have become incorporated into official records. What exactly constitutes an official record in circumstances of this nature is a moot point, but at least the MCC *Diary* publishes a list of county champions from 1873 showing Gloucestershire and Nottinghamshire as joint first Champions. They gave Derbyshire as the winners in 1874, and Middlesex in 1878. But they added the following footnote: 'The winners from 1873-86 are given, in the main, on the basis of fewest matches lost, but contemporary opinion favoured Gloucestershire in 1874 and thought that no one county came first in 1878.' MCC became responsible for awarding the Championship in 1895.

For purposes of bona fide records, therefore, 1895 seems to be the year in which the County Championship was set on a proper footing, but if MCC saw it fit to publish a list from 1873 there seems no point in destroying the decision to do so, even if some of the so termed Champions in those early years might have to be taken with a pinch of salt. In any event, other sources talk of the Championship's receiving official recognition in 1887.

The nine counties which competed against one another in 1873 were Derbyshire, Gloucestershire, Kent, Lancashire, Middlesex, Nottinghamshire, Surrey, Sussex and Yorkshire. These counties remained the combatants until 1887, when Derbyshire dropped out. In these years the northern counties were mainly professional; the southern were principally amateur. The method of deciding the order of merit in this period, with the exception of 1887, was based on the very rough and ready method of 'least matches lost'.

This might have been reasonably fair if each county had played the same number of matches, but in any case it induced counties to play for not losing rather than winning. Yet it is quite surprising that if the existing method of Championship scoring had been in vogue in those early days the results would have been only marginally different.

The basic weakness of the system was clearly apparent in the season of 1886 for it produced questionable champions. Notts. won seven and drew seven of their fourteen matches and were hailed as Champions in a season when Surrey won twelve of their sixteen matches, but because they had lost three matches whereas Notts. were unbeaten, Surrey were deemed to be second best. Was it by coincidence that a county table was not available for this season in most books of the period? Was someone dodging the dubious issue of the identity of Champions? The *Lillywhite Annual* went as far as saying that Nottinghamshire and Surrey should be bracketed. On what basis, one might ask? This looked conspicuously like sitting on the fence.

In 1887 a new system of points scoring was in force. The method adopted allowed one point for a win and half a point for a draw. Surrey's twelve wins on this occasion were properly rewarded with the Championship. Derbyshire, in 1887, had played only six matches compared to Surrey's sixteen, and fourteen by Lancashire and Nottinghamshire. Derbyshire lost all six and withdrew from the competition at the end of the season, despite the fact that they had arranged seven first-class fixtures for 1888. The side was obviously out of its class.

The second phase in the Championship was spread over the next seven years, from 1888 to 1894. In 1895, with the addition of five new counties, the County Championship was moving towards the structure which we know to-day. The years 1888 to 1894 belonged incomparably to Surrey. They were champions in 1888, joint-champions in 1889, champions in 1890, 1891, 1892 and 1894 (they were also winners of the enlarged competition in 1895). These were golden days of Surrey cricket, the first of the two golden eras. Under the leadership of John Shuter Surrey boasted a host of splendid cricketers. George Lohmann; Tom

Richardson, the Lion of Kennington; The Guvnor, Bobby Abel; Walter and Maurice Read, and Bill Lockwood. They achieved an average of three wins for every four matches played in this period. Eight counties competed, but in 1891 Somerset were elevated to first-class status and joined the other eight.

The summer of 1889 produced a triple-tie, Lancashire, Nottinghamshire and Surrey all finishing the season with 10½ points, although Lancashire and Surrey won ten matches, and Nottinghamshire only nine. It was in December 1889 that the county secretaries met and decided on yet another points system; losses to be deducted from wins, drawn games being ignored. In speaking of this change *Wisden* refers to 'the now officially recognized competition for the championship'.

The year 1893 shows Yorkshire as Champions for the first time. It had taken twenty years to achieve their first success – the first of twenty-nine Championships. At a Captain's meeting held in May 1894 it was agreed that four new counties – Derbyshire (now restored again), Essex, Leicestershire, and Warwickshire – should be admitted to the championship in 1895. In October, the name of Hampshire was added to the list (this late election explains why Hampshire's matches in 1894 were deemed not to be first-class, whereas the others were). So 1894 was virtually the end of an era; another began in 1895 with yet another points system – one point for each victory, one point deducted for each loss, the final order being decided by the greatest proportion gained of points to games completed.

Between 1873 and 1894 two counties had emerged head and shoulders above the rest – Nottinghamshire and Surrey. Notts. were Champions on six occasions and Joint-Champions four times. Surrey were six times Champions, too, and Joint-Champions once. The only other county to win even twice was Gloucestershire; inspired by Grace they won in 1876 and 1877.

Who then were the fine players of Nottinghamshire, who in the five years between 1880 and 1886 were five times Champions and Joint-Champions once, surrendering only to Lancashire in 1881? Their triumph of 1880 (twelve matches played; eight won, one lost, and three drawn) was principally the work of three men –

Shaw and Morley, the bowlers, and Barnes, the batsman. Notts. wound up this brilliant season by defeating the Australians – a feat achieved by no other county. Morley's match of the year, in terms of most wickets taken, was that against Yorkshire; he took 7 for 31 and 6 for 52 as Yorkshire were bowled out for 66 and 84, but his most sustained spell of brilliance was his 19·2 overs against Surrey at the Oval, 12 of which were maidens; and he took 7 wickets for 9 runs – Surrey were all out for 16! Of these, Maurice Read scored 9, Pooley 3 and Lucas 2. Jupp managed a single – seven players failed to score. Although rain and sun had produced a treacherous wicket, *Wisden* records that, taking into consideration the calibre of the Surrey team, it is probable that the bowling success of Morley and Shaw in this match stands unsurpassed in the history of the game.

On that July day at the Oval in 1880 the names of Morley and Shaw stood as high in public esteem as did Lock and Laker, Miller and Lindwall, and Statham and Trueman in the years following. Bowlers win matches, and it is particularly noteworthy that in publishing the averages at the end of each county, *Wisden* gave the bowling first – and why not? What prompted the change? Great batsmen have beguiled the connoisseurs with their style and fluency, but matches are won only by bowlers who bowl a side out. All the great Championship sides have possessed a potent attack; usually a twin-spearhead of speed or spin; some had both.

Nottinghamshire took a firm grip on the Championship and won four years in succession from 1883–6, a feat not performed again until Yorkshire were Champions from 1922–5. The Surrey batsmen once again felt the sharp teeth of the Notts. attack in 1883 at Trent Bridge. Abel and Walter Read scored 67 out of a total of 87, and in the second innings Walter Read scored 17 out of 43 (Shaw taking 7 wickets for 22 runs). Barnes and Shrewsbury headed the batting averages with Shaw the leading bowler. Nottinghamshire's domination in 1884 was complete. Out of a programme of ten matches with counties they won nine, and would certainly have been the victors in the tenth had time permitted. Arthur Shrewsbury had a batting average of 37·15, but it was Scotton who made the most remarkable advance. He finished with an average of 31·9. Considering that his average in 1883 for eight completed innings was 12·3, his success in 1884 caused him to be ranked as the best left-handed batsman in England. Alfred Shaw, who reached his forty-second birthday just after the end of the season, again stood at the head of the bowlers. Despite the exceptionally dry summer, Shaw succeeded in capturing 68 wickets at an average cost of only 10·32. Just as Scotton had made an advance in batting, so did Attewell, a young professional, in the bowling department. In 1883 he took 17 wickets at 18·5 each. In 1884 he obtained 71 at 12·35, a season in which Nottinghamshire cricket reached its zenith; although the Championship title was held in the following year their measure of superiority was not as emphatic. Arthur Shrewsbury established himself as the best professional batsman in the country with scores of 224 not out, 137 and 118, culminating in an average of 54·7. So to 1886 and the year in which Surrey contrived twelve wins to Nottinghamshire's seven but ceded the championship because the latter were unbeaten. *Wisden*'s view is this: 'While Surrey, in strictly first-class county matches alone, was three times beaten, it is no more than fair to accord to Nottinghamshire the position of Champion for the year.' This must be a matter of opinion. Support for *Wisden*'s view lies in the result of the two matches played during the season between Notts. and Surrey. The first at Trent Bridge was disrupted by rain and no result was achieved. Surrey were better placed (282 and 100 for 2, Notts. 223) but the die was by no means cast, and no prophet could have been convincing in saying that, but for the weather, Surrey would undoubtedly win in the time available. At the Oval there was a very decisive result – Surrey 99 (Attewell 8 for 56) and 194 (Shaw 4–22), Nottinghamshire 272 and 25 for 3 (all three clean bowled by Bowley).

Although beaten in this match and for the 1886 Championship, the strength of Surrey was becoming eminently clear. They took over the reins from the men from the Midlands in 1887, won the Championship in that year and the next; were Joint-Champions in 1889 with Lancashire and Nottinghamshire, and brought off a triumvirate of successes in 1890, 1891 and 1892. Notts. were not to win a Championship again until 1907. In fact, the last decade of the nineteenth century was an accurate barometer of things to come. Surrey and Yorkshire dominated the Championship between them, winning nine seasons out of ten (Lancashire intervened in 1897). They remain to this day as leaders in championship successes – Yorkshire, twenty-nine, Surrey, seventeen.

Surrey's first Championship success in 1887 was not easily achieved. Roller's health broke down during the season and caused him to give up cricket, and Jones and Beaumont were lost through accidents. Moreover, Wood, a really outstanding wicket-keeper, was severely handicapped by an injured finger, and from time to time had to give up his post behind the stumps to less skilled performers. But the all-round strength of the side swept aside these misfortunes, especially during the month of August when it was reduced to three bowlers. At full strength the victorious eleven was: Shuter, Walter Read, Roller, Key, Lohmann, Maurice Read, Abel, Bowley, Beaumont, Jones and Wood. The trinity of virtues in this splendid side was undoubtedly Lohmann, Key and Walter Read. In the sixteen first-class county matches Lohmann took 108 wickets at less than 14 runs each. Walter Read was in irresistible form during the first half of the season and made a double century in successive matches – a feat of enormous proportions; his average looked like being quite exceptional until he had a surprisingly lean time in August. Key topped the batting averages and, Arthur Shrewsbury apart, was the most prolific run-getter in the country. Surrey's match with Nottinghamshire at Trent Bridge has won a place in cricket history because of an action by John Shuter, the Surrey captain, which was the forerunner of the introduction of a declaration into cricket. It was not until 1889 that there is on record a mention of a declaration – and that was by Mr Shuter, but in this vital contest at Trent Bridge in 1887, Mr Shuter adopted the next best procedure. When Surrey were 250 for 3 in their second innings and a draw seemed absolute, the Captain instructed his batsmen to get out, which they did in rather clumsy fashion. Lohmann then bowled

Nottinghamshire out for a Surrey victory, their first over Notts. since 1870. Shuter's tactics provoked a good deal of discussion in the newspapers; was this the birth of real gamesmanship; was it a breath of the artful dodger; was it just shrewd common sense and a sound cricketing brain? It certainly whetted the appetite of the London crowd when Nottinghamshire came to the Oval for the 'Retribution Match' on August Bank Holiday. Quite emphatically this was the match of the London season; it drew crowds of 24,450 on the first day, 16,943 on the second and 10,243 on the third – an aggregate of 51,636 paying customers. Surrey won by four wickets. There could be no arguing about that result.

The first Surrey success of 1887 was swiftly followed by another in 1888, with an even more impressive playing record than before. Lohmann surpassed every previous brilliant performance. In the fourteen first-class county matches he took 142 wickets at under nine runs apiece, and in all matches exceeded 200 wickets. He bowled 965·2 overs; the rest of the Surrey bowlers between them bowled 1,249·2. Walter Read's innings of 338 against Oxford University was the second highest score ever made in first-class cricket – only six runs short of Grace's 344 for MCC against Kent at Canterbury in 1876.

Surrey's star performance of the season was against Lancashire at Old Trafford; those were days when Hornby and Barlow (Oh my Hornby and my Barlow of long ago) opened for Lancashire. The match was all over in a single day, Lohmann taking 13 wickets for 51 runs when Lancashire's aggregate for the two innings reached only 98 runs. Lancashire, stinging with indignity, came to the Oval and inflicted upon Surrey their only County Championship defeat of the season.

In 1889 Surrey were poised for a hat-trick, but in the end they had to share the spoils equally with Lancashire and Nottinghamshire; this slight set-back was only temporary as they duly accomplished the hat-trick in the next three seasons.

The outstanding feature of Surrey's cricket in 1890 was the astonishing improvement made by Sharpe, who in all matches took 179 wickets, even more than Lohmann. Sharpe, like Lockwood, had been on the staff at Trent Bridge, and when this pair ravaged Notts. in the Bank Holiday game at The Oval (Lockwood made 66 and 28, and Sharpe took 7 for 51 and 4 for 38) there were some boisterous jibes at Surrey for having to recruit players from their now traditional rivals. The jibes surely should have been directed at the other side for having let them go. This sort of thing, however, is as inevitable as night and day – Kent are supposed to have turned down Wally Hammond. Surrey duly won the 1890 Championship but their repeat in 1891 was even more impressive. They took the lead at the start of the season and their position was never seriously threatened. Lohmann and Sharpe were now joined by Lockwood, and the latter's 7 for 19 against Kent was, in the unanimous opinion of the players, one of the most deadly pieces of fast bowling ever seen at the Oval. From a batting standpoint, this was Bobby Abel's season.

Surrey completed a Championship hat-trick in 1892 but only after the pendulum of fortune had swung violently to and fro. At one time it looked pretty certain that Nottinghamshire would sweep Surrey off their feet. When Notts. beat Surrey at the Oval, and then beat Kent at Canterbury and Middlesex at Trent Bridge, they appeared to be certain Champions. But the change which came over the two elevens was quite astonishing. Surrey went on from victory to victory, whilst Nottinghamshire, after defeating Middlesex, did not win another match. Surrey suffered a disappointment in the falling off of Sharpe but there was ample compensation. They found a very effective fast bowler in Tom Richardson, described by Herbert Strudwick (throughout 'Struddy's' lifetime) as the fastest bowler he ever saw. Ranjitsinhji once expressed the view that, on good wickets, Lockwood was more difficult to play than Richardson. Years afterwards, when Bill Lockwood was at the Oval in a bath-chair he was asked to name the greatest fast bowler he remembered during his long association with cricket. 'There is only one,' replied Lockwood, 'Tom Richardson.' 'What about yourself, Bill?' posed the enquirer. 'I wasn't in the same parish as Tom, let alone the same street.'

In 1893 a new page of history received its first entry. The page concerns Yorkshire; they won their first Championship. Their overall record for the next nigh on eighty years is second to none; they have cherished emphatically the tradition that only Yorkshire-born players will play for Yorkshire; preserving this philosophy in the 1970s they stand alone. Their contribution to England in Test cricket has been tremendous, so much so that it was always said that when Yorkshire is strong, England is strong. The Yorkshire side of 1893 contained Lord Hawke, Tunnicliffe and Brown, Wainwright and George Hirst, and F. S. Jackson. Their match of the year was against Surrey, the reigning champions, on a bad wicket at Sheffield. Yorkshire were put out for 98 and 91 (*Wisden* reported that it was a thankless task to stand up to Richardson and Lockwood on such a wicket). But Surrey found Hirst (match figures of 8 for 55) and Wardall (match figures of 9 for 19) an increasingly forbidding proposition. Surrey were toppled over for 72 and 59. Yet the real hero was Moorhouse for Yorkshire who, though knocked about, remained utterly defiant in each innings; his scores of 39 out of 98, and 38 not out, out of 91 were performances showing high courage. Clearly, they won the match. Surrey were waiting for the Yorkshiremen in the return match at the Oval and won by an innings, but no one begrudged Yorkshire their success; for years Nottinghamshire and Surrey had ruled the roost. There was soon more to come of Surrey but at least Yorkshire's triumph ended this first phase in the County Championship on a refreshingly new note.

The Second Phase 1895-1914

The new phase in the County Championship, which began in 1895, proved the competition to be a much more elaborate affair than in previous years. The addition of Derbyshire, Warwickshire, Leicestershire, Essex and Hampshire raised the number of competing counties from nine to fourteen, but produced certain complications with fixtures. It was found to be impossible for all the counties to meet one another; in fact, it was only by the courtesy of Middlesex and Somerset that Essex were able to secure the minimum number of eight home matches insisted upon by the MCC Committee. So with some elevens playing more matches than others, the MCC ruled that, while reckoning one point for each win and deducting one for each loss, the county should be adjudged county champions that had, in finished matches during the summer, obtained the greatest proportionate number of points. In all, 131 matches were played compared with 71 in the previous season. The extension of the Championship was abundantly justified by the results. Derbyshire came fifth, Warwickshire tied for sixth place, Essex were eighth, Hampshire were tenth, and Leicestershire tied for twelfth place. The top and bottom of the table accommodated Surrey and Kent respectively.

A significant wind of change was about to blow through cricket. Batsmen and bowlers had enjoyed comparative equality up until 1893; there were a few great batsmen who held sway, but now, most counties were developing high-quality batsmen and the ultimate result, inevitably, was a large number of drawn games. The method of deciding the County Championship worked quite well for the first few years, but at the turn of the century the number of drawn games was increasing – 70 drawn games out of 166 matches in 1900, for instance. Eventually this new concept led to a further revision and in 1910 the County Championship was determined by percentage of wins to matches played. This dramatically reduced the number of drawn games but, despite this, another change was made in 1911.

The Minor County Championship, organized on a proper basis in 1901, proved that it was difficult to achieve a result in two-day cricket, and in 1902 had adopted a system of points for a side leading on first innings in a drawn match. It seemed only a matter of time before the first-class counties would seize on this piece of common-sense legislation, and in the spring of 1911 Somerset successfully moved that a completely new system of points be adopted for that season. The plan was five points for a win, three points to the county leading on first innings, and one point to their opponent in a drawn match, the order being decided by percentage of points gained to points possible, matches in which a decision on first innings was not reached being ignored for the purposes of compiling a table.

This seemed a sound enough method, but the master-minds soon found a flaw. A county high in the table found that if they had a percentage of more than 60, points for a first innings lead in a drawn match actually reduced their percentage, so that it was more advantageous not to attain a result on first innings if there was no possibility of winning the match. There is no real evidence that this was blatantly abused until as late as 1929, when Nottinghamshire were running for – and won – the Championship. Yorkshire, who were close on their heels, won the toss and batted for 9¾ hours to score 498, so Notts. went for a 'No Result'. They batted 7¼ hours in scoring 190–4, George Gunn batting 320 minutes for 58.

This new era in 1895 began with a Championship win for Surrey but not by any means a convincing one. In fact, the title hinged on their last match of the season against Hampshire which they had to win – and did. Two Surrey cricketers in this season were head and shoulders above their colleagues – Tom Richardson and Bobby Abel – but despite Abel's magnificent batting, it was clearly Richardson's bowling which was the one dominating factor. Richardson, in inter-county matches alone, took 237 wickets at a cost of less than 14 runs each. This 'Italian-looking brigand' as C. B. Fry once described him, never weakened in his attack however hot the day or however much the wicket favoured the batsmen. This was fast bowling supreme; poise, power, unrelenting determination. There was something sadly significant about this season. Surrey were not to win another Championship on great bowling alone for over half a century. Admittedly, they won the championship in 1899 but no bowler took a hundred wickets. It was the batting of Abel (average 64·66), Hayward (average 64·21), Crawford (average 53·50) and Lockwood (average 42·69) which gave the Surrey bowlers so much leeway in bowling sides out. Surrey won another Championship in 1914 but in slightly unsatisfactory circumstances when the season was brought to an end before time because of the 1914 war. They were not to be leading county again until the halcyon days of the 'fifties when they had no less than four great bowlers – Lock and Laker, purveyors of vicious, tantalizing spin, Alec Bedser, and Peter Loader. On the evidence of Surrey's performances over the years bowling strength is clearly the decisive weapon, as for half a century Surrey were never a poor side – how could they be with Hobbs, Sandham, Barling, Gregory, Jardine and Fender – but where were the match-winning bowlers apart from Gover who bowled his heart out on the totally unresponsive Oval wickets of the 'thirties?

This period between 1895 and 1914 was dominated by Yorkshire. History was being made which was to be repeated time and time again. It was Yorkshire who took the title away from Surrey in 1896. In view of the pressure on fixtures with the Australian team in England, it was agreed that a minimum number of six home and six away fixtures should be sufficient to qualify for the Championship, and Middlesex, Somerset and Essex all lightened their programmes, Essex playing only the twelve matches that were needed. For a time it seemed that the Championship was becoming a two-horse race between Yorkshire and Surrey, but whereas Yorkshire retained their consistency, Surrey fell away and in the end had to be content with fourth place. During this whole period between 1895 and the outbreak of war, only twice did Yorkshire fall below fourth place (in 1910 and 1911, when they were eighth and seventh), and in these twenty seasons Yorkshire won the Championship on eight occasions. With batsmen of the calibre of J. T. Brown, D. Denton, G. H. Hirst, F. S. Jackson and J. Tunnicliffe, W. Rhodes and B. B. Taylor, there were always plenty of runs on the board, and what is more, they did have the match-winning bowlers – M. W. Booth, S. Haigh and Hirst, Rhodes and Jackson. Lord Hawke set a standard of leadership which has become a Yorkshire tradition, handed down through the years like a precious family heirloom. Yorkshire is not just a cricket team; it is an institution. Lord Hawke may not have been present at the birth, but he attended the baptism.

In 1897, the title slipped across the Pennines to Lancashire, with Surrey and Essex in pursuit; Yorkshire were fourth. But Yorkshire were back at the top in 1898 with a vengeance. They took the lead at the start of the season, lost to Kent at Maidstone in mid-July, and Surrey and Middlesex in August, but were never then in imminent danger of being deposed. They were deposed, however, in 1899 by Surrey in a year in which five three-day Test matches were played against Australia (up until then only three Tests had been played in a series). Worcestershire were now admitted to the County Championship.

And so to 1900, and a new century. The thirty-seventh edition of *Wisden* contained some six hundred pages and could be bought for a shilling; John Piggott, the city cricket outfitter of Cheapside and Milk Street, offered best match cricket balls at 27/9 a half-dozen, and a square or round tent could be provided by William Curtis of Marylebone for five pounds. Struthers and Company of Finsbury Pavement were selling 'Regal' cricket shirts at half-a-crown a time; a list of leading players from whom the manufacturer had received testimonials is contained in their advertisement. It would be interesting, in this commercial age of the 'seventies, to know what sort of recompense (if any!) the players of 1900 received in return for endorsing the undoubted qualities of the 'Regal' cricket shirt!

Yorkshire began the new century as they intended to carry on. They won the Championship. To date, they have won it twenty-six times in the twentieth century – a total of twenty-nine times in all. In the years between 1900 and the outbreak of the First World War in 1914, Yorkshire won the Championship six times in fourteen seasons. In fact it was during the years 1900, 1901 and 1902 that Yorkshire first seemed to surround themselves with an aura of invincibility. The team was superbly equipped. It was a settled unit (only sixteen players were called upon during the whole of 1901), and there were batting and bowling to match every occasion. In the ninety-nine matches played during the three seasons there were fifty-seven outright victories and six defeats, only two of them in Championship matches. So tremendous grew the Yorkshire reputation that the victories came to be accepted almost without comment; the defeats, by contrast, were headline news. Somerset became the wonder-team of the day by beating Yorkshire both in 1901 and 1902, each time in Yorkshire. The match in 1901 at Leeds was one of the most remarkable ever played in the County Championship. Somerset were bowled out for 87, to which Yorkshire replied with 325. Somerset began their second innings 238 in arrears, whereupon Lionel Palairet and Braund put on 222 for the first wicket in two hours and twenty minutes, and this after it seemed so unlikely that the match would last into the third day, that Somerset had made provisional travelling arrangements to get away early! But such is cricket! Somerset scored 630 (Palairet 173, Braund 107, Phillips 122), and a very weary Yorkshire side were bowled out for 113. They were beaten by 279 runs. Somerset came back to Yorkshire in 1902 (at Sheffield this time) and repeated the dose, although this time there was no extraordinary turn of fortune. Somerset were in control all the time, Braund taking 9 for 41 in Yorkshire's second innings.

Some of Yorkshire's victories during this period, of course, stand equally high in history. Against Worcestershire at Bradford in 1900 they were all out for 99 ... and won by an innings! At Trent Bridge in 1901, Nottinghamshire were dismissed for 13, the lowest total recorded in first-class cricket. Oddly enough, there was a bowling change in this disastrously short innings, Hirst bowling one over for one run before admitting that he could not get a foothold, and leaving the rest to Rhodes, who took 6 wickets for 4 runs, and Haigh who took four for eight. Against Essex at Harrogate in 1900 rain was so persistent that by one o'clock on the third day the match had gone no further than the completion of Yorkshire's first innings for 171. Essex were then dismissed for 65, and Yorkshire declared after hitting 42 in twenty minutes, which left two hours for play, and Essex needing to score 148 for victory. They were put out for 52, Hirst taking 8 for 28.

In the next two seasons, 1903 and 1904, Yorkshire did not head the list, but some people (especially in Yorkshire) think they should have done so in 1903. Middlesex were hailed as Champions, winning eight and losing only one of their eighteen matches, but they did not participate in a full programme of matches, and Yorkshire, with thirteen victories in twenty-six matches, had just as good a record although finishing third. The real drawback of the system of points-scoring in operation at the time was that matches left drawn were ignored for the purpose of calculating the percentage of points gained to points possible. In this context, providing a county could win a few matches they were better placed with a series of drawn games than a few defeats, so that the emphasis was decidedly upon not losing, rather than on winning all the time. In 1904 it was Lancashire's turn with Yorkshire as runners-up, but Yorkshire were back at the top in 1905, reversing the placings with Lancashire. Northamptonshire took their place in the Championship for the first time in 1905.

In 1906 Kent celebrated their first Championship, and although they fell from grace in 1907, this was the beginning of one of the most successful periods in Kent's history. They were second in 1908 to Yorkshire, and they headed the table in both 1909 and 1910. Nottinghamshire's victory in 1907 was their first Championship success since 1886. Kent were to snatch one more victory in 1913 before the world was plunged into total war, as were Yorkshire in 1912. Warwickshire appeared on the honours scene for the first time in 1911 when they became champions, and Surrey rounded off this period of history by winning the Championship in 1914, though not necessarily with unanimous approval. In the wake of war, Surrey cancelled their last two matches because Lord Roberts in a recruiting speech had already made pointed reference to people who went on playing cricket at such a time. Surrey were awarded the Championship even though the campaign was not completed.

In this Surrey side of 1914 was P. G. H. Fender; this was the only time in his long career with the Surrey Club in which Fender played in a championship-winning side. Before, however, passing through the war, and on to the next phase of the County Championship, mention should be made of some of the Kent heroes in this triumphant period. Among these were Hutchings, Seymour, Humphreys, J. R. Mason, A. P. Day, Wally Hardinge, Frank Woolley and Colin Blythe – Blythe, spinner supreme, whose steely fingers were developed through playing the violin. In August 1917 he was drafted to the Western Front, and on

8 November 1917, while attached to the KOYLIs, he was killed by a shell. Two days later the third battle of the Ypres salient was over. The Colin Blythe Memorial stands in the St Lawrence Ground, Canterbury, a testimony to a magnificent cricketer – 'As cricketer, soldier, patriot, he played the game.'

Between the wars
The period between the two wars – 1919-39 – brought the County Championship up to its full complement when Glamorgan were admitted in 1921. Wales, where rugby football is a heritage as revered as man's faith itself, was scarcely thought of as a likely hatchery for cricketers. To keep Glamorgan as a going concern was a great struggle; more than once the county's cricket club was in danger of being disbanded because of lack of public support, and even in the 'thirties it was kept in business only by public subscriptions, sweepstakes and numerous and varied functions designed to raise money.

When Glamorgan reached the heights of winning the County Championship in 1948, many Welsh cricketers, in this moment of triumph, would recall with nostalgia and affection, the two men who did so much for the county in its early years in the County Championship – J. C. Clay and M. J. Turnbull. During Clay's playing career, which extended from 1921 to 1948, he took 1,293 wickets at an average cost of 19·45. Clay headed the Glamorgan bowling averages in eleven seasons and in 1937 took 170 wickets.

Maurice Turnbull, in 1924, played his first innings for Glamorgan when a seventeen-year-old schoolboy at Downside. This magnificent cricketer and leader of men was killed in action when he was leading a company of Welsh Guards into action before the break-through in Normandy in 1944. In all first-class matches he scored nearly 18,000 runs with twenty-nine centuries, a record which is even more commendable when it is borne in mind that he was only thirty-three years old when war brought a tragic end to his cricket career.

It was not only in his cricket, however, that Maurice Turnbull brought lustre to Glamorgan. He was a splendid administrator, and when he was appointed Captain in 1930, and Secretary in 1932, by personal example and sheer hard work he fashioned a new Glamorgan. Surely, had he lived, he would have captained England; by one of the strange inconsistencies allowed in sport, he played for England – at cricket ... and for Wales at rugby football! John Clay and Maurice Turnbull – they nurtured Glamorgan cricket with loving care and with great skill and leadership; without it, the county might not have survived.

The method of administering the County Championship in those years seemed to be on a permanent switchback. In the first forty-two years of the Championship there had been very little change in the method of deciding the title, but in the twenty-one years between 1919 and 1939 no fewer than eight different methods were tried. Some were discarded without a fair trial; others were so unrealistic as to cause doubt as to the intelligence of the inventors. In 1919 the order was decided by the greatest percentage of wins to matches played, but as most of the counties played a curtailed programme this did not get a long enough trial, for in 1920 first-innings points came back, but only for a side leading on first innings in a drawn match. Various changes were rung until the most curious innovation of all was introduced in 1927 when it was decided to ignore all matches in which less than six hours' play had taken place, unless some sort of decision had been reached. This simply meant that any captain on the losing end of the stick in a rain-curtailed match, would do his best to see that six hours' play did not take place; he could argue that the pitch was not fit to play or employ all manner of time-delaying tactics. But at the same time four points were awarded to each side in a match that ended in a 'No Result' so, on the one hand, counties could get something for nothing and, on the other, get nothing for a good deal of hard work and success in a game which lasted five hours and fifty-five minutes! Possibly the most far-reaching decision was that taken in 1933 when it was decided that a side winning on first-innings in a match reduced to play on the third day should gain only ten points, their opponents getting the usual three points awarded to a side behind on first-innings.

This was a move which had been forced on the authorities by

what had happened in a match between Yorkshire and Gloucestershire at Sheffield in 1931, and had stimulated ideas for others to follow. This match could not be started until the third day, and the two captains, F. E. Greenwood and B. H. Lyon, took the law into their own hands with a shrewd piece of thinking which did not actually contravene the laws. In order that the full fifteen points should be available, each side declared their first innings closed after one ball had been bowled straight through to the boundary for four byes, and the match developed into a fight for the full fifteen points in what otherwise would have been, in effect, a single-innings match.

Gloucestershire, who were sent in to bat by Greenwood, scored 171 and left Yorkshire two and a half hours in which to get the runs. Yorkshire were bowled out for 124 and lost by 47 runs, Gloucestershire gratefully taking the full fifteen points.

To the uninitiated, cricket is a most complex game; sometimes it is even to the initiated. For example, this was how the County Championship was decided between 1933 and 1937:

Each county to play 24 matches to qualify for the Championship. Counties allowed to play more matches, but all must be reckoned in the competition. No county to play another more than twice during a season. The county obtaining the greatest proportionate number of points on a percentage basis to be adjudged winner of the Championship. For the purpose of calculating the result, the unit of 100 per cent in all matches was the equivalent of 15 points.

Is it any wonder that a small boy, once asked to compile an essay on the game of cricket, wrote as follows:

You have two sides; one out in the field, one in. Each man on the side that's in, goes out, and when he's out he comes in and the next man goes in until he's out. When they are all out, the side that's been out in the field comes in, and the side that's been in goes out and tries to get those coming in, out. Then, when both sides have been in and out – including not-outs – that's the end of the game.

It sounds for all the world like something from a Gilbert and Sullivan opera, but ironically enough, it's quite true! ...

The cricketing years, from 1919 to 1939 were famous for one

team – Yorkshire. In the twenty-one years, they won the Championship twelve times. Lancashire came second with five successes, Middlesex with two, and Nottinghamshire and Derbyshire gained one each. So in twenty-one years twelve counties failed to win a Championship. Yorkshire's dominance was even more marked towards the end of the period, as Lancashire won three of their five in succession in 1926, 1927 and 1928. In the 'thirties, Yorkshire took seven out of ten.

The decision to restrict all county matches in 1919 to two days, and to let the result be determined by the percentage of actual wins to matches played, robbed the Championship of all its lustre. In an exceptionally dry summer, a long succession of drawn games was inevitable – 56 were drawn out of 124. This was something of a hotch-potch season in which Yorkshire just about deserved to be champions under a new leader, D. C. F. Burton, who hit 142 not out against Hampshire at Dewsbury. Sutcliffe and Holmes topped the batting, and Rhodes took 142 wickets at 12·42 each.

In 1920 the ill-starred experiment of 1919 was abandoned, and the Championship stood on its pre-war footing, and what a Championship it was! At one time or another Yorkshire, Surrey and Kent all seemed well placed to win. In the end, the issue rested between Middlesex and Lancashire. Middlesex had to beat Surrey at Lord's to become champions; they did, and 'Plum' Warner, who had already announced that he would retire as Middlesex Captain at the end of the season, ended his term of office amid unforgettable scenes of emotion. His Middlesex colleagues on that memorable day were: Skeet, H. W. Lee, Hearne, Hendren, Mann, Haigh, Stevens, Longman, Murrell and Durston.

Middlesex became champions again in 1921 with more assurance; it was not a matter of a storming finish. They did not lose a county match until the middle of July, and were always favourites. This was a success in his first season as Captain for Frank Mann, a year in which 'Patsy' Hendren hit six of his seven centuries at Lord's, and Hearne hit five of his six hundreds away from Lord's – an interesting comparison which may or may not infer some deep-rooted phenomenon in technique or psychology.

Comparisons are sometimes odious, sometimes intensely interesting, but no comparison can be fairly made between generations of sportsmen. Was this Yorkshire side of the 'thirties greater than the Surrey team of the 'fifties? We shall never know, but we shall often sit and think. Who were these Yorkshiremen of the early 'twenties who won four victories in a row from 1922 to 1925? In this period there were eighty-six victories and only seven defeats in their complete programme of 141 matches. Yorkshire were not only masters of the Championship but ruthless conquerors, for a large number of their successes were gained with an innings to spare. In 1922 the batting was strong with five players (Oldroyd, Sutcliffe, Rhodes, Holmes and Kilner) scoring over 1,000 runs, but the real strength lay with the bowlers and the fielding. Rhodes, Macaulay, Kilner and Waddington all took 100 wickets, and Macaulay, who had found his original fast bowling beyond his physique, had, by this time, thoroughly established himself as a medium-paced bowler of varied skills. Roy Kilner, in completing the double, was confirming that he was pretty close to being the best left-hander in the country at the time.

The year 1923 brought even greater triumph to Yorkshire. They achieved a record number of victories, winning twenty-five of their thirty-two matches, thirteen of them by an innings, and they averaged twice as many runs per wicket as their opponents. This time six batsmen passed the 1,000-run mark, the usual five now having been joined by Maurice Leyland, playing his first full season in first-class cricket. It was Maurice Leyland who was once asked if he relished very fast bowling. His reply remains a classic – 'None of us really likes it, but some of us doesn't let on.'

Yorkshire were again champions in 1924 but this time not quite as overwhelmingly. There were three defeats, and their number of victories was reduced to sixteen. For quite a long time there was a strong challenge from Middlesex, but the challenge weakened on the final run-in, and Yorkshire were home again. Middlesex beat Yorkshire at Lord's when both sides were without some of their leading players, who were taking part in a Test Trial, and when the return match took place at Sheffield there was so much bad blood that Middlesex announced that they would not play Yorkshire again; this decision was later rescinded. It may have been six to one and half-a-dozen to the other, but *Wisden* quite clearly apportions the blame to the unsporting elements in the Yorkshire crowd. Their correspondent wrote: 'For some reason, the Sheffield crowd, forgetting their old reputation for good sportsmanship, barracked more or less persistently all through the game, making the atmosphere almost unbearable.' Under such conditions cricket could not be played in a proper spirit. Some fine work was done by both sides but no one enjoyed the match. The Middlesex side contained Frank Mann, 'Gubby' Allen, Nigel Haigh, Greville Stevens, Jack Hearne and 'Patsy' Hendren.

There was one shattering blow to Yorkshire's pride in 1924. In the traditional 'Roses' match at Headingley, in front of their own folk, Yorkshire required only 57 runs for victory with all their wickets in hand. They failed by 24 runs. In one hour they were put out by Richard Tyldesley and 'Cec' Parkin for 33, Tyldesley taking 6 for 18 and Parkin 3 for 5.

If 1924 had cast some doubt on Yorkshire as reigning champions, this was removed conclusively in 1925. They won the Championship with twenty-one victories and no defeats. A new captain, A. W. Lupton, kept careful watch on the discipline of the side, and the batting achievements scaled new heights. Holmes and Sutcliffe made over 2,000 runs, and Rhodes, Leyland and Oldroyd exceeded 1,000; Macaulay took 200 wickets, Kilner 123 and Waddington 105. This was Roy Kilner's Benefit Year; so popular was this grand cricketer that contributions from all parts of the cricket world brought him over £4,000 . . . four thousand pounds in 1925, certainly the equivalent of at least forty thousand in 1971!

From 1926 to 1930, however, Yorkshire's name did not appear on the Roll of Honour. They were never far short of final victory, but just far enough. Victory was on the other side of the Pennines for three years; then it moved down to Nottingham before returning to the Lancastrian side of the Pennines again in 1930. From this point onwards, Yorkshire took over again.

In 1926 Lancashire had a good year. They were County Champions for the first time since 1904, the balance sheet showed a surplus of over £10,000, and although the side was not as strong in bowling as in 1925 (Parkin ceased to play after the fourteenth match) it was still a team of many talents. Ernest Tyldesley, Makepeace, Watson and Hallows led the batting. McDonald, fast bowler of grace and immense pace, took 163 wickets, and George Duckworth had many brilliant days behind the wicket. Neville Cardus, whose thread of life was interwoven inextricably through Lancashire cricket and who knew personally every blade of grass at Old Trafford as well as he knew the palm of his own hand, once wrote of Ernest Tyldesley: 'There is in Tyldesley's style a certain graciousness, a touch of what the French call *politesse*. He is never brutal, not even when he is driving and cutting at his fastest and best. He reminds me of the stupid old verse

> He kicks you downstairs with such infinite grace,
> You'd think he was handing you up.

Cardus had this to say of George Duckworth:

Men often tell us by their physical appearance what they do for a living. Lawyers look legal; colonels look belligerent; ostlers look like horses about the mouth; and wicket-keepers look like nothing on earth but stumpers. George Duckworth was made by nature to sit close to the ground; he bends nicely, and his voice would have been wasted in any occupation but the one he adorns so perfectly. Duckworth's appeal is famous at this end and at the other end of the earth; sometimes it is so penetrating that both ends of the earth might well be able to hear it at the same moment.

Ernest Tyldesley had a wonderful summer in 1926. At one stage his consistency recalled the C. B. Fry of 1901. In nine innings from 26 June Tyldesley scored 1,128 runs with an average of 141. He scored seven centuries in consecutive matches – and four in successive innings.

The ebullient spirit and understandable optimism at Old Trafford carried the side on the crest of a wave for the next two seasons. They were champions again in 1927 and 1928 to complete a notable hat-trick. Yet it was a very narrow squeak in 1927.

At one period, Nottinghamshire seemed a racing certainty for the title. Then, inexplicably, they lost their last match to Glamorgan; to have won would have meant the Championship. Not only did Notts. lose – they were murdered. Glamorgan won by an innings and 81 runs, having bowled Notts. out for 61 in their second innings – Jack Mercer, 6 for 31, would treasure the memory of that day for a whole lifetime.

In 1928, however, Lancashire carried off the title in much more decisive fashion. For a long time their right to the honour was seriously challenged by Kent, who took first place in the table at the beginning of June and retained the position until the concluding days of July when three consecutive defeats marred their prospects. Thenceforth Lancashire took over at the top and finished with the handsome record of fifteen victories, no defeats, and a percentage of eight points higher than that of Kent. Memorable indeed were the achievements of a triumvirate of Lancashire batsmen, and outstanding among these was Charles Hallows, who triumphed in equalling the performance of W. G. Grace in 1895, and of Walter Hammond in 1927, by registering 1,000 runs during the month of May. Hallows made his 1,000 runs in eleven innings (three times not out) producing an average of 125.

Another dominant feature of this season was the magnificent record of Hallows and Watson as the county's opening pair. On no fewer than twelve occasions did these two open an innings with a three-figure partnership, and four of these stands yielded 200. For Watson it was a season of rare distinction. He scored 300 not out against Surrey, 236 against Sussex, and 223 against Northamptonshire; he passed 100 nine times and, making 1,000 runs more than in 1927, raised his aggregate to 2,403 – a higher figure than either Hallows or Tyldesley reached. Lancashire had five players with an average of over 50 (Tyldesley, Halliday, Watson, Hallows and Iddon), and once again McDonald bagged a huge crop of wickets – 178.

It seemed that Lancashire were set for a prolonged sequence of successes, but although they won the Championship in 1930, Notts. broke their uninterrupted run by becoming Champions in 1929, their first success since 1907.

Under the new regulations every county had to play twenty-eight matches – no more and no less – and while the division of points on the first innings of a drawn game or for a tie remained the same in either instance, the eight points at stake in every match were halved in all cases in which not even a first-innings issue was reached – irrespective of the duration of play. Furthermore, the Championship fixtures were contested under experimental laws which provided for the heightening and widening of the wicket and made it possible for a batsman, even if he had 'snicked' the ball, to be out lbw.

Led by Arthur Carr, this Nottinghamshire side included Larwood and Voce, George Gunn, Arthur and Sam Staples, Fred Barratt, Whysall, Payton, Lilley and Walker. 'Also batted' – that great wit, raconteur, and salt of the earth, Charlie Harris, and Walter Keeton. Their moment of triumph, however, was short lived. Lancashire were back at the top of the table in 1930, with Ernest Tyldesley, Watson, Iddon and Hopwood at the head of the batting, and Richard Tyldesley taking 121 wickets and McDonald taking 104. In this side, captained by Peter Eckersley, the name of Eddie Paynter appears. Paynter later won everlasting fame by rising from his sick-bed in hospital and batting to save England in a Test match in Australia.

Now to 1931 – the beginning of an era, of a Yorkshire era. They were Champions in 1931, 1932 and 1933; they gave way to Lancashire in 1934, were back as Champions in 1935, lost to Derbyshire in 1936, and then took the last three years before the outbreak of the Second World War – 1937, 1938 and 1939. There have been many essays from time to time on 'The Golden Age of Cricket', but who is competent to judge a golden age? Does distance lend enchantment? Were the days of one's youth as enchanting as they seem in retrospect? Are things not what they used to be? They never were, of course. Were the 'nineties a golden age or the 'thirties? What about the 'fifties, when Surrey boasted one of the finest all-round sides in living memory? Yorkshiremen though (and who better to judge their own players) will tell you that the 'thirties was a golden age of Yorkshire cricket.

Now't else matters – seven championships in nine years speaks for itself.'

This period of marked supremacy began in 1931; there was high drama about it. With practically a third of their fixtures fulfilled, Yorkshire had scored 56 points out of a possible 135; they stood eighth in the table. In this situation they took the field at Lord's against Middlesex on 20 June, and won by an innings. Having acquired the taste they then beat Hampshire, Kent, Somerset and Surrey in swift succession, all by an innings.

After a drawn game with Notts. at Sheffield, Yorkshire continued with another run of victories almost as decisive as that which had begun at Lord's. They again won five consecutive matches beating Essex, Nottinghamshire, Glamorgan, Gloucestershire and Somerset, and of these five victories, one was gained by an innings, two by ten wickets, and two – these after declarations – by nine wickets. The first victory of the second sequence placed Yorkshire at the head of affairs and never afterwards was the team in any danger of losing that position. To interrupt what otherwise might well have been a record number of consecutive wins in the Championship, Yorkshire were held to a draw by Lancashire at Sheffield, but they resumed their winning ways by beating Leicestershire, Northamptonshire and Glamorgan in successive engagements. So in fifteen consecutive matches, Yorkshire had won thirteen and drawn two and took 205 points out of a possible 225.

In regaining the Championship after a period of five years Yorkshire owed their success, in the main, to three men. Herbert Sutcliffe, Hedley Verity and Bill Bowes, each showing the skill of a master in a different craft. Herbert Sutcliffe as a batsman, Hedley Verity as a left-arm spinner (a little quicker than most), and Bill Bowes as a fast bowler. Statistically, their achievements can be seen in true perspective. Sutcliffe scored over 2,000 runs at an average of 97·57 (the next best was Percy Holmes, 1,211 runs at 39·06). Verity took 138 wickets at 12·34 and Bowes 109 wickets at 15·29. George Macaulay took 76. Sutcliffe was not just a supreme craftsman, he was an aristocrat in manner and in technique, polished, ice-cool in temperament; his presence could dominate a situation, and invariably did. It could not be said that Sutcliffe as England's opening partner to Jack Hobbs tended to be eclipsed by Hobbs. He was an admirable foil, but as much an integral part as Hobbs himself. You would never try to separate Rawicz and Landauer in terms of individual skill or interpretation, or Laurel and Hardy in humour, or Rogers and Hammerstein in show production. Hobbs and Sutcliffe were just the same; they were not divisible.

Hedley Verity, killed in the Second World War, ranks as one of the greatest left-hand slow bowlers of all time. Was it Cardus who said of him: 'His run to the wicket, so loose and effortless, was feline in its suggestion of silkiness hiding its claws.' In England, alone, in nine and a half seasons, Verity took 1,558 wickets at an average of 13·71 runs – and overall was only 44 short of becoming the first man to take 2,000 wickets in first-class cricket in ten years. He played in forty Test matches and took 144 wickets. He got Bradman out ten times, more often than any other English bowler; he died, at the age of thirty-eight, in a war hospital at Caserta, near Naples, after an operation had been performed to remove a bullet from his lung. His compatriot and close friend in the Yorkshire side, Bill Bowes, heard the news of Verity's death when he himself was in a prisoner-of-war camp. Bowes later visited Hedley Verity's grave. Bowes, still a familiar and well loved figure on the cricket grounds of England, was a magnificent fast bowler who had more than his share of bowling at Bradman.

In 1932 and 1933 Yorkshire retained their command. In 1932 they were under the same leader, F. E. Greenwood, but in 1933, Brian Sellers took over. Sellers has since become an institution in Yorkshire cricket and is a strong disciplinarian and a dynamic leader.

Yorkshire's win in 1932 followed a pattern similar to their late challenge in 1931. Towards the end of May they stood last but one among the seventeen counties. Half-way through June they were seventh, then second and, following one brief spell at the top, they regained the lead at the beginning of August and never looked back. This was a tremendous season for Herbert Sutcliffe.

He hit 2,624 runs for Yorkshire in County Championship matches including an innings of 313, when he and Percy Holmes staged a marathon opening partnership of 555 against Essex at Leyton. Holmes scored 224 not out. This avalanche was followed by a piece of devastating bowling by Hedley Verity, who took 5 for 8, and Essex were shot out for 78. The timetable of this world-record-breaking partnership was as follows: 100 runs in 105 minutes, 200 in 200 minutes, 300 in 275 minutes, 400 in 325 minutes, 500 in 415 minutes and 555 in 445 minutes. Sutcliffe was finally bowled by Eastman, whereupon Yorkshire declared. But perhaps the Essex wicket-keeper will remember this day more than most – he dropped Holmes when he had scored 3! This was the sixty-fifth century opening partnership for Yorkshire by these two wonderful cricketers – Holmes and Sutcliffe.

Maurice Leyland finished with a batting average of 60 and Verity and Bowes were again the principal wicket-takers – Bowes 169; Verity 163.

Yorkshire completed the hat-trick in 1933 with great authority. They were Champions by as early as 18 August. Not even defeat in each of the four remaining engagements could deprive them of the honour. Leyland topped the batting averages for the first time with Mitchell, Sutcliffe and Barber behind him, and George Macaulay joined Verity and Bowes in the 100-wicket class; these three took just under 400 County Championship wickets between them. Lancashire were fifth in the table and did not appear to be the most likely threat to Yorkshire's dominance in 1934 – but they were. There was still one important aspect of Yorkshire's cricket in 1934. A new young player took his place in the side and *Wisden* wrote of him: 'He is the most promising of the younger brigade with a nice style and showed himself master of most of the strokes.' Master of most of the strokes he certainly was. His name was Leonard Hutton. Hutton hit 196 against Worcester on this lovely Worcester ground in the shadows of the cathedral – his first 100 for Yorkshire at the age of seventeen, and very nearly a double-century at that, falling to the wily old bird, Reg Perks, when one more boundary would have made his first-ever century into a double century. Here was a master player in the making, much of him already made.

But 1934 was basically Lancashire's year. Yet how near and yet how far for Sussex again, who had so often challenged for the leadership over the years, but had always been bridesmaid and never the bride. To this day Sussex have never won the Championship. In 1934 they lost their position at the top on 14 August to Lancashire, and that was that. Although Ernest Tyldesley, Iddon, Hopwood, Watson and Paynter were at the head of the Lancashire batting averages, a little lower down was the name of Cyril Washbrook, one day to become a world-class partner to Hutton. Hopwood had a wonderful all-round season – a splendid double, 1,583 runs at an average of 41·65, and 110 wickets at 17·89.

Yorkshire were swiftly back in the hunt. They were Champions again in 1935. During the latter part of June, Derbyshire figured at the top of the table, but early in July they were ousted by Yorkshire, who never afterwards lost the leadership. It was the old firm again – Bowes and Verity (300 wickets between them). Sutcliffe and Barber both had averages in excess of 50.

Friday, 28 August 1936 is written down as the greatest day in the history of Derbyshire cricket. On that day, under the leadership of A. W. Richardson, they became, beyond all shadow of doubt, Champion county. Yorkshire's desperate, if belated, challenge had failed. This was a triumph for great bowling since only three Derbyshire batsmen had an average of above 30 – Stan Worthington, Leslie Townsend and Denis Smith. The red-haired Copson took 140 wickets, and Tommy Mitchell, arch-spinner, who, legend has it, was discovered spinning billiard balls in a working men's club, took 116. Alf Pope was six short of his 100 wickets. Rarely having large totals at their backs, the Derbyshire bowlers were more often than not under pressure, and they rarely failed. Copson's fiery bowling at the beginning of an innings frequently gave Derbyshire the whip hand, and his exceptional nip off the pitch was always a hazard to an opening pair in the process of getting a sight of the ball. Perhaps it was Copson most of all who brought this first success to the cricketers of Derbyshire.

Yorkshire, once again, would brook only minor interference

with their superiority. They were back as Champions in 1937, and in 1938 and 1939 completed another hat-trick. Yorkshire reigned supreme when Hitler's war put an end to the summer game in 1939 – in that fateful September. In 1937 it was touch and go. The issue remained in doubt until the last week in August, when Yorkshire routed Sussex and settled all doubts with a ten-wicket win over Hampshire at Bournemouth. Only one Yorkshire bowler took 100 wickets – Hedley Verity (157) and Hutton topped the batting averages with 55·74 with Sutcliffe, and a new name, Norman Yardley, behind him. In 1938 it was a well merited success in the face of extensive injuries to Yorkshire players; here was full testimony to their resources; six players hit centuries; two others were only three short, and there was also a score of 93. In October of that year, Yorkshire suffered a great loss in the death of Lord Hawke, for so long President and leader of the County Club.

And so to 1939, another Yorkshire success – and war. Middlesex, who had been striving so hard season after season were foiled once again at the last minute. Not until Surrey drew at Lord's on 29 August was it impossible for Middlesex to win the Championship. On that day Yorkshire beat Hampshire, and this gave them an unassailable advantage. Middlesex had been runners-up since 1936. A Middlesex side with the arch-villain of the piece, Jim Sims, spinner, great character, philosopher, as the principal protagonist taking 142 wickets, and with the inseparable 'twins', Compton and Edrich, astride the batting.

Brian Sellers had led Yorkshire to victory five times in seven seasons. This was a prolific season for Hutton; both he and Sutcliffe hit double centuries. Hedley Verity took 165 wickets but this great Yorkshireman was never to bowl again. The sight of him bowling will forever remain in the mind's eye of those who were fascinated by his artistry, beguiling, tantalizing skill, a master craftsman in a skilled and absorbing trade.

After the Second War

The County Championship in these years following the Second World War has undergone almost continuous and radical changes.

Not that this is anything new. It is a fact that Glamorgan, who won the Championship for the first time in 1948, having been admitted to the Competition only in 1921, had seen either the format of the Championship or its point-scoring system undergo no less than eighteen changes in those forty-three years. There have been ten changes since 1946. Except for the period 1953-6, and the last four seasons, the administrators in their wisdom have come up with some little surprise packet or another; some good, some bad, some indifferent. The number of matches played by each county has varied often enough to render a discussion on the subject pointless; it is sufficient to mention the major revisions, such as the limitation of the leg-side field in 1957 (a splendid piece of legislation designed to discourage defensive leg-side bowling); the abolition of the amateur status in 1963 (other sports preferred to hang on to the 'sham' amateur for much longer); the front-foot, no-ball law introduced in 1963 with various amendments since; the immediate registration of one overseas cricketer authorized in November 1967 and the introduction of the present bonus-points system in 1968 (this had been a tremendous success). There have been a number of scares on the painfully controversial subject of 'throwing' in which Tony Lock and Harold Rhodes for instance, were the subject of camera spying (concealed or in full view) as MCC tried to prove their guilt or innocence.

There have been constant debates on the question of covering wickets – to cover or not to cover, that has been the question, with a fair range of alternatives – full covering, no covering, or a mixture of the two. Similar alternatives have been available to the 'front foot' law disciples – either the whole foot must be behind the line, or the foot is allowed to cut the line and so on. There have been minor innovations which have not survived the passage of time such as the limiting of first innings to sixty-five overs in 1966. In all fairness this was an attempt to get more aggression into the game from the start and was merely the forerunner of the present bonus-points system which has worked well, and under which a winning county gets ten points for a win and the teams five each if they tie. There is nothing for a first-innings lead or for victims of a match ruined by weather. In addition to these points for a win, counties receive a bonus point for every 25 runs over 150 scored in the first eighty-five overs of their first innings, and a point for every two wickets taken in those 85 overs if they are fielding. This has created extra effort on the part of the players and fulfilled the aims of the creators.

The result of the cricket itself in these post-war years has been to produce one of the finest sides in Championship history – Surrey, who won the Championship for seven consecutive years from 1952–8, and the almost total domination of the competition by Surrey and Yorkshire. In these twenty-six years, Yorkshire have won eight, and Surrey eight. This apart, only Worcestershire have been able to win in successive seasons, 1964 and 1965, and only Glamorgan of the remaining counties have won more than once – in 1948 and 1969. With two of the years producing Joint-Champions, only Middlesex, Warwickshire, Hampshire and Kent also appear in the Honours list. Nine counties have striven in vain during this period, and five of them, Essex, Leicestershire, Northamptonshire, Somerset and Sussex are still trying to win the County Championship for the first time.

It was in 1952 that Stuart Surridge took over the captaincy of Surrey. He said at the time that no amount of practice could make him a great bowler or a great batsman, but he firmly believed that by devoting time and application to his fielding as a personal example, he would be making a major contribution to Surrey cricket. This he did, and to all intents and purposes he basically altered the whole technique of fielding. His bowlers were accurate enough to allow his close-to-the-wicket fielders to become an aggressive unit in themselves. Crouching on their haunches near enough to a batsman to pick his pocket, they became almost as great a menace to the batsman as the bowler himself. Surridge would stand so close that unless the umpire watched him like a cat watching a mouse, he would have had his foot on the pitch. Sometimes, I am sure he did – and chanced it! His players could scarcely refuse to occupy the highly dangerous position Surridge sometimes asked of them, because they all knew that Surridge would stand there himself – or even closer. Catches win matches

– they certainly did for Surrey; sometimes during these seven golden years their superiority was overwhelming. Two-day finishes were commonplace, but was there anything to match the audacity of Surridge when he once declared with a score of 92 for 3 against Worcestershire – and won by an innings?

The massive strength of this Surrey team for seven years was its bowling, spearheaded by four great Test bowlers – Bedser and Loader to operate with the new ball, and Lock and Laker, spinners supreme, to follow them; the bowlers knew that ninety-nine times out of a hundred the catches would be held. Arthur McIntyre, a Test match wicket-keeper, missed little behind the stumps, and with Peter May as the principal performer, the batting was nearly always good enough to give the bowlers a task that was well within their compass.

Surridge first led out his Surrey side at Lord's in a fixture against the MCC on 3 May 1952 – E. A. Bedser, Fletcher, Constable, Fishlock, Parker, Whittaker, McIntyre, Laker, A. V. Bedser, Surridge and Lock. The two seasoned campaigners from pre-war days, Laurie Fishlock and Jack Parker were to savour the fruits of becoming Champions in this, their last season. It was touch and go. Was it a flash in the pan? Surrey began 1953 by beating Warwickshire in a day – this had not happened there since 1857. It was the forerunner of another Championship despite calls on Surrey players for representative matches. When the main bowlers were on duty elsewhere, Loader (not then capped), McMahon, Surridge, Clark and Eric Bedser carried on the fight. Champions again, Surrey set out to achieve the hat-trick in 1954; their last hat-trick had been in 1890, 1891 and 1892, and now they did it again. Two young players made their mark that season; much was to be heard of them for years to come – Barrington and Stewart.

Some think that the Surrey side of 1955 was the best in its history; if judged by results this may well be true. They won twenty-three of their twenty-eight County Championship matches and although only one batsman had an average of over 40 (May, 41·86), three bowlers took 368 wickets between them – Lock 149 at 12·34, Alec Bedser 117 at 16·92 and Laker 102 at 18·13.

They were desperately pursued by a fine Yorkshire side (Yorkshire were always Surrey's greatest threat during their successful reign), but when they won the Championship for the fourth successive season, Surridge, as leader, equalled a feat only twice previously accomplished under the same leader – Yorkshire (A. B. Sellers) 1937–46, and Nottinghamshire (Alfred Shaw) 1883–6.

In 1956, Surrey again continued to brush aside all threats to their undoubted superiority. They had now become a cricket machine.

This was Surridge's fifth year; he had decided beforehand that it should be his last; he had also decided that he would go out of cricket as the only captain to have led his side to five Championships in the only five seasons in which he was Captain – and once Surridge had decided something, that was it! Of course Surrey won the Championship again, perhaps not quite as decisively as in 1955, but they won it all the same. Yorkshire, for a change, were well behind in seventh place. This year no Surrey batsman had an average as high as 35. Tom Clark was top with 34·86, but still the bowlers bowled on with amazing success. Lock's 117 wickets cost him as little as 10·46 apiece.

So in 1957 Surridge had gone, but Surrey hadn't! Peter May took over the captaincy. Surrey retained their title and successfully defended it again in 1958. *Wisden* commented on the 1957 season:

For the sixth successive year incomparable Surrey carried all before them. Their high skill, ruthless efficiency, matchless team spirit, and appetite for quick runs, left no reasonable doubt that their record run of Championship victories would be extended. Once they had taken the lead theirs was a lonely supremacy, and in the final table they were separated from Northamptonshire, the runners-up, by the wide margin of 94 points. On 16 August they clinched the title, a date which equalled Warwickshire's post-war record, set in 1951, of winning by the earliest date.

And now to 1958; victory again for Surrey, but the last of the seven. The reign of Surrey as the masters of cricket was to end. Yorkshire were back in control in 1959. In fact, in nearly all these post-war years, Yorkshire had been a good side. They had never accomplished what Surrey had done in terms of continuous Championship success, but they had generally been there or thereabouts. They won the first Championship after the war in 1946 – their fourth in succession; they were Joint-Champions in 1949 with Middlesex, they won again in 1959 and 1960, then in 1962 and 1963, and then did the hat-trick in 1966, 1967 and 1968.

It was as difficult for Yorkshire as for any county to pick up the threads again after the long years of war, but, as so often previously, they found ways to overcome every handicap and maintained the position they held in 1939. Under the leadership of Brian Sellers, the team, as in each summer from 1932, played with the zest and determination common to Yorkshire folk; the reason for playing was winning, and they certainly had to go hard to win. Len Hutton was far and away their best batsman with an average of over 50. Ellis Robinson was the leading bowler. Bill Bowes, still recovering from the arduous days spent in a prisoner-of-war camp, took 56 wickets for as little as 13·89. But surely the most remarkable performance was that by Arthur Booth, who was tried in 1931, then went to Northumberland, and now, after some experience in 1945, found a regular place in first-class Championship cricket. Hitherto unwanted because of the incomparable Hedley Verity, Booth took 84 wickets at 11·90 each, and gained his county cap at the age of forty-three; this may well be a record.

This summer of 1946 brought a post-war boom for sport; long years of the desert, or of dangerous convoy work on the high seas, or Royal Air Force raids deep into the heart of the industrial Ruhr, or of hours of tedious waiting, were over. To be able to watch cricket again was a dream come true for many, and despite the wet and cold season the gate receipts for Yorkshire, amounting to £22,793, constituted a record, and over 5,000 members paid £11,741 in subscriptions. Despite exceptionally heavy expenses, particularly towards renovating grounds, and £3,700 entertainments tax, special grants to players were made without disturbing the county's accumulated fund which then stood at £22,180. Times have changed in the following quarter of a century. Few counties have accumulated funds these days; overdrafts are much more common – and frightening.

In 1947 it was Middlesex – 1947, the Vintage Summer; golden sunshine, and Edrich and Compton, their bats mightier than a sword, their aggression as decisive as a rapier. All roads led to Lord's in this wonderful summer whenever word spread that Edrich and Compton were batting. It was not just a question of the runs they made; it was the way they made them; both seemed to possess an unending repertoire of flowing strokes; orthodoxy on the one hand, and an almost impertinent disregard of the principles of correct teaching on the other; improvization. They placed their own artistic interpretation on basic methods. It was a special transcription of cricket orchestrated by Edrich and Compton, and what a symphony it produced.

The Middlesex batting averages for 1947 tell a formidable story. Compton 96·80, Edrich 77·82, Robertson 65·11, Fairbairn 44·00 and Brown 40·69, and more comforting, too, for the devotees of the subtle craft of slow bowling, it was the two spinners, Jack Young and Jim Sims who took most wickets. So Middlesex, after being runners-up on five successive occasions, were now Champions – worthy reward for Walter Robins in his last year as Captain. In view of the type of cricket they had played, no one (not even in Hampshire or Huddersfield) begrudged them their success.

The year 1948 was a significant one for Wales. Glamorgan, the County Championship Juniors – their career had begun only in 1921 – became Champions for the first time. Once again as they had done with Maurice Turnbull they had a leader who was a rugby International; this time it was Wilf Wooller, one of the finest centres ever to wear the red jersey of Wales. Wooller exerted the same sort of flair into his cricket as he injected into his rugby; he was not always popular with his opponents for one reason or another, but he was popular enough in the Principality on the afternoon of Tuesday, 24 August 1948 when Glamorgan were home and dry as Champions. How fitting that it was J. C. Clay, a member of the original side which entered the Championship in 1921, who played a leading part that day in the victory over Hampshire at Bournemouth. This event ensured them the honours after an exciting race with Surrey, Yorkshire and Derbyshire. John Clay was then aged 51; he took 9 for 79 in this game, and in the preceding game against Surrey he had taken 10 for 66. This was truly a victory out of the blue. No one at the beginning of the season could possibly have considered Glamorgan as potential Champions; all the sweeter when victory came. Another rugby player, Willie Jones, headed the batting, with Emrys Davies, a seasoned campaigner just behind him, and Gilbert Parkhouse, a fine player in the making, third. It was a splendid bowling year for Len Muncer, who had emigrated from Middlesex to Glamorgan; he took 139 wickets, almost double that of anyone else.

In the next two seasons the Championship was not won outright, Middlesex and Yorkshire, and then Surrey and Lancashire sharing the spoils, but in 1951, before Surrey's ruthless machine was set in motion, Warwickshire became Champions, and they set up one record in doing so. In making the title theirs, they used only thirteen players, the last two (making fifteen in all) did not appear until the title was certain. It is interesting that only two of the twelve players forming the backbone of the side were actually born within the county borders – not that this worried the Warwickshire supporters who were hailing their heroes as Champions for the first time since 1911. Warwickshire had been beaten only twice in all matches during the season. Their batting was consistent if not spectacular. Dick Spooner and Tom Dollery, followed by Ray Hitchcock, Fred Gardner and Jimmy Ord, were at the top of the batting averages, the last three all having an average of 31. In bowling the important ingredients were the spin and guile of Eric Hollies and the pace of Charlie Grove, with Tom Pritchard, a New Zealander, close on their heels. Warwickshire set another record. They became the first county to win a Championship with a professional Captain and an all-professional team. They called on only one amateur, E. B. Lewis, a wicket-keeper, and he appeared in only one Championship match. Tom Dollery, the first professional Captain, had proved Warwickshire's point. Many other counties were to follow the example in due course.

During the next twelve seasons, only one county was able to prevent the total domination of Surrey and Yorkshire, and that was Hampshire in 1961. When Yorkshire brought Surrey's marked superiority to an end in 1959, they won, as if to prove their point, in 1960 as well. Their victory in 1959 had no air of the inevitable about it, as many of their previous successes had done. Yorkshire surprised even their most ardent supporters: In the previous season they had finished as low as eleventh in the table. Moreover, this was expected to be a season of transition with the side still recovering from the 'Wardle Affair'. Johnny Wardle had left the county in unhappy circumstances which to an extent had produced divided loyalties within the county. Sellers, now the Club Chairman, had predicted that it would take three years for Yorkshire once again to rise to the top. Certainly, this side was nothing like as strong as many of its great predecessors, but it still had the old fighting spirit, not the least factor in which was that shown when Yorkshire needed a victory at Hove on 29, 31 August and 1 September to make sure of the title. They were set to get 215 to win in one and three-quarter hours. If the author of a schoolboy thriller had ended his story with Yorkshire getting the runs, he would have been accused of over-exaggeration, yet from the first moment Yorkshire made such an onslaught that the runs were hit off in a blaze of glory with seven minutes to spare. The hero was Brian Stott, the left-handed opening batsman. He hit 13 of the 15 obtained off the first over, and the 50 appeared in twenty minutes; the 100 took forty-three minutes. Stott batted for eighty-six minutes to score 96, and his principal aide, Doug Padgett, stayed just over an hour while 141 were scored. Padgett hit 79.

The season was a personal triumph for Ronnie Burnet, who had taken over the leadership in 1958 at one of the most difficult times in the club's history. He was then thirty-nine, had never played first-class cricket, and was obviously never going to be a top-class batsman. But he had done well in building a promising young second eleven, and the Yorkshire Committee placed their faith in him to remould the county eleven. He had to live down the accusation that his own form was weakening the side, but his personality emerged above his multifarious problems to stamp him clearly as a leader of some merit. After this great success he gave up to make way for a younger man. It might perhaps have added to his determination when he lost the toss on no less than twenty occasions. Ray Illingworth had a splendid season doing the double in all matches, Trueman led the bowling with 92 wickets for Yorkshire at 18·60, and Padgett, Illingworth and Bolus topped the batting. Illingworth's performance is especially interesting. Only when he became Captain of England in 1970 did the public think of him seriously as a batsman, yet as far back as 1959 he scored 1,000 runs for Yorkshire with a batting average of 43·16.

In 1960 Yorkshire appointed a professional captain for the first time – Vic Wilson, the Malton farmer. His appointment was a success and Yorkshire again won the Championship, this time without a final flourish of aggression; they won easily, 32 points clear of Lancashire. Jimmy Binks had a memorable summer and became the first Yorkshire wicket-keeper to claim 100 victims in a season. Trueman had a magnificent season taking 132 wickets at 12·79, Padgett again topped the batting averages, and Close, just behind him, also took 66 wickets.

So to 1961 and a new winner. Hampshire, for the first time in their history, won the Championship after a three-cornered struggle with Yorkshire and Middlesex in which the lead frequently changed hands. Hampshire eventually went into first place on 1 August and were not caught, although they rarely had much in hand. It looked as though the Hampshire–Yorkshire match at Bournemouth would be the Championship decider, but the title went to Hampshire in the match before when they beat Derbyshire, and Yorkshire could only draw with Warwickshire. As it happened, Yorkshire won at Bournemouth (this may well have been an anti-climax for Hampshire), but against that they lost twice to Middlesex. Hampshire, who had finished runners-up in 1958 – the first season in which Colin Ingleby-Mackenzie captained the side – dropped to eighth and twelfth in succeeding summers, and gave precious little indication that 1961 would be the greatest year in the club's history.

What satisfaction for their President, Harry Altham, who devoted a lifetime (and a long one at that) to the game of cricket, as player, administrator, and constant admirer of all that was good in the game. There was much satisfaction, too, for their Secretary, Desmond Eagar, who, like Altham, has contributed so much to the game of cricket. On the field of play, Ingleby-Mackenzie's leadership, allied to his humour (he once stated on being asked what conditions he imposed on his players' habits off the field, that he insisted on their being in bed before breakfast!) made Hampshire a happy side. Ingleby-Mackenzie's tactical ability speaks for itself; of Hampshire's nineteen victories in the Championship, ten were the direct result of declarations in their third innings, and only two counties, Northamptonshire and Middlesex, managed to escape defeat – both drawn – after being set a task. The Captain was fortunate in having such a reliable side with which to gamble. The batting, with the exception of Roy Marshall, who was absolutely brilliant, was never spectacular, but consistent; somebody always scored runs when the others failed. Seven players hit centuries – Marshall (including the first double-century of his career and only the second double-century for Hampshire since the war), Henry Horton, Jimmy Gray, Peter Sainsbury, Mike Barnard, Ingleby-Mackenzie and Danny Livingstone. The bowling was spearheaded by the immaculate Derek Shackleton; 'Shack', the man with the ability to pitch on a sixpence from sunrise to sunset – and bowl all that time if necessary! His was a nagging, tantalizing, irritating length for batsmen to cope with; like a mechanical toy, you just wound him up at the start of a day's play and he would keep going until the mechanism ran down. Bowling Hampshire to victory with Shackleton was David White, better known to cricketers, affectionately at that, as 'Butch', a fast bowler who put everything into his performance. It was surprising at times that the follow-through didn't take him to the other end of the pitch with the ball, and Butch arriving first! This pair of marauders took 270 wickets between them in 1961, a season to remember.

For the next seven years, the Championship honours were the prerogative of only two counties – Yorkshire and, for the first time in their history, Worcestershire, who confirmed their performance by winning again the next season. Yorkshire won in 1962 and 1963, Worcester intervened in 1964 and 1965, and

The all-powerful county elevens

Yorkshire 1938. *Standing:* B. Heyhurst, W. Barber, C. Turner, A. Mitchell, L. Hutton, H. Verity, W. E. Bowes, T. F. Smailes, W. Ringrose, A. Johnson. *Seated:* A. Wood, H. Sutcliffe, A. B. Sellers (Captain), P. A. Gibb, M. Leyland

Surrey 1955. *Standing:* A. Sandham (Coach), R. C. E. Pratt, D. F. Cox, P. J. Loader, T. H. Clark, G. A. R. Lock, D. G. W. Fletcher, K. F. Barrington, M. D. Willett, A. J. Tait (Masseur), B. Constable. *Seated:* M. J. Stewart, E. A. Bedser, A. J. McIntyre, P. B. H. May, W. S. Surridge (Captain), A. V. Bedser, J. C. Laker

The legendary
partnerships

Hobbs and Sutcliffe

Edrich and Compton

Touring teams to England

The Australians 1934. *Standing:* W. C. Bull (Treasurer), A. G. Chipperfield, E. H. Bromley, W. J. O'Reilly, H. Bushby (Manager), H. I. Ebeling, T. W. Wall, L. O'B. Fleetwood-Smith, S. J. McCabe, W. Ferguson (Scorer). *Seated:* C. V. Grimmett, L. S. Darling, D. G. Bradman, W. M. Woodfull (Captain), A. F. Kippax, W. H. Ponsford, W. A. Brown. *On ground:* B. A. Barnett, W. A. Oldfield

The Indians 1946 – the first season after World War II *Standing:* P. Gupta, M.B.E. (Manager), V. S. Hazare, V. Mankad, Abdul Hafeez (later known as A. H. Kardar), R. S. Modi, S. W. Sohoni, R. B. Nimbalkar, S. G. Shinde, W. Ferguson (Scorer). *Seated:* S. Bannerjee, Mushtaq Ali, V. M. Merchant, Nawab of Pataudi (Captain), L. Amarnath, D. D. Hindlekar, C. S. Nayudu. *On ground:* Gul Mahomed, C. T. Sarwate

Touring teams to England

The New Zealanders 1949. *Standing:* V. J. Scott, T. B. Burtt, F. L. H. Mooney, J. A. Hayes, G. O. Rabone, H. B. Cave, J. R. Reid, C. C. Burke, F. B. Smith, G. F. Cresswell. *Seated:* M. P. Donnelly, W. M. Wallace, W. A. Hadlee (Captain), J. A. Cowie, B. Sutcliffe

The great West Indies side in 1950. *Standing:* W. Ferguson (Scorer), S. Ramadhin, K. B. Trestrail, A. L. Valentine, L. R. Pierre, H. H. Johnson, C. L. Walcott, A. F. Rae, R. E. Marshall, C. B. Williams. *Seated:* R. J. Christiani, E. D. Weekes, G. E. Gomez, J. M. Kidney (Manager), J. D. Goddard (Captain), J. B. Stollmeyer, P. E. Jones, F. M. Worrell.

then Yorkshire came back with a bang to bring off another hat-trick in 1966, 1967 and 1968. Just two and a half hours remained of the 1962 county season when Yorkshire won the title by beating Glamorgan at Harrogate. This climax was dramatic. Worcestershire had completed their programme and were ten points ahead of Yorkshire. Yorkshire made certain of four points on the first day, but rain washed out the proceedings on the second, so the third day was the all-important one, with the weather likely to play a more vital part than that of any of the cricketers.

Glamorgan had been put in on a drying pitch, and were bowled out by Don Wilson for 65. Wilson, with his left-arm spin, took 6 for 24, then the best figures of his career. Ken Taylor fought a lone fight when Yorkshire batted. He hit 67 out of a total of 101; without him, this could have been a rout. Glamorgan were 13 without loss at the end of the day, 18 behind. Then the rain came; the Yorkshire players spent the next day in mental anguish; not a ball was bowled, but the weather gods were kind to them on the third day; once again Glamorgan's batting broke down in the face of Yorkshire's spin attack and they were all out for 101. Yorkshire scored the prescribed number for victory for the loss of three wickets. John Hampshire was not out 24, and Brian Stott, the hero of Hove, was also in at the death, but there were no hero's acclamations for him this time; his was a modest 9 not out. For Vic Wilson it was the end of his first-class career in triumph.

Yorkshire owed much in this season to Phil Sharpe. During the early weeks when Yorkshire were struggling he often held the side together, and, finishing with over 1,800 runs in the Championship, he also took 71 catches – a new record for a Yorkshire player, beating the 70 held by Tunnicliffe in 1901. Illingworth, too, played a principal role in Yorkshire's success, taking 102 wickets, and being second to Trueman, who took 106. The spin of Wilson was much in evidence, too. It was right and proper that Yorkshire should again win the Championship in 1963. This was their centenary year. Four hundred people celebrated the occasion in the Cutlers' Hall at Sheffield on 24 January, and the team celebrated, under their new Captain, Brian Close, by winning the Championship with twenty points to spare over Glamorgan. Yet it was a triumph over adversity. Injuries which kept Illingworth, Padgett, Stott and Taylor out of the side for several matches, proved a big handicap, and with Close, Sharpe and Trueman often required by England, the side had to lean heavily on lesser known members. This was a Boycott season. Geoff Boycott, who began the season as a middle-order batsman, later opened the innings. He finished second in the national first-class batting averages, averaged 46·64 for Yorkshire and hit three centuries, including one in each of the 'Roses' matches at Sheffield and Manchester. That has always been the real test of a Yorkshireman – what he can do against Lancashire!

The summer of 1964 produced yet another surprising swing of the pendulum with Worcestershire cricket. In 1962 they all but won the Championship. Rain on the last day of that Yorkshire match at Harrogate would have brought the Championship to Worcester. In 1963 they fell to fourteenth place in the table. In 1964 they picked themselves up from the floor to win the Championship. This was the real Worcestershire. They proved it was by winning again in 1965. Furthermore, their success in 1964 was by the emphatic margin of 41 points, the biggest difference between first and second places since 1957 when Surrey had 94 points to spare.

It was at Worcester – delightful Worcester, with the cathedral in all its majesty keeping vigil over the green turf on this most famous ground, on the sunny afternoon of 25 August 1964 that champagne corks popped to celebrate success after sixty-five years of striving for the top, just a few months before the club became 100 years old. Don Kenyon, a professional Captain in the mould of Tom Dollery, set the example of leadership at the top.

Tom Graveney, born at Riding Mill in Northumberland, but bred as a cricketer in Gloucestershire, had left following disagreement and joined Worcestershire in 1961. In this Championship year for Worcestershire his batting burgeoned into its peak; he scored 2,271 runs for Worcestershire at an average of 55·39; Ron Headley, son of the famous West Indian, George Headley, and Kenyon himself were second and third to Graveney, but the bowlers took the lion's share in the proceedings. These were John Flavell and Len Coldwell, names in Worcestershire that had the same ring about them as Statham and Trueman, or Jackson and Gladwin. Norman Gifford all but spun himself to 100 wickets, and Jim Standen, footballing goalkeeper, took 52 wickets at as low a cost as 14·42. But fielding, too, can be a devastating weapon. Dick Richardson and Ron Headley with 51 and 50 catches respectively led the country in this field, and Roy Booth was the leading wicket-keeper. Booth's final figures of 91 catches and 9 stumpings left him 22 victims ahead of the next best, Arnold Long of Surrey, and he surpassed Hugo Yarnold's record for Worcestershire of 709 dismissals.

Just as Yorkshire had done, Worcestershire celebrated their centenary by winning the Championship in 1965; this time it was a rare tussle, and as late as 23 July it looked a forlorn hope for Worcester. They were ninth in the table and appeared to be well out of the hunt, but a transformation followed. They won ten of their last eleven matches, and it was not until 31 August that they headed the table for the first time during the season. It was the right time to be at the top! In 1964 Basil d'Oliveira, a Cape coloured cricketer, who had been playing for Middleton in the Central Lancashire League for four seasons, had joined Worcester and became eligible for County Championship matches in 1965. His performance was a revelation. He even beat Graveney in the number of hundreds, hitting five in Championship cricket to Graveney's four and, with another against Cambridge University, he was second only to Edrich of Surrey in the whole country in the matter of centuries. He also took 99 off Warwickshire and played six other innings of over 50. The part that Basil d'Oliveira was to play in world cricketing affairs was to unfold some four years later. Graveney, too, had another fine season for Worcester in this second Championship year, and Flavell once again bowled magnificently, taking 132 wickets at an average of under 15 each. So Don Kenyon now had two Championships under his belt.

In 1966 Worcestershire were poised for a hat-trick, but it was not to be. Instead, the auld enemy came back and did a hat-trick for themselves. Yorkshire were Champions in 1966, 1967 and

1968. In 1966 there was another close shave and a complete swing of fortunes. Yorkshire looked such a certainty at one time that the Championship was described as a one-horse race. But then Worcester came with a late run and it was all left to the last day of the last game. The final act took place at Worcester, where John Snow and Tony Buss of Sussex took 18 wickets between them to bring victory to Sussex and disastrous defeat for Worcester. While all this was going on, Yorkshire, at Harrogate, took a firm grip of their last game with Kent, and despite Derek Underwood's 11 wickets, Yorkshire won by 25 runs. The cardinal factor here was Wilson's second hat-trick of the season. Boycott again topped the batting averages, and this time, three Yorkshire bowlers, Trueman and Wilson, took over 100 wickets, and they were joined by Tony Nicholson, born in Dewsbury, a former policeman in Rhodesia. Illingworth was only four wickets short of his 100 for Yorkshire; four bowlers taking 100 wickets for their county in the same season would have been something of a rarity.

Once more, in 1967, the Championship decider came on the last day of the season. Yorkshire were home in the end by ten points; they thrashed Gloucestershire by an innings in two days, Illingworth taking 14 wickets for 64 in the match. Boycott, once again, was the principal batsman with an average of practically 50; five batsmen had averages in the thirties – Close, Sharpe, Illingworth, Hampshire and Padgett, but Nicholson was the only bowler to take 100 wickets.

In 1968, when Yorkshire completed another hat-trick, there were portents of things to come. Kent were second for the second year in succession (they were to win the Championship in 1970), and Glamorgan made a spectacular rise in the table (they were to win the Championship in 1969). Yorkshire's margin of success this time was 14 points. It was Boycott, as usual, who was top of the class in batting; this time he had an average of 77·23. Again there was a wide gap between Boycott and the others in the thirties; but it was a triumphant year for Yorkshire's spin, Illingworth and Wilson each taking over 100 wickets. The hat-trick of successes reflects immense credit on the leadership of Brian Close, a cricketer of high spirit, of tremendous courage, and possessing an inbred flair for facing tactical situations. It was one of the game's major tragedies that he had to leave Yorkshire. Two other famous Yorkshiremen to leave had been Wardle and Illingworth. It was a great pity this bountiful talent was allowed (whatever the reason) to migrate to other fields. Illingworth, after his departure, was elevated to the cricket peerage – he became Captain of England, and a highly successful one at that.

For the moment, at any rate, that was the end of Yorkshire's successes – twenty-nine times Champions, a proud record. In 1969 it was Wales' turn again, Glamorgan taking their second Championship. Welshmen say they won it because they were not rated, outside Wales. In the valleys, they were always regarded as being in with a chance. Glamorgan did not have to rely on one or two outstanding players, for they had several, and only thirteen players appeared in Championship matches. There were six bowlers – Malcolm Nash, David Williams, Don Shepherd, Peter Walker, Tony Cordle and 'Ossie' Wheatley. In the field they had a fine close-to-the-wicket squad: Majid Jahanghir (son of Jahanghir Khan, pre-war Cambridge Blue and Indian Test cricketer who achieved fame by killing a sparrow in flight whilst batting at Lord's, the sparrow in question now being a museum piece on view at Lord's), Bryan Davis, Roger Davis, Walker and Cordle, with Eifion Jones an extremely effective wicket-keeper. The success of the batting can be attributed to the two overseas players, Majid and Bryan Davis (Trinidad), the form of Tony Lewis, the Captain (yet another rugby player to lead Glamorgan), and the good starts provided by Roger Davis and Alan Jones. Glamorgan's lead in the end was 31 points over Gloucestershire; Yorkshire, three times Champions in the previous three seasons were unbelievably thirteenth.

History repeated itself yet again in 1970. Still another county won the Championship in its centenary year; this time it was Kent. The belief in any quarter that the other sixteen counties arrange for a county enjoying its centenary to cap it with a Championship victory can be firmly discounted; cricket, by its very nature, throws up coincidences time and time again. Kent's victory was one of the most stimulating in County Championship history. On the first day of July, Kent were bottom of the table. Bookmakers would have offered any odds you liked to name against their winning the Championship, but even bookmakers are wrong sometimes. Kent won despite their loss of most of their leading players at various stages of the season: Colin Cowdrey, Mike Denness, Brian Luckhurst, Alan Knott and Derek Underwood all answering England's call. Luckhurst and Knott played in all five Tests for England against the Rest of the World, and Cowdrey in the last four, after he had recovered from the Achilles tendon injury which struck him down in 1969 and necessitated an operation. In addition, Norman Graham, a bowler on whom Kent pinned great hopes, suffered trouble with his feet and missed half the matches.

Few county sides could have overcome such a drain on their players. Kent took it in their stride, and when all the best players were back at the conclusion of the series, everybody put his shoulder to the wheel and all opposition was brushed aside. Two overseas players, John Shepherd from Barbados, and Asif Iqbal (Pakistan), held the fort with some dynamic performances when the others were away – and when they were there, too. Kent won final victory at the Oval and shortly after they were Champions, the Prime Minister, the Rt Hon. Edward Heath, arrived at the Oval to give their success Cabinet blessing. Mr Heath has always been a great enthusiast for Kent cricket. His election to power and Kent's win in the same year was a double event of great magnitude for him. The team was photographed with the gas holder as a background, but with garlands of hops at their feet. They led the cricket world for the first time since 1913; Cowdrey had achieved a dream. Kent cricket had been his life.

The County Championship in 1971 had a finish as exciting as in 1970. It was not decided until 13 September at Southampton. The new Champions – the old Champions of the 'fifties – were Surrey. They had emerged again after lean years, a personal triumph for their Captain, Micky Stewart, a member of the great team, whose life and soul had been put into winning again for Surrey, and who had announced his retirement as Captain before this success was achieved (although he intended to carry on playing). Surrey cricketers, like Arsenal footballers, had lived for years with the shadow of their great teams of the past hanging over them; it was hard to live down, but in 1971, both did. The new Surrey side playing in the vital Championship match against Hampshire in the Indian summer of mid-September 1971, was: M. J. Stewart (Captain), J. H. Edrich, G. R. J. Roope (surely an England player in the making), Younis Ahmed, S. J. Storey, Intikham Alam, P. I. Pocock, D. R. Owen-Thomas, A. Long, R. G. D. Willis and C. G. Arnold. Three other players, M. J. Edwards, R. D. Jackman and R. M. Lewis had made their contributions to this Championship, Edwards having a particularly unlucky season with injuries. So Surrey at last are back in business. The golden years again? Who knows?

And yet, in one respect, the summer of 1971 did not belong to any single Surrey player. It belonged, instead, to Geoffrey Boycott, as much a part of Yorkshire as the grey stone walls and the talk of Hirst and Rhodes. Boycott, in his vintage summer, became the first Englishman to record an average of over 100 in an English season. In 30 innings' he hit 2403 runs and 13 centuries which produced an average of 100·12. Boycott, a remarkable cricketer – a technological cricketer – bred in a computer age, with a computer ideology.

3 Test Cricket

Australia

It was warm and sunny in Melbourne on 15 March 1877 when Charles Bannerman took guard and prepared to receive the first ball from Alfred Shaw in what has come to be regarded as the first Test Match – the first in a long line of two hundred and nine Tests between England and Australia, of which England has won 68, Australia 80, and 61 have been drawn. Bannerman did not commit his name to history purely because he scored the first run in a Test match – he happened to make 165. Whether or not contemporary historians will fall out over the question of this being the first recognized Test Match is quite immaterial; what cannot be disputed is that this was an England eleven very much below full strength. W. G. Grace was missing to begin with. These early Australian tours were organized by private individuals, and until the MCC took over the management of official touring teams in 1903–4, the sides were never fully representative. In England, the situation was rather different, since the team was chosen by the authority upon whose ground the match was to be played, but even then there was an understandable bias towards that county's own players, and, moreover, there was no continuity of selection.

Australia, in spite of being the home side, had considerable difficulty in selecting a side for this first Test as Evans, Allen and Spofforth all declined to play for various reasons, the latter stating categorically that the absence of Murdoch to keep wicket was his reason for refusing to play. It was, essentially, Bannerman's match. He scored 165 before retiring hurt after receiving a blow on the hand, and a collection to mark this feat produced a pound a run. Australia, 245 and 104, beat England by 45 runs (196 and 108). The contestants in this historic match were;

Australia: C. Bannerman, N. Thompson, T. Horan, D. Gregory, B. B. Cooper, W. Midwinter, E. Gregory, J. M. Blackham, T. W. Garrett, T. Kendall, J. Hodges.
England: H. Jupp, J. Selby, H. Charlwood, G. Ulyett, A. Greenwood, T. Armitage, Alfred Shaw, T. Emmett, A. Hill, James Lillywhite, J. Southerton.

Few detailed accounts of the match have been preserved. *Scores and Biographies* had very little to say on the matter, but what it did say was to the point: 'The defeat of England must candidly be attributed to fatigue, owing principally to the distance they had to travel to each match, to sickness, and to high living. England never were fresh in any of their engagements, and, of course, had not near their best Eleven.'

Best eleven or not, England were obliged to field the same team for the second Test, whereas Australia were strengthened. Murdoch was selected to play this time, so Spofforth took his place alongside him. England, incidentally, were without their wicket-keeper, Pooley, for both these matches, as they had been compelled to leave him in New Zealand after Pooley had become involved in a little contretemps with a gentleman named Ralph Donkin, which culminated in a brush with the law. At least it seems that in 1877 England were sensible enough to go to New Zealand first on a tour of Australasia, instead of as nowadays, when an exhausted team arrives on New Zealand soil after a long and arduous programme in Australia. It seems that, having eliminated their high living, the England players were fresh for this second Test and won by four wickets. So it was honours even; the battle with the real enemy was on!

Both these Tests were of four days duration, and in the second (also at Melbourne), 7,000 people attended on the first day, 3,000 on the second and third, and 2,000 on the fourth.

Lord Harris's side lost the only Test played in 1878-9, but no Test match was originally arranged for the 1880 Australian team to England. In fact the tour was so badly organized that they had to advertise for matches. They played very few first-class games, but did so well that at the end of the season a Test was hurriedly arranged for the Oval. Lord Harris led the England

F

team to its first victory over Australia on English soil. The Surrey authorities chose the England team which, for the first time, was the strongest England could muster. The three brothers Grace all played – W. G., E. M. and G. F.; tragically, G.F. died within a month as the result of a chill. With an innings of 152, W. G. scored the first Test 100 for England, but was still not top scorer of the match, which England won by five wickets. Murdoch carried his bat in Australia's second innings for a valiant 153, when Australia had followed on 271 runs behind. Alfred Shaw took a side to Australia in 1881–2 and played four Test matches, two being lost and two left drawn. After this tour all Test matches in Australia were played to a finish, and it was not until the re-introduction of time-limit matches in 1946-7 that another Test match in Australia resulted in a draw.

And so to 1882, and the now famous match at the Oval. Australia were toppled out in their first innings for 63, and when England set out to make 85 to win in their last innings, it looked a foregone conclusion. But cricket, they say, is a funny game! England were bowled out for 77, the great Spofforth taking 7 for 44. On the following day, the *Sporting Times* produced its now legendary obituary –

IN AFFECTIONATE REMEMBRANCE
OF
ENGLISH CRICKET
WHICH DIED AT THE OVAL, 29th AUGUST, 1882,
DEEPLY LAMENTED BY A LARGE CIRCLE OF
SORROWING FRIENDS AND ACQUAINTANCES.
R.I.P.
N.B. – THE BODY WILL BE CREMATED AND THE
ASHES TAKEN TO AUSTRALIA

In the following winter (1882–3) the Hon. Ivo Bligh took a team to Australia and four Test matches were played. Australia won the first match by nine wickets, but England won the next two and so secured the rubber. At the end of the third match some ladies burnt a bail, sealed the Ashes in an urn, and presented it to the England captain, the Hon. Ivo Bligh, later Earl Darnley. The urn was his private property until his death in 1927, but in his will it was bequeathed to the MCC, and it now rests in the museum at Lord's. It never leaves the museum, irrespective of who technically holds the Ashes. In 1971 the wisdom of preserving this piece of tradition has been questioned, since any team holding the Ashes only has to draw a series to retain them, and this could (and does!) lead to defensive attitudes on the part of captains. But in a fast changing world where values and standards seem to depreciate rather rapidly, is there not some merit in holding on to something from other days, for surely 'The Fight for the Ashes' has produced more magical moments through its twisting and winding paths of fortune and anguish than any other sporting endeavour. Let us cherish those Australian ladies for what they did nearly ninety years ago.

It is fascinating how often England met Australia throughout the 'eighties and 'nineties, through the turn of the century, and up until the outbreak of the First World War. It seemed almost like non-stop traffic between the two countries. The next Australian team to visit England arrived in 1884, and for the first time a series of three Test matches was arranged, although some years were to pass before the word 'Test' became an integral part of the proceedings. The tourists brought nine of the victorious side of 1882, while W. E. Midwinter was again a member of an Australian team. Midwinter was now approaching the sunset of a curious switch-back career. He was born in Gloucestershire, but played his early cricket in Australia. He returned to England to play for the county of his birth in 1877, but joined the 1878 Australians on their arrival in England, apparently to the utter displeasure of W. G. Grace, who later in the tour gave vent to his feelings in a tangible form and lured (or kidnapped!) Midwinter back to the ranks of Gloucestershire, where Grace considered he belonged. In 1881-2, Midwinter was off on another cricket tour, but this time he was in the England party on the way to Australia; then, in 1884, he had switched to Australia again. Never before, or since, has there been such an international case of hunting with the hounds and running with the hare.

An England team under Arthur Shrewsbury arrived in Australia even before the 1884 Australians to England had reached home. This trip was followed by another in 1886-7, also led by Shrewsbury, and two teams went in 1887-8. What an extraordinary state of affairs this was, to send two teams. *Wisden* commented:

> Two English teams visited Australia in the season of 1887-8 but it is certain that such a piece of folly will never be perpetrated again. Having regard to the fact that eleven-a-side matches are only practicable at Melbourne, Sydney, and Adelaide, it was clear from the first that two combinations would not be able to pay their way, and though we do not know the exact result of Shaw, Shrewsbury and Lillywhite's venture, the Melbourne Club frankly admitted a heavy loss over Mr Vernon's team. Wherever the blame lay, the effect was to throw a complete damper on the visits of English cricketers to the Colonies.

It appeared that there was no animosity between the two sides, however, since they joined forces to play a match against Australia, and won it.

It was four years before another English side set foot on Australian soil, this time under the leadership of the Great Man himself, 'W.G.' Meantime, an Australian side had arrived in Manchester for a Test in the summer of 1890 and received its first bitter taste of what Manchester can conjure up in the way of weather. Not a ball was bowled! Grace's tour to Australia was a vital one. The 1884-5, 1886-7 and 1887-8 English teams had lowered cricketing morale in Australia, while the records of Australia's 1888 and 1890 teams did little to inspire support. Australian cricket, therefore, was at the crossroads; further disaster could have impaired its survival. Thankfully, for the future of Australian cricket, they finished top dogs in this series against Grace's team winning two Tests against England's one. The Australian visit to England in 1893, when England won one Test and two were drawn, threw up one of the most extraordinary cricket matches in the game's history, as a result of an incomprehensible flaw in the law concerning declarations, and more incomprehensible still, it was another seven years before it was amended. The wheels of authority grind slowly! Sadly, this has been true of cricket administration for generations.

What happened was this. The Australians, playing Oxford and Cambridge Universities Past and Present on the United Services' Ground at Portsmouth, reached a score of 346 for 4 on the first day, but the law covering declarations, which had been put into effect in 1889, gave authorization to the batting side to declare its innings closed only on the last day of a match. This left the Australians with two options, either to throw their wickets away in order to hasten the end of the innings, or to bat on. Since it has always gone (and always will) very much against the grain for an Australian gladly to throw his wicket away, the instructions given were 'bat on'; this was duly carried out, throughout the whole of the second day. When it came to the third day the Australians decided that there was no possible chance of forcing victory, and that the match to all intents and purposes was dead anyway, so they just carried on batting. They finally amassed a huge total of 843, but still found time to bowl the Universities out for 191 (Ranjitsinhji 44), and the Universities were 82–1 at the close of a long day! All ten University players (bar the wicket-keeper) bowled, and Bainbridge had the remarkably fine analysis of 3 for 122. Berkeley toiled for sixty overs without a wicket, but the gods finally took pity on him and with the second ball of his sixty-first over he bowled Giffen, Australia's No. 10, who had run up a useful little 62! In total, 244 overs were bowled against the formidable visitors. Work began immediately on revising the law to prevent such a farce again; seven years later it was put into effect!

With a pioneer band of cricketers in the West Indies in 1894–5 and with Grace, F. S. Jackson and W. Gunn missing, A. E. Stoddart took a team to Australia, and despite a disastrous start when Australia opened the proceedings with a score of 586 at Sydney, won the series by three matches to two. The Australians were back in England in 1896 to maintain the merry-go-round in perpetual motion. This three-match series went to England 2–1. In 1897–8 Stoddart was back leading his men in Australia, though perhaps 'leading' was an ill-chosen word in the circumstances.

England took the biggest hiding it had been our displeasure to incur. Australia won four games out of five. It was an unhappy tour for Stoddart. An attack of influenza at the outset of the tour, and the shock caused by the news of his mother's death, seriously affected his cricket, and worse still, he complained bitterly of the barracking indulged in by sections of the crowds. On the other hand, the financial success was immense. The Test matches drew record crowds, and the performance of the Australian cricketers was eagerly acclaimed by their supporters. Above all the others in batting stood out the two left-handers, Clem Hill and Joe Darling, while in a group of fine bowlers, Noble shone conspicuously. There was one interesting footnote to this tour: James Phillips accompanied the team throughout the whole tour as umpire, and caused a great sensation by twice no-balling the South Australian bowler, Jones, for throwing. Phillips later came to England and called Mold of Lancashire for throwing in 1906. This action had most to do with wiping out throwing when it seemed likely to infest cricket.

Australia were to repeat this four-to-one margin of victory on the very next England tour to Australia in 1901–2 under Archie MacLaren. By now a Board of Control had been formed to administer Test matches between England and Australia in England, and a decision had been taken to appoint a Selection Committee each season, who would be responsible for choosing the teams for all five Test matches, it having been agreed that five Test matches should be played. The first selectors appointed for the 1899 series were Lord Hawke, as Chairman, W. G. Grace and H. W. Bainbridge; the last-named, of course, had seen the Australians at close quarters for a long time when he had stood in the field for three days at Portsmouth in 1893!

Before MacLaren's side left for Australia in the autumn of 1901, C. B. Fry, probably the greatest all-rounder of his, or any other, generation, set up a new record by scoring six centuries in consecutive innings – a record equalled by Bradman in 1938–9, but never surpassed. Fry was an astonishing man. He was a brilliant scholar, and an accomplished performer in almost every branch of outdoor sport. He captained England in Test matches, and England were never beaten under his captaincy. He played association football for England, he was full-back for Southampton in the Cup Final of 1902, and in 1892 he set up a world long-jump record of 23 ft 5 in, which stood for twenty-one years. But it was at cricket that his outstanding personality found its fullest expression. He played in eighteen Test matches against Australia between 1899 (when he scored 50 on his debut in a great England side of Grace, Jackson, Gunn, Rajitsinhji, Hayward, J. T. Tyldesley, Storer, Hirst, Rhodes and J. T. Hearne) and 1912 in the last Test against Australia before the First World War. In that match at the Oval he scored 79 in England's second innings. This was an England side which now included Jack Hobbs, Reggie Spooner, Frank Woolley, J. W. H. T. (Johnny Won't Hit To-day) Douglas, and the great Sydney Barnes.

After the two serious reverses in Australia another traditional name in cricket was chosen to lead the England side in Australia in 1903–4. It was 'Plum' Warner. He was able to redress the balance. England won the five-match series by three matches to two. But Australia set up an individual record in 1905 when Darling brought an Australian side to England for the third time. He had been captain of the Australians in 1899, in 1902, and now in 1905; this record is likely to stand the test of time unchallenged.

Joe Darling played in thirty-one Test matches against England, the first at Sydney in 1894. His start was a cricketer's nightmare, bowled by Tom Richardson for nought, but he made up for it with a fifty in the second innings. His last was at the Oval in 1905 when he made another 50. In 1907–8, England took another 4–1 hiding in Australia – the third time on four successive tours that such a disastrous result had been the outcome. Noble brought his 1909 Australians to England and won that series 2–1 with two drawn, and so to the last tour of Australia before the first war. The result was 4–1 again, but this time to England – a triumphant tour – the first time that an England side had won four Tests in Australia. Douglas captained the side in the winter of 1911–12 *vice* 'Plum' Warner, who was taken ill after scoring 151 in the opening match against South Australia at Adelaide, and could take no further part in the tour. He recovered in time to watch some of the important matches and sent home his comments to the West-Minster *Gazette*. He wrote:

> The team has had some rare batting triumphs, but the batting of the side never struck me as being relatively so good as the bowling and general out-cricket. I will, therefore, take our bowlers first, and of these Foster and Barnes achieved wonders. Finer bowling than theirs I have never seen on hard, true wickets. In the Test matches alone they took sixty-six wickets (Barnes 34, Foster 32) between them out of the ninety-five that fell, five men being run-out. Match after match their consistency was extraordinary, and it is impossible to praise them too highly.

The full England party was: P. F. Warner, J. W. H. T. Douglas, F. R. Foster, J. B. Hobbs, W. Rhodes, F. E. Woolley, S. F. Barnes, J. W. Hearne, G. Gunn, E. J. Smith, C. P. Mead, W. Hitch, H. Strudwick, S. P. Kinnear, J. Vine and J. Iremonger. Although Warner tended to give highest praise to the bowlers, *Wizden's* representative wrote:

> I have long since exhausted my vocabulary of praise in favour of Rhodes and Hobbs, and, thanks in a very large degree to their superlative work, our batting was eminently successful. Too much stress cannot be laid on what they accomplished, for innings after innings they gave us a wonderful start. Woolley played a great innings in the final Test, and is a beautiful batsman. I would as soon see him bat as anyone in the world. He drives magnificently, he hits the ball when he plays back, and he is very strong on the leg-side. A natural cricketer who has very distinctly arrived.

Gregory's team to England in 1912 contested the last 'Fight for the Ashes' before Europe erupted into a World War in 1914. In the second innings of the last Test at the Oval, Australia were bowled out for 65 of which Macartney made 30. Some thirty-six years later something similar happened at the Oval except that the boot was on the other foot. England were all out for 52, of which Hutton scored 30.

In the dark days of war in 1915 came news of the tragic early death of Victor Trumper, acknowledged by general consent as the best and most brilliant Australian batsman of them all. No one else among the famous group, from Charles Bannerman to

Bardsley and Macartney, Clem Hill, Noble or Murdoch had quite such remarkable powers. Trumper, at the zenith of his fame, challenged comparison with Ranjitsinhji. Trumper paid four visits to England in 1899, 1902, 1905 and 1909, but it was in 1902 that he reached his highest point. In a summer of wretched weather he scored 2,570 runs with an average of 48. Trumper was a fascinating batsman to watch because of his brilliant improvisation which demanded a perfect union of hand and eyes. Sometimes he drove a bowler to despair by dispatching the best ball he had bowled all day for four with a flick of the wrist and the eye of a hawk. Trumper, one of the most popular Australian cricketers of all time, died of Bright's disease at the age of thirty-eight. His name has passed into the common vocabulary as a sheer symbol of cricket; other players remain shadowy images in the pageant of the past; not so Victor Trumper.

Rivalry was resumed after hostilities when Douglas took a side to Australia in the winter of 1920-1. In between the First and Second World Wars ten series of Tests were played between England and Australia and a total of 49 matches (the 50th was the 1938 Test at Manchester which was abandoned without a ball being bowled). Australia won 22, England 15 and 12 drawn. The most successful captain of the period was Warwick Armstrong, the only Captain in the history of Anglo-Australian Tests to win all five Test matches in a series. This he did in 1920-1. Armstrong then won three and drew two when be brought the 1921 Australians to England, so his record in ten Test matches was to win eight and draw two, an unparalleled success. Although faring a little better by winning one Test, Arthur Gilligan's side was beaten 4-1 in 1924-5, so the post-war position then was: Australia twelve wins, England one, and two drawn. England in 1926 won the only match producing a result, but it was Chapman's tour of 1928-9 which put England firmly back on the map in the eyes of the Australians. England won four out of five Tests on Australia's own midden. Bradman apart, this tour produced one of the most magnificent batting performances of a series to date. Wally Hammond's scores in the Test matches were 44, 28, 251, 200, 32, 119 not out, 177, 38, and 16. His 119 not out and 177 were scored in the same match at Adelaide, and his 251 and 200 were consecutive Test innings.

The touring party was: A. P. F. Chapman (Captain), J. C. White (Vice-Captain), D. R. Jardine, J. B. Hobbs, H. Sutcliffe, W. R. Hammond, E. P. Hendren, E. Tyldesley, C. P. Mead, M. Leyland, M. W. Tate, G. Geary, G. Duckworth, L. E. G. Ames, H. Larwood, A. P. Freeman and S. J. Staples. A total of 859,008 spectators watched the five Test matches, paying a total sum of £73,877. The strength of the batting, the herculean bowling endeavours, the stout heart of Maurice Tate, and the splendid leadership of Chapman, inspired this side to the pinnacle of success. Only once since, on the body-line tour of 1932–3, has England won four matches in a series against Australia.

Australia took control again in England in 1930 under the leadership of W. M. Woodfull – they won by two Tests to one with two drawn. In 1930 England first saw Don Bradman (334 at Leeds) – the phenomenon, a living legend, the most prolific run-machine of all time, to whom a special mention is devoted later in this book. It was the invincibility of Bradman which in 1932–3 provoked Jardine's use of Larwood who bowled very fast and short outside the leg-stump with a packed leg-side field. As a result of these tactics England won by four matches to one in circumstances which have had so enormous a bearing upon the whole tactical course of cricket, that this, too, is accorded a chapter of its own in this history.

Woodfull and Bradman and many other great Australian players – Stan McCabe, Bill O'Reilly, 'Clarrie' Grimmett – were back in England in 1934. They again won 2–1 with two drawn. For the England bowlers it was an uphill job. Bradman scored 304 at Leeds and 244 at the Oval. Ponsford 181 at Leeds and 266 at the Oval. Australia won back the Ashes appropriately enough at the Oval on their Captain's birthday. As the result of the rubber depended on this match it was planned to be played to a finish, yet despite Australia's scoring 701 in their first innings and a total of 1,500 runs being scored in the match, it was all over in four days. Frank Woolley, incidentally, at the age of forty-seven, kept wicket when Ames was injured. A word about Stan McCabe.

After Bradman, he was probably the greatest Australian batsman of all time. He played the innings of his life (or anyone else's life for that matter) against Larwood's body-line – 187 not out. Some of the players still talk about it as the finest and most courageous innings in the whole history of Test cricket. There were people who rated his virtuosity above Bradman's – a truly gifted and remarkable player.

In 1936–7 'Gubby' Allen took a side to Australia which gave a pretty good account of itself in spite of losing the series by three matches to two. Only one word stood between them and assured success: that word was Bradman. He scored 810 runs in nine innings, with a highest score of 270, and an average of 90. Hammond, Leyland and Charles Barnett, that flamboyant and exhilarating opening batsman from the W. G. Grace county carried the English batting, and Bill Voce headed the bowling. This was a good Australian side with highly dependable and talented players like Jack Fingleton; Grimmett had gone but Bill O'Reilly and Australia's master 'stumper' Bertie Oldfield were still there. Australia, like England, can boast a pedigree line of world-class wicket-keepers to trace through the ages from the bearded Blackham, who revolutionized wicket-keeping; in 1880 he had stood up to fast bowlers, and in 1882 he even dispensed with a long-stop. He was accused by the clergy of turning cricket into a lethal pastime by introducing an unwarranted risk of injury. Until Blackham came to adorn the game (and retire from it with tapering fingers uninjured) the rough and ready workmanship of Pilling or Sherwin had always been recognized as wicket-keeping in its perfection. Bertie Oldfield may well rank in a Hall of Fame, as the greatest Australian of them all. England had a pretty good keeper on this tour, too. Leslie Ames was probably the greatest batsman-keeper in cricket history – he scored a hundred centuries in a distinguished career.

In 1938, 'The Don' was back, this time as Captain. Manchester hit upon the only way to curb his activities; it rained incessantly, and not a ball was bowled in the match, the second time that this had happened to the Australians in England. The series ended with honours even, a game each with two drawn. Bradman's contribution to the tour was thirteen centuries (including 278, 258 and 202). Bill Brown and Lindsay Hassett hit five; Hassett was the little man who became such a popular character with English cricketers, both on and off the field; no quarter was given when on duty, but off it, he was a comic in the traditional line of Keaton or W. C. Fields; come to think of it, he would have made a good straight man for George Burns – the Hassett-Burns show would have been a riot! Yet an Englishman will be remembered more than any Australian in this series: Len Hutton – 364 for England at the Oval, in a total of 903 for 7 declared. Edrich was out with the score at 12. Leyland joined Hutton to form an all-Yorkshire assault party. The next wicket fell at 411 when Leyland was run out. Hammond made 59 – then Australia got on top – Paynter 0, Denis Compton 1. Then Arthur Wood came in at the crisis to team up with Joe Hardstaff. Wood made 53; Hardstaff soldiered on to score 169. With 50 extras the English total totted up to 903 when Hammond called it a day. In the face of this overwhelming and utterly hopeless task, made more a matter for despair by injuries to Bradman and Fingleton, neither of whom could bat in either innings, Australia were out for 201 and 123 – England thus won by an innings and 579 runs.

Hutton's statistical milestones were as follows; he batted 13 hours and 20 minutes; at the age of twenty-two he had made the highest individual score in Test cricket; his stand of 382 with Leyland was a record for any wicket in England; his stand of 215 with Hardstaff established a new record for England's sixth wicket. The takings for the match were just under £20,000 – a record for a Test match at the Oval – the last between England and Australia for eight years; the bloodstained shadow of war hung over Europe from 1939 until 1945.

No sooner was war over, than England was asked to send a team to Australia in the winter of 1946-7. It was too soon after the harrowing years of war for English cricket to assert itself. Times had been hard for cricket and cricketers; some fine players had died in the service of their country – Hedley Verity, Maurice Turnbull and Kenneth Farnes, to name a distinguished triumvirate who were never seen again on the green fields of England.

But Australia felt that the world had for so long been starved of international cricket that the result was of secondary importance; what mattered most was that Test cricket should burgeon again. that old rivalry be renewed at the earliest possible moment. The leadership of the England party was assigned to Wally Hammond and these were the players who went with him: N. W. D. Yardley, P. A. Gibb, A. V. Bedser, D. C. S. Compton, W. J. Edrich, T. G. Evans, L. B. Fishlock, J. Hardstaff, L. Hutton, J. T. Ikin, James Langridge, R. Pollard, T. P. B. Smith, W. Voce, C. Washbrook, D. V. P. Wright. On 31 August 1947 they left Southampton in the *Stirling Castle* for Fremantle – it was the long sea voyage in those days – there were no jet aeroplanes! English fears as to the result on the field were confirmed – three Tests to Australia and two drawn, but it had been worth while on the part of the Australians for pressing for the tour. The Englishmen were popular wherever they went, and so large were the crowds that flocked to the matches that the MCC's share of the profits reached £50,000. The First Test at Brisbane, beginning on 29 November, was an ominous portent of things to come – Bradman 187, Hassett 128, McCool 95, Miller 79 – Miller 7 for 60.

What a great cricketer this fellow Miller was. Keith Miller was probably one of the hardest hitters of a cricket ball in the game – controlled, calculated hitting, displayed as a distinct art, not chance. Miller's techniques recalled some of the great hitters of bygone years – Alletson, Trott, Jessop, Fender. Alletson's innings, of course, has become a legend. He went in at No. 9 for Nottinghamshire against Sussex at the Hove Ground, Brighton in May 1911 and scored 189 out of 227 in 90 minutes. At one point after lunch, he scored 115 out of 120 in seven overs; in one over from Killick he hit 22, and in another – which included two no-balls – 34 (4, 6, 6, 4, 4, 4, 6). Alletson's innings is referred in the same tones as, say, the White Horse Cup Final at Wembley, or the Suffragette's Derby, or Obolensky's try against the All-Blacks at Twickenham.

Another hitter, Albert Trott, delivered one of the most powerful blows ever to be seen on a cricket ground when he smote a ball over the pavilion at Lord's in 1907 – an enormous carry. Gilbert Jessop, crouching over his bat, and as quick on his feet as a panther, scored six centuries, each in under an hour. Once, against a West Indies side not counted as first class, he made 157 in an hour at the end of which the helpless fieldsmen were rolling about on the ground in laughter; above all, he made, in seventy-five minutes, the 104 runs which made possible England's famous one-wicket victory at the Oval in 1902. Jessop came in when 5 wickets were down for 48 – he left when 187 of the 263 had been made. Yet despite Alletson, Trott and Jessop, mighty men to be sure, it was Percy Fender who hit a hundred in 35 minutes at Northampton in 1921, still the fastest first-class hundred on record. Keith Miller belongs to this sort of company, as part and parcel, by universal acclaim. These were the men who made cricket. Keith was a law unto himself – yet lawless – a man's man, and a ladies man; Miller is Miller and remains unique.

Thirteen series between England and Australia have now taken place since the Second World War. Australia has won twenty-three, England thirteen with thirty drawn. What is significant, however, is that Australia's lead of ten Test matches was built in the first three series – in 1946–7, 1948 and 1950–1, when Australia led by eleven games to one. Since then, despite the pendulum swinging (violently at times) to and fro, the honours are even. Any minute, one side or the other, could make matters decisive, for the time being, at any rate. To deal with these thirteen series in depth would call for a book of some length. To précis them is immensely difficult but a necessity.

Bradman's tour to England in 1948 does bear examination in rather closer detail from an Australian point of view, because it was considered as the best Australian team ever sent to England. When this view was freely bandied about the elder statesmen rushed to the defence of Warwick Armstrong's 1921 side. The 1921 bowling was formidable, headed by that great pair of fast bowlers, Gregory and McDonald, with Mailey and Armstrong in reserve. Mailey's autobiography was like its author's bowling, full of zest, varied, quick, shifting the point of attack, sometimes extravagant, frequently brilliant and always thoughtful; he believed so utterly in calling a spade a spade that he wrote: 'It is almost unbelievable that Australia has produced only three great slow spin bowlers since World War 1. Call it what you wish – vanity, conceit, egoism, pride, or any form of self-aggrandizement – I feel obliged to add my name to those of Clarrie Grimmett and 'Chuck' Fleetwood-Smith.' Two other bowlers of the kind, Doug Ring and Colin McCool, and a third, in the less experienced [Mailey's book was published in 1958] Richie Benaud, have visited England with the Australian team, but their value as batsmen was responsible to a great degree for their selection in Tests. On the other hand, Fleetwood-Smith as a batsman was a rank outsider, Mailey wasn't much better, and Clarrie, the 'Scarlet Pimpernel', although the best of the three, never rose as a batsman to the heights he himself thought commensurate with his skill.

The record of Bradman's side in 1948 seems to me to provide the indisputable proof of its greatness – the greatest of them all, yes, even taking into account those valiant warriors of 1921. When announcing his retirement from first-class cricket, Bradman claimed that the 1948 side bore comparison with any of its predecessors. He was absolutely right. In fact, it led its predecessors, because this was not a weak England side by any standards. How could it be with Compton, Washbrook, Hutton, Edrich, Evans, Laker and Alec Bedser? Compton had a batting average of 62, Washbrook 50, Hutton 42, but Australia had seven players with an average of over 40 in the Test matches – Morris (87), Barnes (82), Bradman (72), Harvey, that majestic left-hander (66), Toshack (51), Loxton (48), Hassett (44). Three bowlers, Lindwall and Miller and Bill Johnston, took 67 Test wickets between them. Throw in Don Tallon behind the stumps, and the efficiency of the side was seen in its performance. Lindwall was at his most magnificent in the Oval Test match, when he took 6 for 20. I think now of the regal Frank Woolley and the waving flags above the tents at Canterbury, of Jack Hobbs, the Master, or the fluency and culture of Hammond, but to me the most enthralling sight that cricket has ever provided was Lindwall, lithe of limb, gathering momentum with every step, that delivery stride of absolute technical perfection, bowling from the hips, and then the thunderbolt let loose: sheer undiluted pace, too swift to allow much variation in flight, but straight as a die; he hit the stumps four times in that 6 for 20 when Hutton alone had the slightest idea of how to play him. The superb Australians of 1948 and Lindwall, of blessed memory.

Never since has an Australian side given the impression of having such batting strength. Nor, indeed, for that matter, has either side. In the years since England teams have done battle in Australia under the leadership of Freddie Brown, Len Hutton, Peter May, Mike Smith and Ray Illingworth. Two of these teams were successful, those led by Yorkshiremen, Hutton, in 1954-5, and Illingworth in 1970-1. Australian sides have come to England under Lindsay Hassett, Ian Johnson, Richie Benaud, Bobby Simpson and Bill Lawry; Benaud and Simpson were successful. Overall, there has been nothing in it, though this is not to say the battles have lost any of their lustre, nor that they have lacked tremendous feats of skill and endurance; indeed in the case of Jim Laker's performance at Manchester in 1956 there was sheer magic in it. Laker, taking no fewer than nineteen wickets in a single Test match must reign supreme as the sort of *Victor Ludorum* of all Test cricket. I can say with pride and gratitude that I was there. How could it happen that Lock, bowling as well as he was, could take only one wicket? Laker, having already taken all ten in an innings for Surrey against the Australians, did it again, and captured the whole bag, bar one. His figures in the two innings were: 16·4, 4, 37, 9, and 51·2, 23, 53, 10. The only variation was Burke, caught Cowdrey bowled Lock for 22. What made this whole fairy tale even more astonishing was that Australia, in reply to England's 459, were 48 without loss. McDonald and Burke seemed to be going well with no suggestion that utter destruction was lurking just round the corner, but it was, and Australia were 84 all out – Harvey 0, Craig 8, Miller 6, Mackay 0, Archer 6, Benaud 0, Lindwall 6 not out, Maddocks 4, Johnson 0.

So England were level in the series instead of being two down as they might well have been at Leeds. It was here that Cyril

Washbrook, a Selector who was persuaded by his colleagues to play, came in to bat when England were 17 for 3. May stood at the other end, watching the imperturbable Washbrook, cap at a jaunty angle, making his way out as if he had all the time in the world. If everybody else on the ground thought that this was a crisis, Washbrook, by his air of confidence, did not share that view. He made 98. May, having admitted afterwards, that Washbrook's whole bearing completely soothed the tension he felt himself, scored 101. In my mind's eye, I can see Washbrook coming out now. Here was a great cricketer; here, too, was a memory to be cherished.

I remember the Oval in 1953 when Edrich and Compton were in at the kill as England regained the Ashes and the hordes swarmed across the Oval turf to pay tribute to a fine England side – Hutton, Edrich, May, Compton, Graveney, Bailey, Evans, Laker, Lock, Trueman, and Bedser. Godfrey Evans, human dynamo, dismissed sixteen batsmen in the series, a new record for a wicket-keeper in any Test series in England. Hassett, incidentally, won the toss in all five matches in the series but in doing so created a record he could well have done without. He was the first Captain to win the toss all five times and then lose the series.

In the winter of 1954–5, Len Hutton became the first (and only) England Captain to win three Test matches in a series against Australia since the Second World War. He pinned his faith absolutely on speed. He reflected on Lindwall and Miller in their prime and what England batsmen had suffered at the hands of these two great exponents of pace. After an overwhelming defeat in the first game at Brisbane by an innings and 154 runs. Frank Tyson and Brian Statham formed a speed combination even more potent than the two great Australians. England won the next three Tests. Tyson soon given the apt title of 'Typhoon', shattered Australia; he took twenty-eight wickets, and Statham eighteen; they were admirably supported by Trevor Bailey, Bob Appleyard and Johnny Wardle. There was a hero's welcome awaiting Hutton and his men on their return. Hutton, of course, was later to receive a Knighthood for his services to English cricket.

The Laker year – 1956 – saw England retain the Ashes against Ian Johnson's side, but the blow was to come in the winter of 1958–9 when May's team was beaten in Australia 4–0 with one drawn, the worst thrashing since Australia made a clean sweep of all five against Douglas's side in 1920–1. May himself and Cowdrey did all that could be asked of them. Two players in the classic mould of English cricketers and blessed with more natural skill than most. May scored 113 in the first innings of the Second Test at Melbourne – the first century by an England Captain in Australia since MacLaren scored 116 at Sydney in 1901–2. Australia dominated with their trio of bowlers – Benaud 31 wickets, the left-handed Alan Davidson 24, and Ian Meckiff 17. Benaud, after this success, was to be Australia's next Captain to England; he enjoyed more success on that trip. Australia won 2–1 with one drawn. The classical innings of that series was 180 by Ted Dexter at Birmingham, when Subba Row also got 100 runs, but Burge topped Dexter's figure at the Oval by one run; O'Neill scored 117. But bowlers win matches – the trio this time was made up of Benaud, Davidson and McKenzie.

In 1962–3 Ted Dexter took an England side to Australia which drew the series at one each with three drawn, so the Ashes still stayed with Australia. This was a fine tour for Ken Barrington, with Dexter and Cowdrey just behind in the batting averages. Australia's real advantage lay in the bowling of Davidson and McKenzie. There was no change in the destination of the Ashes in 1964 when Bobby Simpson's team to England won the only decisive Test at Leeds, all the others being drawn. The match to remember for those who thrive on runs was the Fourth Test at Old Trafford – Bobby Simpson scored 311. With Lawry also getting a hundred and Booth 98 Australia accumulated the massive total of 656 for 8 declared, but England had the answer for it. Barrington hit 256, Dexter 174, Geoff Boycott 58 and Jim Parks 60. England scored 611.

Mike Smith's team to Australia in 1965–6 were able to draw the series with a game each and three drawn, but this was an absorbing series made memorable not least by an innings of 185 by Bob Barber in the Third Test. Frank Tyson wrote: 'Barber's lordly 185 made the Australian bowlers perpetually afraid of his gaining a toe-hold in the remaining Tests.' This tour was a batting feast. A treble century was hit (by Bob Cowper), a double century (by Bobby Simpson), and twelve centuries, Edrich and Barrington getting two each for England, and Bill Lawry, the barn door, the great run-grafter, making three for Australia. Ken Barrington would have been proud of himself on this tour – he topped the England Test match bowling averages; he was very keen on his bowling; just as an afterthought, he topped the batting averages as well!

There was another drawn series in 1968 when Lawry had assumed the mantle of Australia's leadership. D'Oliveira had arrived to take his place in the unending panorama; so had Alan Knott, and Colin Milburn, a cavalier cricketer until fate struck him down in his cricketing prime when he lost an eye in a motor accident. Underwood had begun to weave a spell; Snow was developing as a world-class fast bowler; here was the nucleus of the side which would regain the Ashes. Connolly had a good bowling tour for Australia, but palpably lacked support, his accomplice, McKenzie, having a rough time and buying his wickets at 46 apiece.

And so to the winter of 1970–1 and the England controversy over the captaincy which was headline news for so long. Would it be Cowdrey or Illingworth, the man in possession, the man who had filled the breach when Cowdrey was out of action after an operation on an Achilles tendon, and had done so well? Finally Illingworth was appointed and, following in the tradition of another resolute Yorkshireman, Illingworth did the job that he had been sent to do. It was a hard tour; few top professional sporting endeavours these days are anything else. There was tension and some bad feeling, accentuated by the microscopic analysis of television cameras and Press; this, too, must be accepted. They all have a job to do, but it all makes the Captain's job harder. Boycott, in a moment of anger, threw his bat away having been given run-out. This was reprehensible, of course, and no excuses can be found for him. Douglas Jardine might even have sent him home for it, but was this tantrum really a world issue? Was it not magnified far beyond its context? Illingworth led his team off the field in the last Test when beer cans were thrown, and had he not brought them back under instruction from the umpires, England would have ceded the match, a dangerous course to have adopted especially when Hutton and Cowdrey have stood their ground in much more inflamed situations in the West Indies. Nevertheless it is easy to sit in judgement on Illingworth from a critic's arm-chair in the cool, clear, relaxed light of afterwards. Illingworth showed that he has many qualities of great merit; he created a tremendous team spirit which saw the side through its many moments of adversity – and there were many, especially in terms of injuries. Illingworth knew that Lawry would play it hard; the latter has made it clear throughout his career that he doesn't give himself out, he considers that to be the umpire's prerogative; Illingworth had to play it the same way or perish, and for those purists (and they shall be nameless) who considered that this simply 'wasn't cricket', one might ponder on whether some of the incidents on the 1932–3 tour were cricket. It provides food for thought if nothing else; it does prove that, in many ways, times have changed, for better or for worse.

For the first time since 1888, Australia failed to win a single Test in a Home series against England. England won two, so the Ashes mythically changed hands. The tour proved several points. First, that in Geoff Boycott, England has a dedicated batsman, who in approach and technique could one day recall memories of Bradman. Second, that John Edrich is not far behind him, and Brian Luckhurst has all the ingredients of following suit. Third, that in John Snow, England has the finest fast-bowler in the world, and in Alan Knott, the best wicket-keeper. Like the film serials of the silent days, the series ended in a gripping situation which has whetted the appetite for next time. And next time is this summer.

South Africa

The British Army spread the gospel of the game of cricket in far distant corners of the earth. It was certainly the Army who first pitched their wickets at Pietermaritzburg a year after the first occupation of Natal in 1843. A few years after, British settlers at Bloemfontein started a club. In 1864 a Western Province Cricket Club was founded, but it was not until the winter of 1888–9 that the first English team set foot on South African soil; it was the turning point in South Africa's cricketing affairs, because Frank Hearne, one of the party, stayed behind afterwards on a coaching engagement. This tour was the joint enterprise of a Major Warton and Sir Donald Currie, the founder of the Castle Line (later Union Castle). Sir Donald also founded the Currie Cup which has been competed for ever since by the South African Provinces – the equivalent of the County Championship or the Sheffield Shield in Australia.

There was a touch of the romantic about this first tour – it was captained by C. Aubrey Smith, later to become the portrayer of the perfect English gentleman in so many Hollywood films. Because of his curious bowling action he was known as 'Round the Corner' Smith. His team was a very strong one indeed including three stalwarts of Surrey, Abel, Bowden and Wood, but it was the bowling of Johnny Briggs which was a complete eye-opener to the South Africans. Briggs was not far short of 300 wickets at the end of the tour, and these cost him about five apiece; in one match alone he dismissed twenty-seven batsmen for twenty-three runs. To the chagrin of some historians this tour is included in official Test match records.

In 1894 the first South African team came to England. The fixtures were only second-class and the tour was a financial failure, but at least the players enjoyed the pleasure of beating an MCC team at Lord's captained by the renowned Doctor – 'W.G.' It was all invaluable experience. Five England sides had visited South Africa (playing Test matches according to the records – Aubrey Smith's team in 1888–9, Walter Read's team in 1891–2, Lord Hawke in 1895–6 and 1898–9, and 'Plum' Warner in 1905–6) before South Africa contested the first Test match in England. This recognition surely sprang from the terrible hiding the South Africans had inflicted upon 'Plum'

Warner. They won four matches out of five.

Perhaps one of the most surprising aspects of England v South Africa Tests, especially in view of the fine players which South Africa has produced, is that out of the 102 Test matches played between the two countries, South Africa has won only 18. Seven of these victories were achieved before the First World War, so that in 70 matches played after the First War, South Africa has won only 11, and only 5 in England. In this same period, South Africa won only three series – against Champan's team in South Africa in 1930–1, Wade's team in England in 1935 and Van der Merwe's team in England in 1965. The performance of Van der Merwe's team, and their massacre of Australia afterwards, placed South Africa at the head of the cricketing nations; never had she been as strong. What a macabre twist of fate that events described in detail in another chapter have isolated South Africa and robbed its cricketers of world renown such as they had never known before. We may never see another South African team in England; the link in this eighty-year-old chain may have been irretrievably broken. More is the pity, as we reflect on some of the great names in South Africa's cricket cavalcade. The eleven, for instance (and the same eleven played in all five Test matches), who gave 'Plum' Warner such a caning in 1905–6 – P. W. Sherwell (Captain), L. J. Tancred, W. A. Shalders, M. Hathorn, G. C. White, S. J. Snooke, J. H. Sinclair, G. A. Faulkner, A. D. Nourse, A. E. E. Vogler, and R. O. Schwarz. This team forged South Africa's first victory over England at the ninth attempt with a dramatic one-wicket victory at Johannesburg. Has there ever been a more exciting Test match? South Africa, bowled out for 91 in their first innings, were set to score 287 to win. They were 239 for 9 when Sherwell joined Nourse. Amid mounting tension and excitement they crept nearer and nearer to their goal; undaunted the two defied all attempts to dislodge them – victory was theirs – and what a victory! Who could possibly have foreseen then that South Africa would win three more matches on this tour? South Africa's batting was eminently sound, but it was the googly which really proved to be England's undoing. Schwarz, Faulkner, Vogler and White provided a severe Test on the matting wicket in Johannesburg. Schwarz was the most successful of them all; he did not bowl the leg-break but his googly turned sharply and whipped across, and Faulkner's off-breaks and leg-breaks needed Maigret qualities to detect them. Never again were South Africa to win four matches in a single series, although they won three comparatively soon afterwards when Leveson-Gower took an England side out in 1909–10.

But this 1905–6 side provided strong foundations for South Africa's cricket future. Dave Nourse who, with Percy Sherwell, had won the first match, became a famous left-handed batsman, and his years in cricket spanned the period from 1896–1936; his son, Dudley Nourse, was to become equally famous. Dave Nourse, incidentally, arrived in South Africa with the Army as a trumpet boy of eighteen; he stayed to appear in forty-five consecutive Tests. Aubrey Faulkner is recognized as the best left-hander that South Africa ever produced. Sid Pegler, who played his first Test against Leveson-Gower's side, took the record number of 189 wickets on the tour of England in 1912. 'Herby' Taylor, who had a disappointing first tour of England in 1912 became South Africa's finest batsman and Captain. He brought the first post-First-World-War South African team to England in 1924. They were dismissed for 30 in the First Test match, bowled out by the Sussex yeomen, Arthur Gilligan and Maurice Tate, Gilligan taking 6 for 7. At this point, South African cricket was in the doldrums. In this and later periods, E. P. Nupen who ranked with Vogler as South Africa's most accomplished matting-wicket bowler, formed the nucleus of players who were to turn the tide. With Nupen there was Catterall and Siedle; Taylor and Nourse were improving; C. L. Vincent and H. B. Cameron, a splendidly aggressive batsman, and D. P. Morkel. In 1929, H. G. Owen-Smith, the youngest member of the tour party, scored 129 at Leeds, a curious match in which South Africa scored 236 and 275, yet England used eight bowlers – Larwood, Tate, Freeman, Hammond, White, Bowley, Woolley and Leyland. Bruce Mitchell was now emerging as a master defensive batsman who could claim that his was the hardest wicket to get in two decades of international cricket. He was discovered at the age of six, batting with a tin-can for a wicket to his sister's bowling on a dust-caked road near a Johannesburg mine.

The fruits of experimenting with young players on an English tour in 1929 were reaped in 1935, when Mitchell, Cameron, Vincent, Siedle, Dalton and Bell returned with H. F. Wade's team and made history after twenty-eight years by winning a Test match in England. Where better to make history than Lord's itself? This team had a remarkable record, for they played forty matches, including one in Holland, and lost only two, to Essex and Gloucestershire. In the victory Test, Bruce Mitchell played a masterly innings of 164 not out, and the leg-spin bowler, Xenophon Balaskas, took 9 wickets for 93. For Balaskas, it was one fleeting moment of fame; he damaged his elbow so severely against Notts that he dropped off the active list at once, but fame was assuredly his; his impeccable length googlies off a jaunty step or two, and spinning like a top, were too much for the flower of England's batting. The South African side who will cherish the memory of 2 July 1935 as one of their most prized possessions consisted of: B. Mitchell, I. J. Siedle, E. A. B. Rowan, A. D. Nourse, H. F. Wade, H. B. Cameron, E. L. Dalton, X. C. Balaskas, A. B. C. Langton, R. J. Crisp, A. J. Bell.

This was the highest standard so far reached by South African batsmen, and it was maintained when Wally Hammond's team undertook the first all-turf wicket tour of 1938–9. The scoring on both sides was exceptionally high – England: 422 (Paynter 117) and 291 for 4 declared (Paynter 100, Gibb 106); South Africa: 390 (Dalton 102) and 108 for 1; England: 559 for 9 declared (Hammond 181, Ames 115, Valentine 112); South Africa: 286 (Dudley Nourse 120) and 201 for 2; England: 469 for 4 declared (Paynter 243, Hammond 120); South Africa: 103 and 353 (Mitchell 109); England: 215 and 203 for 4; South Africa: 349 for 8 declared ... and so to the most extraordinary game in Test history – 'The Timeless Test' of Durban. This was the statisticians' Paradise – it produced whole pages of highest and lowest and longest and 'Never Befores'. Yet the cardinal question to ask is a very simple one. Why was it a timeless Test? The series was not level pegging. South Africa were one match down, so that at best,

South Africa could only draw the series. You don't play extra time in a football match if the Home team is one goal down, hoping that they might be able to draw level. In the end, the match was not timeless. After ten days – and on no one of them did play continue until the time arranged for the drawing of stumps (bad light ended play on seven occasions, rain on one, there was no play on the eighth day because of rain – and rain caused the end of play and the abandonment of the match on the tenth) – the England party just had to catch a boat home when 42 runs short of victory and 5 wickets in hand. A few snippets from the pages of the statisticians are;

1. The match aggregate of 1981 runs for 35 wickets was a new record for first-class and Test cricket
2. During the match a record number of sixteen batsmen scored innings of 50 or over. Six centuries were scored in the match. Edrich hit a double century (and a tree was planted in his honour which blossoms to this day)
3. Hedley Verity bowled 766 balls in the match – a new record
4. It seems to have been a game of cricket to have read about rather than to have watched – Gibb took 451 minutes in scoring 120; less than 200 runs were scored on the second day of the match; less than 50 runs were scored before lunch on the first two days.

Whoever thought up this idea of a timeless Test should either have been hanged, drawn and quartered, or assigned to the Bertram Mills organization which was flourishing at the time! The twenty-two players who got sick to death of the sight of each other were;

South Africa: P. G. Van der Byl, A. Melville, E. A. B. Rowan, B. Mitchell, A. D. Nourse, K. G. Viljoen, E. L. Dalton, R. E. Grieveson, A. B. C. Langton, E. S. Newson, N. Gordon.
England: L. Hutton, P. A. Gibb, E. Paynter, W. R. Hammond, L. E. G. Ames, W. J. Edrich, B. H. Valentine, H. Verity, D. V. P. Wright, K. Farnes, R. T. D. Perks.

At least they contributed to one unique piece of cricket history! The scores were: South Africa: 530 (Van der Byl 125, Nourse 103) and 481 (Melville 103); England: 316 and 654–5 (Edrich

219, Hammond 140, Gibb 120) ... match drawn!

Since that marathon contest ended, England and South Africa have met in only eight series; another World War prevented a resumption of rivalry until 1947, and world affairs brought down the curtain with a depressing air of finality after 1965. In those eight series (five in England and three in South Africa) England won seventeen matches, South Africa six, and fifteen were drawn. The only series actually won by South Africa was the mini-series of 1965, when South Africa and New Zealand shared the English summer.

From the results it would seem that South Africa took longer to pick up the threads again after the war than England. Alan Melville's team to England in 1947 was beaten 3-0, George Mann's team in South Africa won 2-0, and Dudley Nourse's team to England in 1951 were beaten 3-1. It was a vintage summer – vintage Edrich and Compton that is – in 1947, a never-to-be-forgotten summer, particularly by every single member of Alan Melville's team. Their scores in the Test matches were: Edrich: 57, 50, 189, 191, 22 not out, 43 (luckily for the South Africans he missed the Oval Test because of a strain); Compton: 65, 163, 208, 115, 6, 30, 53, 113. South Africa began this series brilliantly with Alan Melville hitting 189 and Dudley Nourse 149 in their first innings in the First Test; Melville hit a hundred in the second Test, but the bowlers could rarely cope with England's batting which, in addition to the 'Middlesex Twins', boasted Hutton and Washbrook, two inseparable combinations such as the game has not often seen.

The First Test on George Mann's tour in Durban was the 'Cometh the hour cometh the man' Test; the man who 'cameth' was Cliff Gladwin! The closing stages of the match would probably have provided enough saleable material for a Metro-Goldwyn-Mayer feature film. When the last over was about to be bowled England needed 8 runs to win; 8 wickets were down, Doug Wright was padded up in the pavilion, Alec Bedser and Cliff Gladwin were at the centre of the arena poised to face 8 balls, from which 8 runs were needed. A ball-by-ball commentary provided this information: first ball: Bedser – a leg-bye; second ball: Gladwin – a pull for four; third ball: Gladwin – a leg-bye; fourth ball: Bedser – no score; fifth ball: Bedser – no score; sixth ball: Bedser – a single to cover; seventh ball: Gladwin – no score. And so it came to pass that upon the eighth ball England needed one run for victory. Bedser summoned Gladwin for a board meeting and the minutes of that meeting record that it was agreed that both batsmen should run whatever happened. The ball hit Gladwin on the thigh; Bedser had already started his run as Gladwin was heaving unsuccessfully at the ball. Gladwin went off like a shot out of a gun and, to the everlasting sorrow of the South African team, had arrived safely at the other end before anything could be done about it. England had won. Our two heroes marched off; Gladwin and Durban are as indivisible as Gilbert and Sullivan or as famous in victory as Nelson and Trafalgar. To rub salt into the wound Hutton and Washbrook put on 359 for the first wicket in the next Test, and Compton also threw in a century for good measure. England were 516 for 3! Dudley Nourse hit two hundreds in the series then brought the next South African team to England in 1951 – and won the First Test. Nourse's courage at Trent Bridge had to be seen to be believed. Painfully handicapped by a broken thumb, which had been pinned a few weeks before, he batted 550 minutes to score 208 before being run out – and every stroke he made must have jarred his thumb. There was to be another double century maker for South Africa – Eric Rowan hit 236 at Leeds.

But there is little doubt that the most popular South African side ever to come to England was that led by Jack Cheetham in 1955. A green tie with a single Springbok head embroidered on it, worn every Tuesday, will mark – so long as ties endure – the members of this team. On Tuesdays, because on Tuesday, 12 July at Old Trafford and on Tuesday, 26 July at Headingley, the Springboks won the Third and Fourth Tests – after England had won the first two – to go all square in the final match at the Oval. They lost the rubber; they won the admiration and affection of a nation, and I think most of all of this side as we ponder on the problems which have engulfed South African cricket. We may never see their like again; all very sad.

Waite and Winslow formed the pair who did the trick at Old Trafford. Waite at No. 7 and Winslow at No. 8 both hit centuries. The 'Winslow Boy' scored 108 out of 171 in 191 minutes, and hit three sixes, completing his century in the truly grand manner by lifting a ball into the television stand over the sight-screen. 'Jackie' McGlew, who had also hit a hundred at Old Trafford, repeated the performance at Leeds. Russell Endean hit a century, too, and South Africa's second innings total of 500 paved the way for a notable victory; all was set for a titanic match at the Oval; but the Oval was the feared home of Lock and Laker. They had to be feared. South Africa were spun to defeat as many sides had been before and after them. Lock and Laker were magical names. But what a wonderful series! Cheetham was a great Captain and this was a summer of the happiest of memories.

Peter May's team to South Africa in 1956–7 was held to a two-all draw; once again it represented a great fight back by South Africa after being two down after two Tests. This time the boot was on the other foot. South Africa had a world-class off-spinner, Hugh Tayfield, titled 'Toey' Tayfield because of his undying mannerism of toeing the ground before he delivered each ball. At Johannesburg he took 4 for 79 and 9 for 113, and his 6 for 76 in England's second innings in the Fifth Test brought South Africa a sweet victory. This, too, was a very good South African side – Roy McLean, Trevor Goddard, Peter Heine and Neil Adcock. The 1960 team to England was not as good; was it that they were unlucky to face Statham and Trueman in their most devastating mood or were unsettled by the throwing controversy which enveloped Griffin? England won the first three Tests and so tied up the series.

South Africa had no answer this time, nor indeed could they register one single victory against Mike Smith's team in South Africa in 1964–5. England won the First Test; the remaining four were drawn. But the nucleus was there of the 1965 South Africans under Van der Merwe – Eddie Barlow, Graeme and Peter Pollock Colin Bland, who added an entirely new dimension to the art of fielding; he hit the stumps not by pot luck but by dedicated practice. This was a wonderful tour for Ken Barrington.

And so ... to the last chapter ... perhaps even the epilogue, though one hopes not. South Africa beat England at Trent Bridge in the second of this three-match series in 1965. Graeme Pollock hit a hundred; his style and majesty conjured up nostalgic memories of the great Frank Woolley. Despite Cowdrey's hundred for England South Africa won by 94 runs. Peter Pollock took ten of the wickets; a brotherly triumph. In the last Test England were 308 for 4, within 91 runs of their winning target when time was up. Cowdrey and Smith left the field, followed by these eleven South Africans – P. L. Van Der Merwe, E. J. Barlow, H. R. Lance, J. D. Lindsay, R. G. Pollock, K. C. Bland, A. Bacher, R. Dumbrill, J. T. Botten, P. M. Pollock, A. H. McKinnon. Looking back, that may be a most poignant moment in cricket's history.

West Indies

How notable a contribution have the West Indies made to world cricket? Surely, the following eleven names, set down as a team, purely from memory and without recourse to history books – and at risk of having left out an obvious choice is the most forceful answer: 1. Stollmeyer, 2. Marshall, 3. George Headley, 4. Weekes, 5. Worrell, 6. Walcott, 7. Sobers, 8. Constantine, 9. Hall, 10. Ramadhin, 11. Valentine. What world eleven would not be chary of Sobers coming in at 7, with Constantine to follow him, with an opening pace attack of Hall and Constantine, with Sobers first change, and Worrell second, and Ramadhin and Valentine to weave the spinners spell?

By the very nature of things, West Indies cricket is different in character. It has been called cavalier cricket; to an extent it is, but a more down-to-earth assessment is surely that West Indian cricketers, on their own fast wickets, have learned (or better still, have taught themselves) to play the full range of strokes available to a batsman; and what they have learned, they practise, in Test cricket if needs be. To play flamboyant shots is an expression of their own national heritage. Learie Constantine and Frank Worrell, Everton Weekes, Clyde Walcott, Gary Sobers – they were all expressive of a strong and exhilarating freedom, but they were all great players with a high enough degree of technical ability to defend as skilfully as they could attack. Of them all Everton Weekes had the greatest killer instinct; he could murder bowling, with or without gay abandon! You could never imagine his allowing the bowlers to get up off the floor any more than Joe Louis or Marciano would allow any one of their tottering opponents to come back.

Yet England have been playing Test matches against the West Indies for only a little over forty years. Admittedly, there were encounters of some sort before this, even as long ago as 1895, when R. Slade Lucas of Middlesex took a team to the West Indies. Two years later Lord Hawke and Arthur Priestly took teams to the Caribbean and helped to stimulate the inherent love of cricket there. Lord Hawke's team included 'Plum' Warner, himself from Port of Spain, Trinidad. In fact, in 1900, when the first West Indies side came to England, it was captained by his brother, R. S. A. Warner. In the early months of 1902 another team of English amateurs headed for the West Indies captained by B. J. T. Bosanquet; Lord Brackley's side followed two years later. In 1906 H. B. G. Austin brought a very useful side to England, and during the winter of 1912–13 a fairly strong MCC team toured West Indies under the captaincy of A. F. Somerset, who had been a member of Lord Brackley's team seven years previously. Because of the break brought about by war, it was not until 1923 that another West Indies side came to England, and included in it were two players who had come in 1906 – Austin himself, and G. Challenor. The party also included Karl Nunes, later to lead the West Indies in the First Test match against England, and Learie Constantine, great all-rounder who established West Indies cricket in world affairs, and did so much for the cause of his people in all other walks of life. West Indies lost a great champion when he died of a heart attack in July 1971.

Encouraged by the form shown on this 1923 tour, the MCC decided to send a really strong side to the West Indies in the winter of 1925–6. It was captained by the Hon. F. S. G. Calthorpe, and included a strong contingent of eight well known professionals – Percy Holmes, Wally Hammond, Frank Watson, Ewart Astill, 'Tiger' Smith, Roy Kilner, Fred Root and the Kent all-rounder, George Collins. This was the supreme test for West Indies cricket; their future was in the examination room – and they passed. The prize was an official Test series in England in 1928. West Indies cricket had taken its first major step forward, and it has been stepping forward ever since. Of the fifty-eight Tests played against England, West Indies have won sixteen, England twenty, with twenty-two drawn. In fact, after the completion of a successful tour of England in 1966, the West Indies were only one behind to underline their dominance in seven series from 1947-8 to 1966. In this period, West Indies won thirteen Tests to England's nine. This was a golden era of great players in which appeared the famous 'W' Plan – Weekes, Worrell and Walcott. Many great cricketers have hunted in pairs – Hobbs and Sutcliffe, Hutton and Washbrook, Lock and Laker – but it is rare to have an inseparable triumvirate such as this. They will, however, always be remembered together for batting such as we had not seen the like before. Ramadhin, who brought a certain mystique with him when he arrived unheralded for the first time, made the finest England batsmen confess that the only hope of spotting what he was going to bowl was in the bright light of the Caribbean; in England you simply played him off the pitch and took him on the face value of each ball, hoping you would be there to face the next one. Cowdrey, after his marathon partnership with May at Edgbaston, admitted that this is how he played Ramadhin, and gave up trying to spot him. Then there is Sobers; the complete one-man cricket team; like a member of a famous symphony orchestra able to play every instrument on the platform. Sobers is a batsman, a fast bowler, a slow bowler and a wicket-keeper; a cricketer extraordinary.

There were five series between England and West Indies before the 1939 war and in these England led by eight matches to three. Not unnaturally they had won the three played in 1928 when the West Indies had come very much as the new boy, feeling their feet, as it were, although seven of them – Challenor, Nunes (the Captain), Constantine, Browne, Francis, Fernandes and Small had been to England before. The newcomers were: E. L. Bartlett, H. C. Griffith, W. St. Hill, E. L. G. Hoad, J. N. Neblett, F. R. Martin, E. A. Rae, C. A. Roach, O. C. Scott and C. V. Wight. The First Test match was played at Lord's when the teams were:

England: H. Sutcliffe, C. Hallows, E. Tyldesley, W. R. Hammond, D. R. Jardine, A. P. F. Champan (Captain), V. W. C. Jupp, M. W. Tate, H. Smith, H. Larwood, A. P. Freeman.

West Indies: G. Challenor, F. R. Martin, M. P. Fernandes, R. K. Nunes (Captain), W. H. St. Hill, C. A. Roach, L. N. Constantine, J. A. Small, C. R. Browne, G. N. Francis, H. C. Griffith.

England won, as was expected, by an innings and 58 runs. Constantine took 4 wickets for 82 and held three catches in England's total of 401; West Indies' batting was never the equal to the occasion. At Old Trafford it was very little different. The West Indies batted first but again lost by an innings, and precisely the same course was followed at the Oval which resulted in three wins for England – all by an innings. But for West Indies, there was still a good deal on the credit side. They had now experienced the atmosphere of Test cricket and were bound to be all the better for it. Constantine did the double – a magnificent performance – 1,381 runs and 107 wickets, and seven West Indian batsmen hit hundreds.

The West Indies were not to wait long for success against England, although when it is considered that in the winter of 1929–30 MCC also had a strong side in Australia and New Zealand, and that players of the calibre of Hobbs, Sutcliffe, Hammond, Ernest Tyldesley, Tate and Larwood were taking a winter's rest after a strenuous summer, the side in the West Indies could be hardly described as a Test team in the accepted sense. In fact, although four matches are categorized as Tests in the records, *Wisden*, at the time, referred to these games as: MCC *v* West Indies in a Representative match.

There were four such matches, each side winning one and two being drawn. Not that this series did not put some very fine players on display – the Hon. F. S. G. Calthorpe, as Captain,

Nigel Haig, Bob Wyatt, Wilfred Rhodes, George Gunn, Patsy Hendren, Andrew Sandham, Leslie Townsend and Bill Voce for the MCC, and George Headley, Roach, Constantine and Griffith for the West Indies. Roach and Headley hit hundreds in the First Test as did Sandham; Hendren with a double century and Ames with a century were the batting stars of the second match.

It was the third game at Georgetown which gave the West Indies their first win. A double-century by Roach and a century in each innings by the masterful Headley produced scores of 471 and 290 for the West Indies. But MCC could manage only 145 and 327. The fourth game was memorable for England and for Andrew Sandham – he hit 325, and tells a wonderful story about this innings. Sandham, with that rare twinkle in his eye which many of us knew well, said that when he reached a hundred quite often he failed to get many more, and after reaching his century in this match he said to the umpire: 'Well, I suppose I had better be going.' The umpire replied: 'Oh, don't go, you're the only one I know out here.' Sandham acceded to the request and stayed to make a triple-century! With Ames making 149, England amassed 849. They might have won had the West Indies not possessed another edition of Bradman – George Headley scored 223, and in their second innings, West Indies were 408 for 5 when the match was left drawn. So that was the end of a Test series – at least the records say that it was!

The West Indies failed to win a Test in England in 1933, but in the winter of 1934-5 they won two against Wyatt's side after England had gained one of the most dramatic victories imaginable in the First Test (duly given the title of Test by *Wisden* this time). On a pitch seriously affected by rain, the West Indies were bowled out for 102. England, faring no better, surprisingly declared at 81 for 7; the West Indies replied with an even more startling declaration – 51 for 6, England making the 73 runs required for victory for the loss of six wickets; a remarkable match indeed. The fast bowlers who made hay on this wicket were Farnes, 'Big' Jim Smith, the ferocious hitter, who emptied the Tavern every time he strode to the wicket at Lord's, and 'Manny Martindale for the West Indies. Ken Farnes was a magnificent fast bowler who lost his life in a war-time air crash, taking off in a Wellington bomber one night; this I know because I was in hospital with his air-gunner, the only survivor of the crash.

England once again felt the sharp edge of Headley's rapier in the Fourth Test – 270 not out; his average for the four Test matches was 97. This was the series which placed the seal of genuine Test match authority on West Indian cricket. They were never to look back and their players were to give enormous pleasure with their glittering stroke-play. George Headley touched greatness: his inspiration fired many a young West Indian with the desire and determination to emulate him. Rolf Grant's team to England in 1939 were dogged by miserable weather, and the final imminence of the catastrophe of war caused the cancellation of their last few matches. England won one Test and two were drawn. Headley was to distinguish himself still further. He hit a hundred in each innings of the Lord's Test, as he had done against Calthorpe's side. Constantine, at the age of thirty-seven, had lost little of his magic; he was the most unflagging member of a very alert side.

It was nine years before England and West Indies met again on the cricket-field. Europe, instead, was plunged headlong into war, and it was not until G. O. 'Gubby' Allen took a side to the Caribbean in the winter of 1947–8 that the West Indies began to emerge as the principal world power in cricket. This was a memorable series for them, but not for the MCC, who created the unenviable record of being the first MCC touring side to complete an overseas tour without a single victory. The West Indies, by winning two and drawing two matches, gave the prestige of English cricket a nasty jolt, although this was a side well below full strength. This was because of the absence of Edrich, Compton, Yardley, Bedser and Wright all of whom stayed at home, and of Hutton who joined the party only halfway through the tour when Allen implored the MCC in an urgent cable to send reinforcements for his beleaguered garrison – beleaguered in terms of illness and injuries and, not a little, by the skill of the opponents.

The situation was so bad for the Second Test that if you were walking wounded ... you played! The Captain was at his wits' end for an opening batsmen and decided that it should be the next man who walked into the dressing-room. It happened to be S. C. 'Billy' Griffith, playing in his first Test match. Griffith shaped so well as an opening batsman that he immediately ran out Jack Robertson, the only man in the side likely to make a really big score! Griffith has said since, that he was so afraid of facing the full impact of Allen's wrath that he dared not get out, and preferred the safety of what the West Indies attack could hurl at him! He remained firm in his intentions and scored 140; what a magnificent performance in his first Test match; he saved the match for England, but centuries by Worrell in the Third Test and Weekes in the Fourth produced West Indian victories. Now the lesson had been driven home; never again could England afford to send a below-par side to the Caribbean. Their best was as good as ours ... and better.

And so to 1950, and incomparably the best West Indies side to face England at any time. This was an unforgettable tour; calypso music and oil drums, gaiety and joy; cricket was bursting at the seams with a wonderful competitive spirit. We had been warned before the team arrived to keep a weather eye out for the fast bowlers; this, it was felt, was where the West Indies held the trump card. We had no such warning of Ramadhin and Valentine; to the outside world they were untried, unsung and almost unheard of. They were not only sung about afterwards, but a calypso was written specially in their honour. Ramadhin, like some little mystery man from the Orient had a mixed bag in his repertoire. Valentine merely trundled his left-arm spin just as left-arm spinners had trundled before him, but there was something different, somehow. It just wanted a few snake-charmers dotted round the ground providing background music and the whole performance would have been completely set in its own strange environment. As it was their success chilled the spine a number of times. Ramadhin and Valentine took fifty-nine wickets between them; Goddard and Worrell were next with six apiece. Where were the much trumpeted fast bowlers? They barely got a look in! The 'W' formation hammered the English bowling, there were two superb opening batsmen in the left-handed Alan Rae and Jeff Stollmeyer – the 'Palairet of the Lovely Isles' to give balance, poise and unrelenting power. The West Indies won at Lord's to achieve their first Test victory in England, and took the series 3–1. The lingering memory of this tour for those who were privileged to see it was Worrell and Weekes at Trent Bridge – batting that was sheer poetry. They were happy days for all of us.

The players on this highly memorable tour were: J. D. C. Goddard (Captain), J. B. Stollmeyer, A. F. Rae, E. Weekes, F. M. Worrell, C. L. Walcott, R. E. Marshall, C. B. Williams, G. E. Gomez, P. E. Jones, L. R. Pierre, S. Ramadhin, K. B. Trestrail, H. H. Johnson, R. J. Christiani and A. L. Valentine.

Since 1950 there have been seven series between England and the West Indies and thirty-three Test matches. England have won eleven to the West Indies' eight, with fourteen drawn. In 1953-4 Len Hutton took a side to the West Indies which prompted Alex Bannister's book on the tour to be titled *Cricket Cauldron*. Hutton considerably enhanced his reputation for leadership and courage. When faced with bottles being thrown at Georgetown he refused to take his side off the field because he said that England could not afford to waste time. The West Indies won the first two Tests. A great innings of 169 by Hutton himself paved the way for an England victory in the Third; supreme batting by the 'W' Plan – Weekes (206), Worrell (167) and Walcott (124) – put the West Indies far beyond the possibility of defeat in the Fourth, which meant that England had to win the last to save the series – and save it they did. Trevor Bailey (an astonishing and courageous cricketer) took 7 for 34 – what a magnificent bowling performance – and West Indies were all out for 139. Hutton replied with a double century – he just kept soldiering on, despite the intense heat of Kingston, Jamaica. Trueman and Laker bagged seven wickets between them in the West Indies' second innings, and a wonderful victory was achieved.

In 1957 John Goddard revived memories of 1950 when he captained another West Indies side to England. History did not repeat itself as the West Indies failed to win a single Test, England winning three with two drawn. To those who saw it (happily,

I was one of them) the abiding memory of this tour was an innings of 258 by Tom Graveney at Trent Bridge. This innings showed this player at his most elegant. Cardus wrote of him: 'Few batsmen, in my experience, have concealed forcibility as subtly, as sinuously, as delightfully as Graveney. There is no English-born batsman in view at the moment who is Graveney's equal in point of natural skill, unexhibited grace, all done and revealed with the unselfconsciousness which is the proof of the born artist whether his instrument be a cricket bat or Yehudi Menuhin's violin.' Graveney on those two summer days at Trent Bridge will linger in memory for a lifetime. That is what I remember most about the 1957 West Indians. Their fine players will know exactly what I mean.

In 1959-60 May took a side to the Caribbean and for the first time England won a series in the West Indies, winning the Second Test, the other four being drawn. The First Test produced an exhilarating partnership between Sobers and Worrell; personification of West Indies temperament and the culture of cricket. Sobers made 226 and Worrell 197 not out. Barrington and Dexter had already hit hundreds for England; here was the backbone of a really strong England side: Barrington, the perfectionist, the thorough professional, and Dexter, perhaps one of the last of the Dandies, with his personality, aggression and flamboyant skill. The Second Test, which England won, had everything, and sensation followed sensation. On the first day umpire Lloyd warned Hall under Law 46; on the second day umpire Lee Kow took the same steps with Watson, and on the third the bottles flew again. To make up for the time lost when stumps were drawn early, extra time was added to the last three days. Barrington and Dexter repeated their performances with centuries, and the best fast-bowling firm in the business, Statham and Trueman, bowled the West Indies out. Rohan Kanhai was the only West Indies batsman to pass fifty in either innings; he scored 110 in the second. There were plenty more hundreds to come in the series – Cowdrey (twice), Sobers (twice), Subba Row, Dexter and Jim Parks – but no decisive result emerged either way. Cowdrey, incidentally, took over the Captaincy when May was forced to return home after the Third Test to undergo an operation. The presence of the mighty Sobers was evident in the batting averages – his average was 101·28.

In the next two series in England, the West Indies contrived a sizeable advantage; they won three Tests to one under Frank Worrell in 1963, and Gary Sobers repeated the performance precisely in 1966. The tremendous success of the 1963 tour prompted immediate action to bring the West Indies back to England as soon as possible. The Test at Lord's was probably the greatest drawn Test match in the history of cricket. Cowdrey appeared at the wicket with one arm in plaster (smashed by a short ball from Wes Hall). He was not called upon to face a ball, but his presence saved the match. No England player made a century in the series – for the first time since 1888. Conrad Hunte (two), Basil Butcher and Gary Sobers hit hundreds for the West Indies. Trueman bowled magnificently for England, but so did Charlie Griffith for the West Indies. This series belonged incomparably to the West Indies.

In 1966 the West Indies were back, as powerful as ever. England won the last Test but this kind of result comes as something of an anticlimax when a side is already three down! The West Indies had their usual complement of prolific run-scorers – Hunte, Sobers, Butcher, Seymour Nurse and, in addition, Sobers' cousin, David Holford, who held West Indies intact at Lord's when everything seemed to have gone overboard; his partnership with Sobers is one of the most famous rearguard actions in cricket history. There was still a final flourish to the match – a 126 not out by Colin Milburn, a swashbuckling, bruising innings, that made the blood tingle; this happy cavalier was at his happiest; the memory of it makes his tragedy all the more sombre. Culture and agression took first and second place in the England batting averages – Graveney first, and Milburn second. Sobers, yet again, registered another average of over 100, and Lance Gibbs was spinning his way to fame.

Yet in the next two series the West Indies failed to win a game, neither against Cowdrey's team in West Indies, when England won one, and four were drawn, nor on the truncated three-match tour in 1969, with Sobers at the helm again; this time England won two. Cowdrey's tour produced an absorbing series in which the pendulum swung first one way and then the other; rearguard actions were the order of the day, and the only success, ironically, came as the result of a declaration by Sobers, in the Fourth Test when he set England 215 to make in 165 minutes and England made them. Thirteen centuries were scored, but John Snow's taking of twenty-seven wickets was the heralding of a world-class fast bowler; he ultimately emerged as the best in the world. Clive Lloyd, later to enchant the habitués at Old Trafford, and in many parts of the world, hit a hundred at Port of Spain.

And so the West Indies story is brought up to date with a 2–0 win for England in 1969. From the West Indies' point of view this was a particularly disappointing performance all round. It was, however, a significant series for England. Their captain was Ray Illingworth. He came as a makeshift because Cowdrey was out of action following an operation on his Achilles tendon; Illingworth has stayed to prove himself a Captain in his own right. For me, the most touching moment of it all, was in October 1970 when, on holiday in Barbados, I stood beside the grave of Frank Worrell – Knight, cricketer, gentleman and a great ambassador. He graced the world's cricket grounds by his very presence.

New Zealand

New Zealand, in the mind's eye of the sporting devotee in England, is the home of the famous All-Blacks – George Nepia, Bob Scott, Colin Meads – the mighty man. Rugby football is the religion of New Zealand. Cricket is a game, secondary in nature and in achievement. New Zealand, for instance, is the only Test-playing country never to have beaten England. Their record in forty-two Tests is twenty to England and twenty-two drawn, but they have still produced world-class players, though not in great enough profusion ever to produce a really strong side. Martin Donnelly, a left-handed batsman in the classic mould is able to stand comparison with any company in any age. His 206 at Lord's in 1949 was a cricketing masterpiece; the first hundred was hard grafting. It had to be; circumstances demanded that he trod carefully, but Donnelly added his last ninety runs in eighty minutes. Frank Woolley or Neil Harvey would have been proud to have had this innings in their records.

Bert Sutcliffe, another left-hander, was out of the top drawer. Wherever he went in that summer of 1949 – the happy summer of Wally Hadlee's team – he faced the bowlers with the light of battle in his eyes, and unleashed that swinging stroke through extra-cover that was about the most breathtaking spectacle to be seen anywhere. Then, of course, there is John Reid, one of the most popular cricketers ever to come to these shores – and what a fine player. John Reid did everything for New Zealand – made most runs, took most wickets, held the most catches, scored the most centuries, and played in the Test wins against the West Indies in 1955–6 and South Africa (twice) in 1961–2. He was not just the backbone of New Zealand cricket; he was its mainstay as well. His broad shoulders were frequently called upon to bear one burden or another; he rarely failed, however heavy the load. Eleven Reids would have done for any World Eleven!

Although the first English team to play in New Zealand did so more than a century ago – George Parr captained an all-professional side which paid a brief visit after a tour of Australia in 1864, and a comparatively strong New Zealand side came to England in 1927 – official Test matches between the two countries did not begin until Harold Gilligan (who took over the Captaincy from his brother, Arthur, who was ill) took an England side out in the winter of 1929–30. Tom Lowry brought the first New Zealand Test side to England in 1931.

That first-ever Test match at Christchurch, beginning on 10 January 1930, produced a most extraordinary morning's cricket. New Zealand won the toss and lost 3 wickets for 15 runs. When the score was 21, Maurice Allom took 4 wickets in 5 balls, including the hat-trick. New Zealand were 21 for 7 – something to remember the First Test match by! The Second Test at Wellington was memorable from New Zealand's point of view; J. W. E. Mills and C. S. Dempster, both scoring hundreds, put on 276 for the first wicket. A century in two hours by Kumar Shri

Touring teams to England

The first Pakistan team in 1954. *Back row:* Wazir Mohammed, Khalid Hassan, Shujauddin, Shakoor Ahmed, Zulfiqar Ahmed. *Middle row:* Khalid Wazir, Waqar Hassan, Ikram Elahi, Mohammad Aslam, Mahmood Hussain, Alimuddin, Hanif Mohammad. *Seated:* M. E. Z. Ghazali, Fazal Mahmood, A. H. Kardar (Captain), Imtiaz Ahmed, Maqsood Ahmed

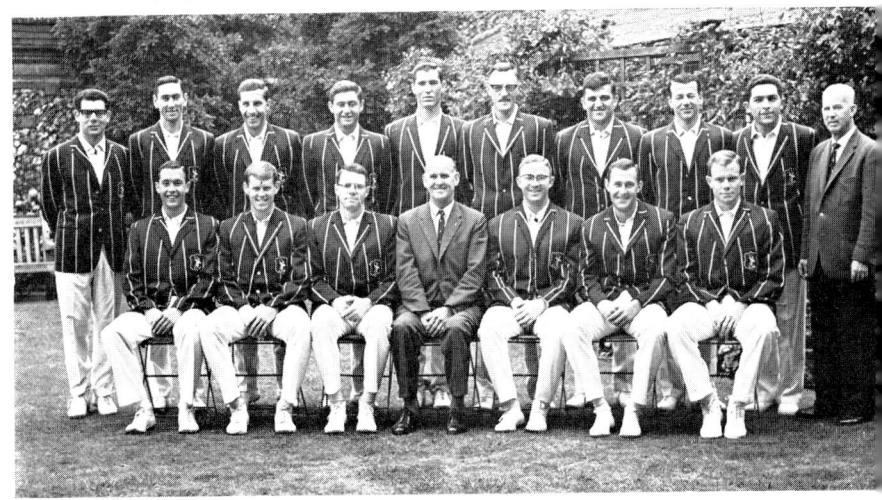

1965 – tragically, the last South African team to be seen in England for some time. *Standing:* D. Gamsy, N. S. Crookes, R. Dumbrill, M. J. Macaulay, H. R. Lance, H. D. Bromfield, A. H. McKinnon, J. T. Botten, A. Bacher, M. McLennan (Scorer). *Seated:* D. Lindsay, R. G. Pollock, P. L. van der Merwe (Captain), J. B. Plimsoll (Manager), E. J. Barlow, K. C. Bland, P. M. Pollock

Master batsmen

Frank Woolley

Geoff Boycott

Colin Cowdrey

Peter May

Great fast bowlers

Harold Larwood

Ray Lindwall

Brian Statham

'Wes' Hall

Great all-rounders

Wilfred Rhodes

Wally Hammond

Keith Miller

Gary Sobers

Duleepsinhji, nephew of the great 'Ranji', a chip off the old block and a cricketer with a wonderful eye and tremendous flexibility of wrist, was a feature of the Third Test, and an innings of 196 by G. B. Legge rounded off the series.

From that day to this, New Zealand have striven for that first elusive victory, so far in vain. One encouraging moment was when New Zealand had England's opening batsmen – Herbert Sutcliffe and Eddie Paynter – out for nought at Christchurch in 1933. Hammond, however, chose this moment to hit 227. Hammond followed this superb innings with something even better – 336 not out in his next innings. He batted for 315 minutes, hit ten sixes, three off successive balls from Newman, and thirty-three fours. Is it any wonder when you talk to players like Charles Barnett or Cyril Washbrook and ask them. 'Who was the greatest player you ever saw?' they answer, without having to think – 'Wally, of course.'

Hammond completed a prodigious Test hat-trick. In his next innings against New Zealand at Lord's in 1937, he hit 140. What a moment of joy for Jack Cowie to get him for nought at Old Trafford!

After Hammond came Len Hutton. He scored 206 in the Oval Test of 1949. At Auckland, under Hutton's leadership in 1955, New Zealand suffered the rock bottom in indignity when they were bowled out for 26 – the lowest total in Test cricket. Bert Sutcliffe made 11, the other 10 players scoring 15 between them; Bob Appleyard took 4 for 7 and Brian Statham 3 for 9; Frank Tyson was rather more expensive at 2 for 10! New Zealand were to suffer cruelly at the hands of England's bowlers on the next tour – all out 47 and 74 at Lord's. Lock and Laker, the cruellest henchmen in the land when the wickets were responsive to their steely fingers, wrought complete devastation. They did it again at Leeds – New Zealand all out for 67, and all out 85 at Old Trafford. If cricketers have nightmares and the science of man seems to suggest that they do, then an ogre-sized figure of the Machiavellian Lock must taunt many a New Zealand cricketer, and will harass them until their dying day.

Dexter and May put their batting techniques on view in New

Zealand in 1959, each hitting centuries. Both were the products of Cambridge University, nurtured on one of the most beautiful batting strips in the world – Fenners. Both cricketers had absorbed the basic teachings, and then had super-imposed their own variations on top of the mundane; neither could abide relentless routine; each was creative and each was blessed with the necessary flair and touch of genius to allow their creative instincts to burgeon. Dexter led the next side to New Zealand after an Australian tour in 1962-3. Once again, England were much too strong. Ken Barrington, Peter Parfitt and Barry Knight hit hundreds in the First Test, Colin Cowdrey scored 128 in the Second, but the performance of the series was surely the courage and fighting qualities shown by batsman John Reid – he hit 100 out of a total of 159.

In 1965 New Zealand participated in the first split-tour of England, playing in three Test matches, the last ending in the middle of July. England then took on South Africa in a three-Test series. England beat New Zealand with a clean sweep of the pen; the weather was abysmal. In the First Test at Edgbaston hot tea was taken out on to the field, and the players warmed their hands on the tea-pot! In spite of scoring 413 in their second innings, a herculean feat, New Zealand lost by nine wickets. At Lord's England won by seven wickets; Trueman was hit for 69 runs in New Zealand's second innings without getting a wicket. 'Fiery' Fred, great bowler, great character (no wonder he ended up on the music hall stage) had bowled for England for the last time. We'll never see another quite like him, this son of the real Yorkshire soil; a spade was a spade in his language. The Third Test at Headingley belonged to John Edrich – he scored 310 not out, a gritty, fighting innings, and he was master of all he surveyed. In nine consecutive innings he had scored 1,311 runs, being three times not out and with a batting average in that period of 218·5. Shades of Bradman, or even better! On 'Mike' Smith's tour to New Zealand in 1965-6 two New Zealanders scored hundreds – Bevan Congdon and Barry Sinclair, but in England in 1969 they felt the whiplash of Edrich again. They still seek that first taste of victory. As far as New Zealand are concerned, England always seem to have the men for the occasion. Derek Underwood ravaged New Zealand's batsmen and bowled them out for 65 on Illingworth's tour. Basil d'Oliveira and Alan Knott came up with centuries just at the right time. England are just too strong – all the time.

India

India – 'Ranji', the germinal power of all Indian cricket, his nephew, Duleepsinhji, Merchant (the Jack Hobbs of India), Nayudu, Nissar, Amar Singh, Mankad, Mushtaq Ali, Hazare, Nawab of Pataudi (father and son), right through to the present triumvirate of spin bowlers – Bedi, Venkataraghavan, Chandrasekhar – and that mercurial wicket-keeper, batsman Farokh Engineer – all players of character and skill, some with a magical touch of the East about them. Who could fail to be enthralled by the turbanned Bedi trundling his left-arm spin with all the cunning of his noble craft, or 'Chandra', with his uncanny ability to bounce the ball more than any other slow bowler I can ever remember?

'Chandra' – no doubt India's teeming millions would willingly give him the Taj Mahal as small reward for what he did at the Oval in August 1971. His bowling gave India her first victory on English soil. The Oval, packed with Indian supporters, live elephants and all, saw once again unforgettable scenes of rejoicing. The Indian players took curtain call after curtain call on their balcony. This great victory was conjured out of nothing. India had been saved from defeat by rain at Lord's and Old Trafford. At the Oval England scored 355 in their first innings. India replied with 284. An England victory was on the cards, almost routine, yet in fact the stage had been cleared for 'Chandra' to give the performance of his life – he took 6 for 38 and England were shot out for 101. India grafted to victory, a victory that meant so much that any fragment of risk was out of the question. England fought tooth and nail to the death, but if we talk of fight, this Indian side fought as few other Indian sides have fought before. Sometimes their cricketers have been suspect in a tight corner but not any more. These eleven players will take the memory of Tuesday, 24 August with them into eternity; A. L. Wadekar, a splendid Captain, A. V. Mankad, S. Gavaskar, D. N. Sardesai, G. R. Wiswanath, E. D. Solkar, F. M. Engineer, S. Abid Ali, S. Venkataraghavan, B. S. Bedi, B. S. Chandrasekhar. Within six months India had beaten West Indies and England away from home; what a pity they could not have a crack at South Africa in search of the grand slam.

I think if I were allowed only one of these players to appear in my side against another planet, I would choose Engineer. To me, he epitomizes every virtue that makes the game of cricket what it is, both on and off the field: cricketer, team-man supreme, gentlemen – an unchallengeable trinity of assets.

Cricket in India stretches far back into history, the first recorded match having taken place as long ago as 1751, yet the first Test match between England and India was not until 1932, and even now only forty matches have taken place between us. India has won four of them. C. K. Nayudu brought the first Indian Test team to England in 1932, when only one Test match was played. Jardine took an England side to India in the winter of 1933-4 when Amarnath became the first Indian to score a Test hundred against England. The Maharajah Kumar of Vizianagram led the 1936 Indians to England.

In India's second innings at Old Trafford, Merchant and Mushtaq Ali put on 203 for the first wicket. Hammond's three Test innings against this side were 167, 217 and 5 not out. I saw Hammond's double-century at the Oval and his partnership with Worthington which put on 266. I took with me a mild cricket enthusiast whose one joy in the game was to see wickets falling; he finally went to sleep behind the sightscreen at the Vauxhall end! I sat, my eyes drawn to Hammond's bat like a magnet, missing not a single run that flowed from it; wonderful stuff it was, absolute poetry.

The Nawab of Pataudi brought an Indian side to England in that joyous summer of 1946 – the first breath of cricket after many war-torn years of suffering and nostalgia. Here at last was Test cricket again. Pataudi, incidentally, having played for England, was given special permission to lead India. I saw the First Test at Lord's when a young bowler named Bedser took 7 for 64 and 4 for 96, and Joe Hardstaff hit a double-century; here was another cultured stroke-master out of the top drawer. Merchant hit 128 at the Oval, an innings which clearly demonstrated his class.

When Nigel Howard took a side to India in the winter of 1951–2, India tasted the first fruits of victory. India showed tremendous strength in batting in the first three Tests. In the First at New Delhi, Merchant scored 154 and Hazare 164 not out; a weakened England side was threatened with disaster until Alan Watkins kept the wolf at bay with a fighting innings of 138 not out. Hazare hit another hundred in the Second Test, as did Roy. This time Graveney kept England's head above water with a majestic 175 not out. In the Third Test, Phadkar maintained India's run of centuries. In the Fourth Test, however, Kanpur produced a spinner's wicket, and Roy Tattersall and Malcolm Hilton spun India to an astonishing collapse – 39 for no wicket – 76 for 6, and all out 121. The same pair produced something similar in India's second innings and England were one up in the series. India's prolific batting in the first three Tests had availed them little; it looked as though the bird had flown, but in the last Test at Madras on 6, 8, 9 and 10 February 1952 the following eleven players inflicted India's first defeat upon England: Mushtaq Ali, Roy, Hazare, Mankad, Amarnath, Phadkar, Umrigar, Gopinath, Divecha, Sen and Ghulam Ahmed. It was Mankad the bowler (8 for 55 in 38·5 overs and 4 for 53 in 30·4 overs) and Roy (111) and Umrigar (130 not out) who were the prime architects of this elusive victory at the twenty-fifth attempt, and by the sizeable margin of an innings and 8 runs.

In 1952, under Hazare, the Indians felt the full weight of England with her very best in the field. The side in India had been a long way from England's strongest; now, things were different. The England team at Leeds was: Hutton, Simpson, May, Compton, Graveney, Watkins, Evans, Jenkins, Laker, Bedser, Trueman. Despite a capital hundred by Manjrekar, they won by seven wickets. England won at Lord's, too, in one of the most remarkable 'one man' cricket matches of all time. The was Mankad Vinoo, that master of versatility and abounding talents. His one-man orchestra at Lord's produced this statistical symphony – 72 and 184, and in England's mammoth first-innings total of 537, Mankad bowled 73 overs and took 5 for 196; he bowled another 24 overs when England were knocking off the seventy-odd runs needed to win. For England, Hutton hit 150 and Godfrey Evans 104. Evans – could he be the greatest entertainer the game has ever known? Certainly, he could be the greatest wicket-keeper, with dashing, cavalier, flamboyant batting thrown in for good measure, but every minute he was on the field the crowd were drawn to him, as they were by Danny Kaye. Come to think of it, you could imagine Danny Kaye keeping wicket and swinging a pretty hearty bat, and would Godfrey have looked all that much out of place singing 'Five Pennies' with the late Louis Armstrong? Not really! But it was not Evans, but Trueman, who gave the 1952 Indians their real headaches. In their second innings at Leeds, India made the most macabre start ever known in Test cricket history – no runs – four wickets! Trueman, whose speed simply shattered India's batting, finished the Test series with 29 wickets at 13·31 apiece. How good a bowler was Fred Trueman ... just ask any member of that Indian team; the answer will be that he was a good one alright.

In 1959, under Gaekwad, India suffered a complete whitewash – England won all five Test matches. May's expertise as Captain and the strength of the players gathered round him were far too good for the opposition. England won by an innings and 59 runs, 8 wickets, an innings and 173 runs, 171 runs, and an innings and 27 runs. Statham and Trueman bowled them out, and eight England batsmen had averages of over 50. 'Who topped the England batting averages?' could be the catch question on any cricket quiz programme. It was Brian Statham, with a batting average of 70 contrived by being twice not out in his three innings!

India were swift to claim revenge and won two Test matches against Dexter's side in 1961–2, after the first three Tests had been drawn, with huge scores the order of the day. In these first three Tests there were eight centuries; Barrington 151 not out,

Umrigar 147 not out, Barrington 172, Dexter 126 not out, Pullar 119, Manjrekar 189 not out, Jaisimha 127, Barrington 113 not out. Barrington's purple patch in these three games produced scores of 151 not out, 52 not out, 21, 172, 113 not out. His average for three Tests was 254·5. But at Calcutta, India forged a notable victory which they repeated at Madras, the young Nawab of Pataudi scoring the only hundred of these last two Tests. Never before had India ever won two matches in a single series.

M. J. K. Smith's tour in 1963–4 produced five drawn games on wickets which were calculated to produce permanent heartbreaks for bowlers. *Playfair Cricket Annual* called this abysmal series a mockery of cricket, and so it was.

Pataudi's three-match Test series in 1967 was decisive for England; they won all three Tests despite a herculean innings of 148 at Leeds by Pataudi himself when India scored 510 in the second innings – and lost! And so to Ajit Wadekar and his triumph of 1971.

Pakistan

Pakistan, as an Independent Sovereign State, was inaugurated on 14 August 1947, so it is young as a State, but is still an ancient land and one of the cradles of civilization. In 1954 Abdul Hafeez Kardar brought the first Pakistan cricket team to England for a four-match Test series, having previously been a member of the 1946 Indian party – and Kardar's Pakistanis won a Test match at the Oval. Many think that this was still the best Pakistan touring side. It consisted of: A. H. Kardar, Fazal Mahmood, Maqsood Ahmed, Khan Mohammad, Imtiaz Ahmed, Hanif Mohammad, Alim-ud-Din, Shuja-ud-Din, M. E. Z. Ghazali, Wizzir Mohammad, Mahmood Hussain, Waqar Hassan, Zulfiqar Ahmed, Khalid Hassan, Ikram Elahi, Khalid Wazir, Mohammad Aslam and Shakoor Ahmed. E. M. Wellings, writing in the *Playfair Cricket Annual* in 1955, said of this team: 'The 1954 Pakistan team will always be remembered in England for the good humour and sportsmanship displayed on all occasions. Kardar and his men may well take most pleasure in the reputation they gained in that direction.'

The fast-medium bowling of Fazal was one of the dominating factors of the series, but this tour was just another stage in the development of Hanif, the 'Little Wonder', as one of the world's outstanding players. He was to become a collector of vast numbers of runs and probably had more patience than any other cricketer – Bradman included. Hanif holds the record for the longest innings in first-class cricket – 999 minutes in scoring 337 for Pakistan *v* West Indies in Barbados in 1957–8. He holds the world record score of 499 for Karachi *v* Bahawalpur in 1958–9, being run-out off the last ball of the day when going for his 500th run. He holds the world record for the slowest century in first-class cricket – 100 not out in 525 minutes for a Pakistan XI *v* the MCC at Lahore in 1955–6; not surprisingly he has scored more runs and centuries than any other Pakistan player. In the first fifty Test matches played by Pakistan, Hanif appeared forty-eight times, having made his Test début at the age of sixteen. Rarely, was he the delight of the crowd; never, was he the delight of bowlers! Never, surely, will there ever be an approach to cricket quite like this.

In 1954 Pakistan had to contend with thoroughly depressing weather, and when the sun did shine it shone the warmest on the back of Denis Compton, who scored 278 in the Second Test at Trent Bridge. England's batting on the second day was described as being 'out of this world' with three supreme stroke-makers, Reg Simpson (101), Denis Compton (278) and Tom Graveney (84); in 290 minutes 437 runs were added. In 125 minutes between lunch and tea 245 runs were scored, 173 of them by Compton. Simpson, Compton and Graveney in this sort of form produced some golden memories of cricket. Rain ruined the games at Lord's and Old Trafford, but at no time had Pakistan given any inkling that they were capable of holding England in any conditions, so England went to the Oval one-up to contest a foregone conclusion. To this day, many critics believe that it was because England's players treated the game as a foregone conclusion that they finally threw it away, unbelievably, almost nonchalantly, but even if the bags were packed and the railway timetables were out, then this was no way to play a Test match. Let us give all credit to Pakistan for seizing the chance offered to them. They might easily have been so surprised that they failed to take it. Pakistan began disastrously by losing Hanif for a duck; Tyson, Loader and Statham bowled them out for 133. Superb bowling by Fazal shot England out for 130; still, no one worried, and when Johnny Wardle spun Pakistan out a second time for 164 (Wardle 7 for 56), a composed calm descended upon the proceedings. When England were 109 for 2 in the second innings the writing was so clearly on the wall that spectators began preparing for home; worse still, so did some of the England players. Then it happened – 109 for 2 became 143 all out – Fazal took 6 for 46 for a match analysis of 12 for 99, and Pakistan had beaten an England team consisting of: Hutton, Simpson, May, Compton, Graveney, Evans, Wardle, Tyson, McConnon, Statham, Loader. He who laughs last laughs longest. England have never been caught napping by Pakistan again, but at least this young country has achieved what New Zealand have failed to accomplish. Of the twenty-one Tests between England and Pakistan, England have won nine, eleven have been drawn, and Pakistan cherish that famous victory.

Five series have taken place since 1954. Dexter and Cowdrey have led teams in Pakistan, and Javed Burki, Hanif and Intikhab Alam have captained Pakistan teams in England. Dexter's three-match series produced a plethora of runs – Burki 138, Barrington 139, Mike Smith – run-out 99, Hanif a century in each innings of the Second Test – 111 and 104, Burki 140, Pullar 165, Alim-ud-Din 109, Dexter 205, and Parfitt 111 – and all in three matches. England won the first and two were drawn.

Burki's team in England in 1962 were crushed 4-0 with one drawn. England's batting averages can seldom have looked more impressive – Parfitt 113, Graveney 100, Dexter 89, Cowdrey 81, Stewart 79, Sheppard 74, Allen 71. England had eight century-makers compared to Pakistan's three (Nasimul Ghani at Lord's, Burki at Lord's, and Mushtaq Mohammad at Trent Bridge).

Five years later, in 1967, Pakistan were back for a three-match tour, having the second half of the season after a three-match series between England and India. Their Captain was Hanif. His own score of 187 not out in the First Test placed Pakistan beyond the possibility of defeat in the match, but they lost the next two. Barringon, at his absolute best, scored a hundred in each Test, but there was nothing quite as exhilarating as Asif Iqbal's innings at the Oval when, going in at number eight, he hit 146, including two sixes and twenty-one fours. This performance had Kent rushing for his signature, since a limited number of overseas players per side could be registered to play without a qualification period.

Cowdrey's team in Pakistan in 1969 faced political upheaval and riots. When England were 502 for 7 in the Third Test rioting caused the abandonment of the match and must raise considerable doubts as to whether or not an England team will be prepared to go to Pakistan again, unless the country's affairs are more stable, and the players' safety is assured. This will be a pity but understandable. At the moment, as they showed in England in a three-match series in 1971, Pakistan have a very good side in the making. The name of Zahir Abbas could remain a shining light in world cricket for years to come. His innings of 274 against England at Edgbaston, when Asif and Mushtaq also made hundreds, will be talked about for generations to come. At Leeds, Pakistan were within sight of their second victory against England until Peter Lever, with a new ball, snapped up the last three wickets in the nick of time. In a very short space of time, this young country has produced some fine cricketers; their characteristics are essentially and diametrically different from those of the cricketers from West Indies in mood and basic temperament, but they have that same inherent love of cricket that stimulates their natural desire to play it well.

4 Grace and Bradman

One of cricket's most absorbing pastimes, usually attempted in a mood of nostalgia, is to pick the best eleven of all time. A history of the game, however, is not the occasion for indulging in playful fantasies, because this eleven can never be more than fantasy. We shall never know whether the spin of Gleeson would have cut any ice with Hobbs; whether Hammond would have majestically driven Tom Richardson through the covers time and time again, or flicked him off his toes through a thin on-side field, or whether Strudwick would have taken Alec Bedser's cutter standing up. Nevertheless, it is no conjecture, it is inescapable fact, that Grace and Bradman are integral ingredients in any chronicle of the game of cricket. Not for their aesthetic qualities (qualities which produce an extravagant appreciation of the beautiful in nature and art and cricket) – neither was especially interested in cricket as a thing of beauty, but because their ability to make runs in such quantities forged a new shape in cricket's destinies. Bradman, even more than Grace, altered the whole strategy of the game for generations to come.

Grace has become a cricketing legend, but would he have done so if, instead of his huge frame, a flowing beard, and a little cap perched on top of his head like a cork bobbing on the waves, he had been a clean-shaven little man, built, shall we say, in the mould of Lindsay Hassett? Without detracting one iota from Grace's herculean feats, it must be admitted that his memory would not have been quite so vividly cherished. How could such a character ever be forgotten – the painter's delight? What an admirable subject to set on canvas, what a figure of awe for small boys to wonder at ceaselessly! How easy for stories, many of them apocryphal, to survive the passing years! Yet, in the light of his performances on the cricket field, Grace must still be revered as a cricketer extraordinary.

Bradman changed cricket as Montgomery changed Alamein; as John Logie Baird ultimately changed the living habits of mankind, or as Cassius Clay gave a new dimension to prize-fighting. The change which Bradman brought about was two-fold – immediate and lasting. The immediate was the invention of body-line bowling, a questionable method of attack because bowlers could find no other way of keeping Bradman quiet. The lasting effect was the developed psychology that a good second best to not getting a batsman out was to stop him from scoring; defensive bowling to defensively set fields has become a cancer stifling free rein in the post-Second World War years. Maurice Tate used to bowl all day believing that every ball he let go from morning to evening on a hot day was likely to produce a wicket; not so to-day. The mean, stingy approach to a situation has replaced the boisterous attack which once never waned throughout a long battle.

At times, cricket can be as boring as shelling peas; it could never be that during a Grace or a Bradman innings. Their influences, however, have left their indelible mark. This is not to venture the opinion that contemporary players are better, worse, or their equals. It is the character of the game that has changed; not men's ingenuity, but what they harbour in their souls. The technique nowadays sets out to contain a batsman, not so much to get him out. This can be done successfully by mediocre performers, bowlers not worthy of tying the shoe-strings of the great – they turn their arms like a rotor (the rotating part of a machine – a particularly apt description of some of them!). Grace and Bradman's mastery was the hatchery for most of it. Both of them, therefore, though they could hardly have known it at the time, were re-moulding the game – for better or for worse. Some say, for worse!

William Gilbert Grace

Born 18 July 1848

Died 23 October 1915

Inevitably, Dr William Gilbert Grace has inspired the writing of thousands of words about him. From a purely cricketing point of view, one of the most interesting facets of his career is that he enjoyed his best season when he was only twenty-three. The statistics alone put his tremendous feats in that summer of 1871 in sharp outline. He scored 2,739 runs in thirty-nine innings, with ten centuries, for an average of 78·25. Never again did he reach this statistical peak; in fact, no player did for a quarter of a century until Ranjitsinhji amassed a total of 2,780 runs in 1896. By comparison, the feat of Grace was infinitely superior. Whereas Grace had hit his runs in thirty-nine innings, 'Ranji' required fifty-five innings to score his runs at an average of 57·91.

The cardinal question in relation to this phenomenal scoring must be: 'What was the standard of the bowling?' It can never be answered. There can be no yard-stick by which to compare bowlers who performed a century apart, but in this fine summer there were quite a number of comparatively low scores. In a match at Nottingham between the two 'Cracks' – Nottinghamshire and Yorkshire – all four innings produced only 438 runs, it being said that all the best bowlers in the north contended. Yorkshire made 117 and 101 and Nottinghamshire 78 and 142, the Yorkshire bowlers, Freeman and Emmett, taking 13 wickets between them. In a Nottinghamshire v Surrey contest, also at Nottingham, Surrey were bowled out for 48 and 63. J. C. Shaw and A. Shaw took 18 of the wickets after Southerton had taken 8 for 63 for Surrey. Lancashire were put out for 25 by Derbyshire, and in a Kent v Sussex match at Maidstone Sussex made 65 and 156, and Kent 62 and 56. Bennett and Willsher took 19 wickets for Kent, and Southerton (who played for Surrey as well as Sussex before the qualification laws were laid down) and Lillywhite took 19 for Sussex. So, although we cannot take Lillywhite or Southerton or the Shaws and look at them in the light of a Statham or a Laker, there were sufficient moderate and low scores about in 1871 to suggest that the bowlers had some merit, certainly enough to highlight Grace's batting as something quite out of the ordinary.

Whether the wickets were good, bad or indifferent does not affect the issue. Even if they were consistently good, it was still a superb performance. If they were bad or indifferent, it puts it on a higher plane still. One aspect of Grace's character which has survived with the living legend is that this huge man was something of a bully and intimidated umpires. Whether we believe this, in part or total, whether we take it with a pinch of salt or dismiss it altogether, it can have had little bearing on the summer of 1871. Grace is hardly likely to have begun intimidating umpires at the age of twenty-three.

Another part of the legend is the constant reference to the 'Grand Old Man' – yet he was only sixty-seven when he died. Once he was a young man, not a bearded giant. Born into a cricket family he admitted to having had a bat in his hand for the first time when he was two. He saw his first cricket match in the year of the Crimean War; by the time he was nine he had mastered the technique of the defensive straight bat and was now learning to play forward as well as back. He was nurtured in a cricketing family. He was nurtured, too, in an atmosphere of medicine. He and his father and four brothers were doctors. At the age of ten he was a tall, leggy boy. In his fifteenth year W.G. suffered a serious attack of pneumonia which at one time put his life in danger. When he recovered he began to grow taller at an alarming rate, so that, although his elder brothers were stocky, he became a six-footer. Just before his fifteenth birthday he was thrown in at the deep end of cricket. He played for Twenty-two of Bristol against the All-England Eleven. He scored 32 against England's best – as a lad of fifteen. When Tinley, the lob bowler, was set in motion to have a go at this youngster, Grace promptly hit him for six. The beard, which became an inescapable part of the English landscape, came into being in his twenties. It was the most famous beard in world history. It put cricket to the forefront of the nation's affairs. W.G. was recognized with every step he took; only Her Majesty, Queen Victoria, and possibly Mr Gladstone could claim greater fame. The nation at large wanted to shake his hand; W.G. seldom refused the request.

Certainly in this summer of 1871 Grace would have won any Sportsman of the Year contest hands down. Since racing was then largely a Sport of Kings, Fordham and Maidment, two prominent jockeys, would have polled less votes, even though Maidment rode the filly, Hannah, to victory in the One Thousand Guineas, Oaks and St Leger. Grace was as symbolic of cricket as Brahms was of music, Napoleon of France, or Columbus of the New World. No other single figure in cricketing history has done as much to foster interest and promote the game of cricket to the same extent.

On his death in 1915 it was generally accepted that no such players would ever be seen again. He first appeared at Lord's in July 1864 for the South Wales Club against the MCC. He played in the Gentlemen and Players' match at the Oval in 1906 and scored 74 at the age of fifty-eight, and it was at the Oval in 1908 that he made his last appearance on a cricket field. To mark that historic occasion, the weather put on something special for him, and it snowed during the luncheon interval!

Grace's career can be sharply divided into two portions. His early fame as a batsman culminated in the season of 1876, when in the month of August he scored in three successive innings 344 against Kent at Canterbury (the highest score of his career), 177 against Nottinghamshire at Clifton and 318 not out against Yorkshire at Cheltenham. Soon after that, having passed his examination at Edinburgh as a surgeon, he thought of gradually retiring from cricket and settling down like his elder brothers to the busy life of a general practitioner. In point of fact, he did for many years hold a parish appointment at Bristol, a *locum tenens* doing his work in the summer months. Once he sat up all night by the bedside of a patient desperately ill; he was not then a young man but next day he stepped on to the College ground at Clifton and hit a double-century. When he was in his prime no sun was too hot and no day too long for him.

His change of plans to concentrate on cricket was due mainly to the appearance in England of the 1878 Australians, and the sensation caused by the victories of that eleven, and in particular by Spofforth's bowling and Blackham's wicket-keeping. Englishmen realized, with an excusable shock of surprise, that in the cricket field there were serious rivals to be faced.

Grace did very little against the Australians in 1878, but what he did whetted his appetite for the game and though the most brilliant part of his career had ended before the invasion of 1878, the Australians found him for the best part of twenty years the most formidable of their opponents.

The second part of his career as a batsman began towards the end of the season of 1880. Following some fine performances for Gloucestershire he played a great innings of 152 at the Oval against Australia. Even then, though only in his thirty-third year, he laboured under one serious disadvantage. In the four years following his triumphs of 1876, he had put on a lot of weight and was very heavy for so young a man.

He had to battle against increasing bulk for the rest of his cricketing life. For a long time he retained his activity to a surprising extent, but as the years went on his once splendid fielding left him. His batting never waned, and his success in what may be called his second period in cricket was reached in 1895 when he scored a thousand runs in first-class cricket in the month of May. He was nearly forty-seven and the first man ever to perform the feat. It has been done only seven times in cricket history. Twice by Bradman, and once by Hayward, Hammond, Hallows and Edrich. Grace's golden month was all the more remarkable because he did not play in a first-class match until as late as 9 May. His time of twenty-two days has been equalled only once, by his natural successor in the Gloucestershire team, Wally Hammond, thirty-two years later.

Grace arrived at Lord's on the morning of Thursday, 30 May 1895 with 847 runs to his credit. When he made out the batting order he is alleged to have remarked: 'I see we are very much below full-strength, so I had better win the toss and make a few.' He won the toss and made a few; 169 to be precise! The One Thousand Runs in May was his.

Grace played his cricket to win and he was sometimes heard to quip when a new batsman arrived at the wicket: 'Oh, he's a young one, I think I ought to do for him.' He usually did. In contrast to the bullying, intimidating qualities often attributed to Grace, Lord Harris once said: 'The old man is the kindest and most sympathetic cricketer I have ever played with.' At a banquet given by Kent in Grace's honour the proposer of W.G.'s health said: 'I never knew a man make a mistake in the field but what W.G. had a kind word to say to him.'

There seems little additional proof required to show that Grace was a cricketer extraordinary. Neville Cardus, describing Tom Graveney's cricket, wrote: 'I would no more estimate Graveney's cricket statistically than I would estimate Schubert by counting the crochets and quavers.' It is easy to see what he meant; Cardus was seeing Graveney's technique as a thing of intrinsic beauty, but to those who come afterwards only the actual deeds that men perform live into history; a cricketer's deeds are runs and wickets. For Grace, runs and wickets tell the unique story of a unique man.

Grace's greatest tribute must surely be the fact that *Wisden* devoted 39 pages to his Obituary and the detailed records of his achievements, a more detailed report than has ever been compiled for any other player. There is even a complete list of men who have clean bowled the maestro; even this apparently was considered a sufficient achievement to warrant a record for posterity. Seven bowlers bowled him ten times or more, A. Shaw, in fact, bowled him twenty times, then comes Richardson (14), Barlow (13), Morley (11) and Briggs, Emmett and Hill, ten times each. But this next short sentence crystalizes the greatness of his career. He scored 54,896 runs at an average of 39·55 and took 2,864 wickets at 17·99 apiece. He appeared in first-class cricket from 1865 until 1908, and hit 126 first-class centuries.

During W.G.'s lifetime the game of cricket grew from a simple rural pastime to those developments of technical skill and popularity that have lasted into our time. W. G. Grace played a part unchallengeably greater than that played by any other man, not only by reason of his unparalleled skill in batting, bowling and fielding, but of his personality, his dominating simplicity and by his unswerving devotion to the game for the game's sake. His place, therefore, in a history of cricket is assured.

Donald George Bradman

Born 27 August 1908

The year 1908 had a dual significance for cricket. It was the year in which W. G. Grace made his farewell appearance. It was the year in which Don Bradman was born. Bradman in his heyday, like Grace, was a world figure, known in every walk of life, a master sportsman, a phenomenon. He was diametrically opposite to Grace in everything (especially physique) except in an uncanny ability to score runs in greater profusion than anyone else before or after him. Cardus once wrote of him: 'If he ever edged a fast new ball through the slips, he seemed to use the middle of the bat's edge. Seldom did he lift the ball. He was a superb and ferocious hooker but he hooked down to the ground, judging perfectly the length of contact of hooked ball to the earth. On a fast ground the speed of his strokes apparently reduced fieldsmen positioned deep to pillars of stone.'

'What is your secret?' Bradman was once asked. He replied: 'Concentration; every ball is the first ball whether I have just come to the wicket or I have reached 200.' After a pause he surprised his questioner by adding: 'And I never consider the possibility that anybody will ever get me out.' Bradman meant every word of this analysis with deep sincerity. He was able to condition himself in the end to the belief that no bowler should ever be capable of getting him out; more important still, the bowlers believed it, too, and this ultimately and inevitably led to the body-line attack.

Bradman was the complete master in every legitimate situation. The introduction of this bitter form of attack was in itself a tribute to Bradman's greatness. All that could be done to reduce his sovereignty was to produce fast bowling aimed outside or just on the leg-stump, pitched short, and calculated to rise breast high at least – with six or seven fieldsmen on the leg-side. Was it body-line, or was it head-line! The Jardinian theory when implemented brought Bradman's Test match average down from a hundred per innings to half. In the body-line Tests his scores were 0, 103 not out, 8, 66, 76, 24, 48 and 71. I doubt if any other batsman, alive or dead, could have equalled Bradman's ability to score consistently on these terms against Larwood. It was said at the time that Bradman was running away from Larwood. He was, towards square-leg, but only so that he could hit the rising, whizzing ball to the off-side, where only one fieldsman was positioned. Larwood admitted himself: 'Some of Bradman's shots to the off from the fastest balls aimed on or outside the leg-stump were marvellous, unbelievable.'

Donald George Bradman was born in Cootamundra, in New South Wales, and spent most of his early life at Bowral, some eighty miles from Sydney. His introduction into first-class cricket came at the age of nineteen. He scored a hundred in his first match for New South Wales against South Australia. He went in just before tea on the first day at number seven when the score was 250 for four wickets (Kippax had previously retired ill). Bowling at him was the best bowler in Australia at that time, 'Clarrie' Grimmett. Bradman hit him for two fours in his first over. He reached fifty in sixty-seven minutes, was sixty-five not out at the close of play, and went on to make 118 next day. What was it most of all that the critics liked about this young fledgling? It was the way he used his feet when playing Grimmett. His quick feet and his piercing eye were his stock in trade as he savaged the world's best bowlers for years.

As for his style, he had none by the generally accepted principles of style. His style was Bradman, exclusive to him. In a revealing study on the subject, R. C. Robertson-Glasgow once wrote: 'About his batting there was to be no style for style's sake. If there was to be any charm, that was for the spectator to find. It was not Bradman's concern. His aim was the making of runs, and he made them in staggering profusion.' The writer could have added: 'But he was never guilty of boring play, simply because no bowler could ever keep him quiet.'

Bradman's career spanned the years between 1927 and 1949, broken by the years of war. One single line in the record book tells the whole remarkable story. Matches – 234. Innings – 338. Not out – 43. Highest score – 452 not out. Runs – 28,067. Average – 95·14. Centuries – 117. One hundred and seventeen centuries in three hundred and thirty-eight innings – he scored a century every third time he went to the wicket. A breakdown of these figures has produced a book in itself; countless records were set up by this genius, and surely he was nothing less. His career average of 95·14 is easily the highest of any batsman in history; his career total of thirty-seven double-centuries is greater than any batsman in history. His total of six treble-centuries is unsurpassed, and he was within a fraction of having a century average in Test cricket.

When he went out to bat at the Oval just before six o'clock on 14 August 1948 in what was his last Test match for Australia, he needed only four runs to average one hundred in Test cricket. This was an unforgettable occasion. The crowd rose to this great cricketer and roars of acclamation accompanied him down the pavilion steps and all the way to the wicket, where Yardley, England's captain, shook him by the hand, and called for three cheers from the England players. Sport occasionally captures a magic moment to be treasured for a lifetime. This was one of them. Bradman, this master of concentration, externally unemotional almost to the point of indifference, was clearly caught in the wave of emotion. Playing forward to the second ball he received from Eric Hollies he was clean bowled by a sharply turning break-back, possibly the googly. The crescendo of cheers, not in defeat, but acknowledging again his greatness rose with each step he took back to the pavilion; it echoed and re-echoed. Then, in the sunlight, he was gone. The end of a legend.

For Bradman this 1948 tour of England provided the most fitting climax to an illustrious career. He scored more hundreds than any batsman in the country and for the second time – he hit thirteen in 1938 – he emulated Trumper's performance of 1902 with eleven first-class centuries. In addition to his supreme batting ability, Bradman demonstrated his knowledge of the game in captaincy and generalship; yet this knowledge, and certainly this concentration, seems to have been inbred. In the summer of 1925, at the age of seventeen, he played for Bowral against Moss Vale, in a match which had to be played to a finish on consecutive Saturday afternoons from two o'clock until six. Bradman's uncle, George Whatman, who was Captain of the Bowral team, won the toss and sent young Don in first. The openers were together until just before close of play when Bradman's partner was out for 52. Bradman was 80 not out. At the end of play on the second Saturday, Bowral for 475 for 1, Bradman 279 not out, and Uncle George 119 not out. Between them they added 323 runs in three and a half hours! Bradman was out on the third Saturday, caught Prigg, bowled Ryder, for 300. Bowral were 672 for 9. They won by an innings, the match lasting five Saturday afternoons!

Before this match, Mrs Bradman had promised her son a bat if he made a hundred. For most Mothers, this sort of promise is usually fairly safe; for Mrs Bradman, however, it was a treble risk!

So even at seventeen, Bradman had this extraordinary gift of dedication and application, the ability, as has been said so often about him, to reach a century and then take guard ready for the second one – the thought that he might at some time or another get out being farthest from his mind.

On 1 January 1949 came the news of Bradman's Knighthood. The boy who had come a long way from Bowral wrote:

> No man had less ambitions in that direction. I neither desired nor anticipated any recognition of my services. They had been spontaneously given. There was no thought of reward. However, it was clear that I was the medium through which was to be expressed England's appreciation of what Australian cricket has meant to the British Empire. In that way it was a compliment to Australia and to the game of cricket.

It was, indeed, a compliment to Australia, and to a cricketer supreme. We shall never see the like again, wrote Cardus. We never shall; he dominated his age like a huge giant; he caused a complete re-thinking among bowlers, and from the point of view of tactics he changed the whole course of the game.

5 Body-Line

In the winter of 1932–3, the expression: 'It isn't cricket' took the hardest knock of its life. Events in the Test series between Australia and England threatened the very existence of the Commonwealth and prompted the Australian Captain, Bill Woodfull to remark: 'There are two teams out there and only one of them is playing cricket.'

The focal point of all this was Bradman. Unless England's bowlers could get him out for much less than his average score in Test matches, then England had no hope of winning the series. Douglas Jardine, the England Captain, had given deep thought to this problem long before the side ever left England. He formed the opinion after prolonged study of the great man, that if he was vulnerable at all, it was to a fast rising ball pitched on the leg-stump or thereabouts. In Harold Larwood, Jardine had the fastest and most accurate bowler in the world – the ideal man to implement this form of attack, with a packed leg-side field and an inner ring close to the wicket to pick up the half-shot or a ball that went up in the air as the batsmen fended off anything around his head. In addition he had men deep in the field to pick-up the successful hook. The off-side was virtually open country with a solitary fieldsman patrolling it.

The plan certainly worked. Bradman's Test average was reduced by half from a hundred to fifty (how many batsmen would be proud to average fifty in a Test Series?), and England won the series by four matches to one. The Australians, and who can blame them, were hostile to the English methods from the start. In the third Test, when Woodfull was struck two body blows under the heart, and Bertie Oldfield was hit straight between the eyes, this hostility almost became open warfare. England claimed that Woodfull was struck when positioned outside the off-stump, and Oldfield was hit when mistiming a straightforward hook shot. Whether this was so is not the real crux of the matter. What mattered was: 'Was this cricket?'

The simple answer, spoken from man's heart, must be 'No.' Nearly forty years afterwards, I asked a member of that England team what he thought would have happened if the boot had been on the other foot, and the Australians had employed the same sort of methods in a Test match at Lord's. He thought for a moment and then replied: 'I think there would have been a riot, and I am sure that MCC would have sent for the Manager and the Captain and insisted that it be stopped at once.' But he stressed that, although in their souls most of the England players were not in favour of what they were doing, they were utterly loyal to their Captain. Only G. O. Allen showed his distaste publicly for body-line by not bowling it. Bill Voce did. Harold Larwood was loyal to Jardine and suffered for it.

During the tour Larwood received three telegrams from the MCC. They read: 'Well Bowled Notts!' 'Bravo!' 'Well bowled congratulations.' When the tour was all over and Larwood was back home, he was then asked to apologise to MCC for what he had done ... Apologise! ... apologise for what? ... for doing what he was told by his Captain, and for continuing to do so although there were genuine fears at one time that he might be lynched? How could there be such a hideous change of heart? It probably lay in the fact that with no satellite television, and with a comparatively small number of English journalists on the spot, the MCC had precious little conception of what was really going on, until the team came home. Then, all the senior professionals were quizzed for every fragment of information, and their confidential views painted a much truer picture than the one which the MCC had received at the time, and to save their own face Larwood had to be the scapegoat. It was the end of his Test cricket and the incident left him a very bitter man.

Jardine, who had precious little to say at any time, made no attempt to conceal his dislike of Australians and his even greater dislike for the Australian Press. This hardly helped the English cause. Jardine had apparently said that body-line was introduced not with Bradman specifically in mind, but that it was aimed at the whole of Australia's batting. This can be taken with a pinch of salt. Larwood himself is the authority for the denial. It was Bradman ... and Bradman alone. The plan was born at the Piccadilly Hotel in the summer of 1932. Nottinghamshire were playing in London and Arthur Carr, the Notts. skipper, invited Larwood and Voce out to dinner. Jardine went, too. Leg-theory was nothing new; it was discussed at length and Jardine's decision to use this form of attack was obviously taken that night. Other members of the team knew nothing of it and were not told anything on the voyage out. Larwood himself regarded leg-theory as a known and legitimate weapon in any fast bowler's armoury, and had no idea that anything untoward would result from its use. The fast wickets suited Larwood; he probably never bowled faster at any time in his career. Yet in the first match when Bradman was not playing, body-line was used and Stan McCabe scored 187 not out in what ranks as one of the greatest Test innings of all time. How was he successful? Well, he simply stood up and hooked.

It is ludicrous to suggest that there was an element of luck about an innings of this magnitude and courage. It is significant, however, that McCabe's scores afterwards were 32 in the second innings, 32 and 0 in the Second Test, 8 and 7 in the Third, 20 and 22 in the Fourth and 73 and 4 in the last.

Bradman was accused of being frightened. Are these really the scores of a frightened man – 0, 103 not out, 8, 66, 76, 24, 48, 71? No batsman of any age would have done better. What prompted this adverse comment on a great cricketer was a photograph of Bradman being bowled by Larwood when he was standing a couple of feet away from the wicket on the leg-side. Why was he? Simply because Bradman was not prepared to risk hooking and getting caught, so he was stepping right across on the leg-side to give himself room to cut or drive on the off-side. Larwood, himself, said that some of Bradman's shots in the off-side had to be seen to be believed. The fact that Larwood bowled Bradman prompted people at home to suggest that the Australian's accusations against Larwood were entirely unfounded since he

Great personalities – great moments

H.H. the Jam Sahib of Nawanagar, K. S. Ranjitsinhji: master batsman

Freddie Trueman: fast bowler supreme, and wit and raconteur par excellence. An honest-to-goodness product of Yorkshire, the natural home of great cricketers

Len Hutton: England have won the Ashes at The Oval in 1953

Jim Laker: holds the silver salver presented to him for taking 19 wickets in a Test Match in 1956. With him is Lord Tedder and Earl Alexander of Tunis

The glamour of Gillette Cup final day

Sussex – the first winners in 1963. L. J. Lenham, J. M. Parks, A. S. M. Oakman, G. C. Cooper, E. R. Dexter (Captain), R. J. Langridge, K. G. Suttle, A. Buss, N. I. Thomson, D. L. Bates, J. A. Snow

Lancashire, 1970 and 1971 – masters of the one-day game. *Standing:* B. Wood, J. Simmons, D. Lloyd, D. P. Hughes, J. Sullivan, F. C. Hayes, K. Shuttleworth. *Seated:* P. Lever, H. Pilling, J. D. Bond (Captain), Farokh Engineer, C. H. Lloyd

was hitting the stumps. He was, but probably four balls an over were of the fast rising variety. To-day four bouncers an over would be stopped immediately by the umpires, as intimidating the batsman. Larwood was doing just this.

The score was one Test each when the teams met in the Third Test at Adelaide. England won the toss and were soon on the brink of total disaster – Sutcliffe 9, Jardine 3, Hammond 2, Ames 3, but Leyland, Wyatt, Paynter and Verity shaped a respectable score of 341. Australia struggled even more. Woodfull was struck two blows in the body by Larwood, and with five wickets down for 130, Oldfield began to fight a brave rearguard action. When he had made 41 he tried to hook a fast rising ball from Larwood and was hit smack between the eyes. Pandemonium broke loose as the little wicket-keeper dropped his bat, staggered away from the wicket and fell to his knees, blood streaming from the wound. Woodfull vaulted the picket-fence and rushed to Oldfield's aid, shouting: 'This isn't cricket, it's war.' Never has there been, before or since, a scene as ugly as this one.

The England team feared that if one spectator jumped the fence then the whole mob would come on, and Larwood moved towards the stumps intending to grab one for protection if he was attacked. The noise was deafening. Larwood described by the Australian Press as 'Larwood the Killer', 'The Silent Killer' and 'Murder on Tiptoe', stood motionless. Jardine's reaction when the Australian innings closed at 222, was to open for England wearing the most gaily coloured cap imaginable; to the Australian a Harlequin or similar cap represented typically English snobbery, and they hated Jardine all the more for it. By wearing such millinery on this occasion Jardine was taunting an angry crowd; he taunted them for four and a quarter hours and scored 56; whatever you may think of Jardine, his courage is unquestioned.

The Australian Board of Control cabled MCC protesting that body-line was unsportsmanlike, was a menace to the game, and threatened the relations between England and Australian players. MCC suggested that the situation was not at all as serious as had been claimed, and offered to cancel the rest of the tour. The attitude of MCC must surely confirm what I have

K

written on a previous page, that while they were busy sending Larwood cables of congratulations, they really had no idea of the tenseness of the situation on the spot. It was only on receiving first-hand reports when the team returned that they realized the true position. So, far from becoming their hero, Larwood was now seen by them as the villain of the piece. How did they see Jardine?

Of course Larwood was not bowling in order deliberately to maim batsmen. He was a cricketer (and a very fine one) not a sadist. But on his own admission he was bowling to frighten and intimidate, and excessive use of this form of attack could only be detrimental to the game, but I do not attach one iota of the responsibility to Larwood himself. In one vicious letter Larwood received (and he received many) the writer said: 'The Hangman's name is Larwood.' Poor Harold – he has never forgotten those words. He said himself: 'In my heart I feel I must take the blame for all the trouble that occurred. I know I shouldn't but the position is similar to the hangman's. If the Judge orders him to hang a man, he has to do so.' But just supposing, for one moment, that Larwood had flatly refused Jardine's request to use this form of attack, or refused to continue with it after the crowd's hostile reactions, what would have happened? Would he have been sent home for defying his captain's orders? He could have been – we will never know, but it is a thought worth considering in the overall analysis.

How do we see 'Plum' Warner's role? How well does he come out of it? As Joint-Manager, he is reported always to have confessed that it was outside his province and was entirely a matter for the Captain. Was it? Did Warner have no responsibility at all? If not then what is a Manager? What would Warner's attitude have been as an MCC official at Lord's if the Australians had adopted similar tactics at Headquarters? Again, we will never know, but this was another point which should have been examined at the time, instead of simply condemning the Australians for being frightened. Were they frightened? Can I quote again Maurice Leyland's immortal remark about fast bowling? 'None of us likes it, but some of us doesn't let on!'

Not even a brave man could have relished this form of attack with a bowler of Larwood's pace and consistent accuracy, and with the number of short-pitched balls delivered in each over.

What view did the umpires take of Larwood's bowling? Is not an umpire's task to ensure fair play. Was there nothing the umpires could have done if they considered Larwood's methods of attack unfair? As they did nothing, was that tantamount to open admission that they regarded Larwood's bowling as being within the framework of the laws of the game, and so did not warrant any intervention by them. That, surely, is what one must assume. On the other hand, did they regard the issue as one of such moment that they felt it should be dealt with at a higher level? They kept out of it, as some English umpires have done since with the throwing controversy. An umpire's lot is not a happy one, in any case, without wishing to be the central figure in an international crisis; these two at Adelaide deserve sympathy whatever they thought.

But with the Third Test completed the troubles surrounding the tour were certainly not over. Jardine had objected to the Australian Board's reference in their cable to the MCC to 'unsportsmanlike play', and had cabled the latter asking for their influence in seeing that this reference was withdrawn. It was hinted that Jardine went so far as to refuse to lead England in the Fourth Test until this implication had been withdrawn. The MCC duly cabled the Australian Board asking for its withdrawal. Meetings took place in Queensland, where the team were staying at the time, between the Queensland representatives on the Australian Board, and two Joint-Managers, Warner and Palairet. The Press had their ears to the ground. A British Government official in Australia, Mr E. T. Crutchley, was used as an intermediary in the dispute; rumour was rife; the tour was in danger of being called off, and so the situation remained until two days before the Test was due to begin. Finally, the Australian Board of Control sent a cable to the MCC saying 'We do not regard the sportsmanship of your team as being in question.' A settlement had been reached; unanimous approval of it by some sections of Australian opinion had not; bitterness remained.

England won the Fourth Test and the Ashes when Eddie Paynter rose from his hospital bed whither he had been suffering from tonsilitis. Paynter heard the England score and knew the side needed him; this was true heroism. He went back to hospital when he was 12 not out, and returned the next day to score 83. England, from 264-8, reached 356, and led Australia on first innings by 16 runs. Larwood and Allen then bowled Australia out for 175 and England won by 6 wickets. England won the last Test by 8 wickets. In the five Test matches, Harold Larwood took 33 wickets at under twenty runs apiece, bowling extraordinary in the light of the huge scores which were frequently made on Australian wickets in those halcyon days of tremendously powerful Australian batting.

Recriminations went on and on. Larwood, by the terms of his contract, was obliged to remain silent despite approaches by almost all the newspapers, who were prepared to pay handsomely for his story. The feeling was still abroad when the Australians arrived in England in 1934; it lingered on. Larwood was omitted from the England side for the First Test at Trent Bridge – his home ground. This surely meant that the writing was on the wall. In an article in the *Sunday Dispatch* of 17 June 1934 Harold Larwood wrote: 'England Selectors meet to-morrow to choose a team for the Second Test Match. My friends tell me I am certain to be asked to play. It will not matter. I have definitely made up my mind not to play against the Australians in this or any of the Tests. I doubt if I shall ever play against them again – at least in big cricket.'

The Larwood Story ended with a curious twist of fate. On 28 April 1950 Harold Larwood and his family sailed in the *Orontes*, the same ship which took him on tour in 1932, for Australia, where he was to settle for the rest of his life.

But in a way, the legacy of that unpleasant tour has had its full impact on the game of cricket. It convinced bowlers that the short-pitched fast ball (now known as a bumper) was fair game; it also convinced the authorities that this weapon, used in excess, could ruin the spirit of cricket, and ultimately, the game itself. The bowler has striven for equality between bat and ball, a situation often denied bowlers on the shirt-front wickets of the 'thirties, especially in Australia. Leg-theory, as such, has disappeared, but sometimes it appears on the scene tied up in different packaging, but never on the scale of 1932–3. Cricket has changed; crowd behaviour has changed with it. Whatever the rights or wrongs of the events of close on forty years ago, the modern partisan supporters would not easily stomach their favourite players being consistently hit. Why should they? Cricket certainly wasn't devised as a blood-sport! The proper preparation of wickets should help more than anything to achieve equality. But I still think of Harold Larwood as a great bowler, whose loyalty brought him some pretty miserable moments – and everlasting memories of the cruellest kind.

6   One-Day Cricket and Sponsorship

'With a view to promote county cricket, and to bring counties into contact which might not otherwise have an opportunity of competing with each other, and to establish a series of first-class matches on a neutral ground, the Committee propose to offer a silver cup for competition. The matches will be arranged by lot, and the ties drawn by the Committee of the MCC, as soon as possible after the acceptances are received. The winner of the final tie will hold the cup for one year. The winner of the final tie for three years successively shall hold the cup in perpetuity. The name of the winning county, with the date of the match, shall be engraved on the cup at the cost of the MCC.'

This resolution has nothing to do with the Gillette Cup! It was passed by MCC back in January 1873. The venture was a complete failure; only six counties were among the original contenders; Kent beat Sussex in the first match at Lord's, but the other counties had withdrawn and the competition floundered. It took ninety years to revive it!

It was in 1963 that the First-class Counties' Knock-out Competition for the Gillette Cup began. It was to be one-day cricket on a limited-over basis on a knock-out principle with the Final at Lord's. Endless discussion and heart-searching had gone into these proposals. Many doubted its possible success. The expense involved in taking players round the country for one-day matches which could be seriously disrupted by the weather, involving players in hotel bills for several days with a small financial take at the end was a major source of concern to the county treasurers. It was at this point that the question of sponsorship was raised; the opposition to this in Committee was understandable. Although the name of Spiers and Pond had been directly associated with the first England tour to Australia in the distant past of 1861, sponsorship was something well outside the realms of the game of cricket. No one knew precisely what sponsorship meant, or how far it would go. Did it mean that cricket was selling its soul to brash and distasteful commercialism? It was this undercurrent of opinion which had prompted MCC to tread cautiously. I have good reason to know this to be true, since I have been a Consultant to Gillette Industries in sporting matters since 1952, as well as an MCC member, and was directly involved in these delicate negotiations between the Gillette Company and MCC.

As the result of an experimental Midlands Knock-out competition in May 1962 at Leicester, in which, curiously enough, I was also involved in another context, the counties were of the opinion that the competition did have a reasonable chance of success. This Midlands competition was between Leicestershire, Derbyshire, Nottinghamshire, and Northants. When Leicestershire played Derbyshire, I was sent by *The Times* to report on it. I wrote:

> This enterprise experiment arises from a desire expressed by all the counties to acquire a practical knowledge, before 1963, of just how one-day cricket can operate successfully, and how different is its image from the accepted format for county cricket. The Leicestershire Secretary, turning this over in his mind, discovered that Leicestershire, Derbyshire, Nottinghamshire and Northamptonshire had these available dates, and took swift action. The geographical position of these four means that no hotel accommodation is involved (and as it turned out, the fees received from the Independent Television Authority defrayed all the expenses of the competition, including the purchase of a cup – the Midland Counties Knock-out Cup. Laws framed for this match limit each innings to sixty-five overs, prevent any one bowler from bowling more than fifteen overs, restrict the off-side field to six players, and authorize the umpires to be the sole judges as to whether or not extra time shall be played in order to finish the match.

My assessment of the day's play, and of the future, was as follows:

> In a finish which would have gripped the most unemotional and carping critic, Leicestershire beat Derbyshire by seven runs in the one-day Midlands knock-out competition. This absorbing day's cricket – which clearly stamps the experiment with considerable success, a happy augury for the future – produced 493 runs in a little under seven hours,

yet at no time did the proceedings give the impression of prostituting the basic skills of the game. There was no suggestion of a carnival. In fact, only three sixes were struck. It was just a question of bowlers' bowling a liberal ration of overs in the time and batsmen's getting on with it by playing strokes and using their pads only for protection.

In those days it was the tradition of *The Times* not to name its correspondents, and it was only sometime afterwards that I found out that my report had been studied at length by the appropriate committee at Lord's, without, of course their knowing who had written it!

But even having agreed on the merits of the competition there were still doubts on the main financial issues; rain and cricket have been the deadliest of enemies for centuries; rain could deal one-day cricket a mortal blow. It was, therefore, ultimately decided to enlist the help of a sponsor, and at a meeting of the counties at Lord's, on 26 November 1962 it was decided to accept a block grant of £6,500 by the Gillette Safety Razor Company, who would also provide the cup, and give an award to the 'Man of the Match' in each of the ties.

Now, in 1972, Gillette's block grant has been periodically increased to reach a figure of £30,000 per season; cricket will do well to know, and remember, the facts of the first year, and the part played by Henry Garnett, then the Company's Managing Director, and by his successor, George Robinson.

Henry Garnett saw Gillette's contribution as being solely an insurance against bad weather and loss of revenue. He thought it important that the competition should be able to stand on its own feet without leaning too heavily on someone's arm. He believed that if the counties had to make a success of it, there was a better chance of their doing so, than if it didn't matter too much. For cricket's sake, the competition had to be a success. He asked nothing whatsoever in return. He believed that if the competition achieved success, then Gillette would ride on its back. He believed that Gillette's primary function at this stage was to establish confidence and goodwill with MCC, and as he knew the apprehension on their part that a sponsor might turn a cricket ground into a supermarket, he would not even allow Gillette advertising to be exhibited on the grounds. In that first year, since the competition was officially known as 'The First-Class Counties' Knock-out competition for the Gillette Cup', and the newspapers understandably condensed all this to the 'KO Cup', Gillette got precious little identification. But Henry Garnett achieved exactly what he set out to do. He cemented a strong bond of confidence and friendship with MCC who were thus very happy, for 1964, to rename the competition 'The Gillette Cup'.

In that first year success for cricket and Gillette was assured, and I can vividly remember to this day what Henry Garnett said to me when we were having dinner in the Midland Hotel, Manchester, on the eve of the first Gillette match at Old Trafford in 1963. It was simply this: 'I am going to give you a specific instruction now, and I hope I don't have to give you another one. You are an MCC member and very much involved in the game – don't ever put a foot wrong with cricket.'

That first year is one of very happy memories. Henry Garnett's direction for the conduct of affairs was admirable for someone like myself with such an affection for the game of cricket. In addition, the Managing Director of Gillette's Public Relations Consultants, Alan Campbell-Johnson, was also a devoted cricket enthusiast who frequently recounted to me his own deeds in the 'Butterflies' colours. I think he once hit a five (his first scoring stroke) at Lord's, a feat almost certainly never performed by Bradman or Hutton or Constantine. Campbell-Johnson, therefore, commits his name to posterity!

Between us we worked out the details of the 'Man of the Match' awards. We decided against the somewhat hackneyed awards of the past – best bowler, best batsman, ad infinitum. We decided on a sort of *Victor Ludorum* – a 'Man of the Match'. 'How,' said our critics, 'can anyone decide whether 57 not out is better than 4 wickets for 31?' 'They would have to judge it in the context of the result,' we replied, although we did agree that it was a pretty hard assignment for any judge; there were bound to be some ticklish situations. In the light of this, we hit upon the idea of asking England Test cricketers to undertake the task of becoming adjudicators. If at any time the public did not agree with their decisions they could hardly question their qualifications for doing the job, or their integrity. This, happily, has proved to be the case. Having decided on the principle, we then invited a number of distinguished cricketers from other days; in every case they welcomed the opportunity of 'being back in cricket', as it were. Several of them were still operating nine years afterwards.

So it was, then, in 1963 that this great adventure began. The terms of reference for the competition were as follows:

Duration of matches

The normal hours will be 11.0 to 7.30, though umpires may order extra time, if, in their opinion, a finish can be obtained. Lunch normally from 1.0 to 1.40, and tea after one and a half hour's batting by the side going in second or at 4.30, whichever is earlier.

Each match shall consist of one innings per side with each innings limited to sixty-five overs. No bowler may bowl more than fifteen overs in an innings, and the existing leg-side limitation of fieldsmen shall apply. The pitch shall be completely covered throughout in the event of rain.

The result

(a) A tie

In the event of a tie, the result shall be decided in favour of the side losing the least number of wickets. If both sides have lost the same number of wickets, the result shall be decided on the higher rate of scoring in the first 20 overs of each innings. In the event of both sides being all out in, or under, 65 overs, the overall scoring rate of both sides shall be the deciding factor.

(b) Unfinished match

If a match remains unfinished after three days, the winner shall be the side which has scored the faster in runs per over throughout the innings, provided that at least twenty overs have been bowled at the side batting second. If the scoring rate is the same, the side losing the least number of wickets in the first twenty overs of each innings shall be the winner.

If, however, at 3 pm on the third day, in the opinion of the umpires, no result can be achieved in the match, whatever the weather, the umpires shall order a match of ten overs each side to be started, if to do so is humanly possible.

If no play is possible on the first and second days, the Captains, bearing in mind the time remaining, shall be empowered to re-arrange the number of overs to be bowled by each side to achieve a result. In the event of the number of overs being re-arranged, a minimum of ten overs for each innings shall apply.

If, owing to conditions, it is not possible to obtain a result, the two Captains will arrange another match of a minimum of ten overs each side, to be played within ten days on a ground to be mutually agreed.

Basically, these rules have remained, and have worked well. There were a number of 'dusk' finishes in this first year, and the number of overs was reduced to sixty, with the limitation on each bowler being accordingly reduced to twelve; only once has the weather so ruined a match for days on end, that it had to be decided over the minimum of ten overs. The players of Yorkshire and Cambridgeshire had sat for three days watching rain at Bradford, and ultimately fixed another match at Leeds. An overnight thunderstorm set the Headingley ground awash, and I remember John Nash, Yorkshire's Secretary, Brian Close, and myself, telephoning a number of grounds in Yorkshire before being told by the groundsman at Castleford that play would be possible there. We agreed on a two o'clock start, had lunch at Headingley, and set out. A thunderstorm hit Castleford within moments of our arriving; the lights in the pavilion were fused; the situation looked hopeless, but the groundsman was determined to be able to tell his descendants that he once prepared a wicket that Yorkshire played on, so all the drying equipment was rushed over from Leeds, and we finally got a start about four o'clock – in pouring rain; both Captains, heartily sick of the waiting, agreed to continue regardless of the weather. They did, and were dripping wet when they came off the field. Yorkshire won.

There was another case of a match at Taunton which dragged on over a week-end for four days, and Freddie Brown, the adjudicator, was compelled for business reasons to return to London after three days, and left me with the task of adjudicating. The Taunton ground staged dog-racing on Tuesday nights in those days, and as the cricket match dragged on and on between the squalls, I had visions of giving the award to the favourite in the first race! Fortunately, the cricket finished in the nick of time with Roy Virgin the recipient of my considered judgement!

Tremendous interest centred upon the first match in the knock-out competition between Lancashire and Leicestershire at Old Trafford on 1 May 1963. This was a preliminary round match made necessary by the need to reduce the odd number of seventeen counties to sixteen in order to facilitate the draw. Lancashire and Leicestershire were chosen because they had been the two bottom counties in the County Championship table the previous season. The place, Old Trafford, lived up to its reputation, apocryphal or not – it rained! Play did not begin until three o'clock. I can see Frank Woolley now, scarf and gloves, cold to the marrow, but insisting on sitting behind the bowler's arm and scorning the comfort of the Committee room, situated roughly on a line with mid-wicket and cover. Maurice Hallam, Captain of Leicestershire, won the toss and put Lancashire in (this was a move widely adopted in the early days, but revised later as the technique of the game evolved with experience). Lancashire scored 304 for 9, of which Peter Marner hit 121 in under two hours. Hallam did his bit the next day to atone for his tactical error and scored a hundred himself, but Leicestershire were all out for 203. Lancashire had become the first winners of a Gillette Cup-tie, and Peter Marner was the first 'Man of the Match'.

The Press, overall, were enthusiastic, although there was quite a heavy body of opinion against this new style cricket. 'A prostitution of the art,' some said; 'just not cricket,' said others. Probably the most forthright statement against the new idea was made by the Assistant-Secretary of Essex. Under the heading 'KO Cup – not for us! says Don Watt,' the following appeared in a local Essex newspaper:

The county cricket fraternity up and down the country is wildly enthusiastic about the knock-out cup competition introduced this season, but not so Essex Assistant-Secretary Don Watt.

'We got knocked out by Lancashire in the first round at Old Trafford I'm happy to say,' he said this week, as he watched Essex fielding against Leicester at Valentine's Park. Don believes that as far as Essex is concerned the knock-out competition is a waste of time financially because of the extra expenses involved.

If one county was not very interested, another most certainly was. That county was Sussex, and their Captain Ted Dexter. They carried off the Gillette Cup both in 1963 and 1964 and did not lose their first Cup-tie until their tenth match in the competition against Middlesex at Lord's in 1965. I wrote in the Cup Final programme in 1970:

> I have seen Sussex play twelve Gillette Cup-ties spread across some of England's loveliest cricket grounds; Taunton, Worcester, Canterbury, Hove, not to mention their trio of appearances at Lord's. Now, they come here for the fourth time in eight years, a record for the competition. I have always believed that one of the cardinal factors in establishing the Gillette Cup as an instantaneous success was Ted Dexter's liking for it as a serious competition from the outset. If I harboured any doubts in those early days of negotiation it was that the players might treat this type of cricket as a new toy to be taken lightheartedly. Had that been the case it would never have got off the ground. Dexter saw it as a challenge. It was not long before the others saw it the same way.

And so the Gillette Cup was home and dried. The big day in that summer of 1963 was 22 May. Eight matches were scheduled across the country. Prayers were offered for a fine day; they were answered! Some splendid cricket was played. Middlesex beat Gloucestershire at Bristol by 39 runs. Yorkshire beat Notts at Middlesbrough by 4 wickets. Glamorgan won a cliff-hanger at Cardiff beating Somerset by 10 runs. Derbyshire won an even closer one at Bournemouth, beating Hampshire by 6 runs. Worcestershire beat Surrey easily at Worcester by 114 runs. In a match where 556 runs were scored at Tunbridge Wells, Sussex beat Kent by 72 runs, while Lancashire beat Essex at Old Trafford by 81 runs. The following eight players received a cheque for £50 and a gold medal, their reward for being adjudged by a panel of Test cricketers as 'Man of the Match': D. Bennett (Middlesex), J. B. Bolus (Nottinghamshire), B. Hedges (Glamorganshire), D. C. Morgan (Derbyshire), J. A. Standen (Worcestershire), R. M. Prideaux (Northamptonshire), P. E. Richardson (Kent) and J. Dyson (Lancashire). The distinguished adjudicators, all with considerable Test match experience were: George Geary, Charles Barnett, Herbert Sutcliffe, Jack Robertson, Frank Woolley, Cyril Washbrook, Alec Bedser and Joe Hardstaff.

The weather was bounteous again for the next round on 12 June. Fifteen thousand people packed Hove to overflowing to see Sussex contrive a magnificent win against Yorkshire by 22 runs. Over 500 runs were scored and Yorkshire died gloriously in appalling light at a quarter to eight. Tom Graveney rallied Worcestershire to win against Glamorganshire at Neath with an innings of 93, described by *The Times* correspondent as being 'all sweetness and light'. It was Colin Milburn day at Lord's. He took 4 for 34 against Middlesex and then hit 84, as Northamptonshire coasted home by 6 wickets. Lancashire comfortably disposed of Derbyshire at Old Trafford.

The draw for the Semi-Finals was: Northamptonshire *v* Sussex at Northampton; Worcestershire *v* Lancashire at Worcester. The heavens were certainly giving their blessing to this new competition. It was fine on 10 July, although one of the matches showed that even on a fine day, Gillette Cup cricket can be very disappointing. A good crowd at Worcester were wending their way homewards at ten minutes past two. Forty-one overs and two balls were all that the Worcester bowlers required to bowl out Lancashire. Flavell taking six wickets for fourteen runs. Worcester reached 60–1 in double-quick time, and it was all over. Some of the real enthusiasts were quickly at the wheel of their cars and on the way to Northamptonshire where there had been one or two minor intrusions because of rain, and Herbert Sutcliffe presented the 'Man of the Match' award to Ted Dexter as night was falling fast – it was after eight o'clock. Sussex won this one by 105 runs, so that Sussex met Worcestershire in this first historic Cup Final at Lord's on 7 September.

The weather was fine only to the extent that it did allow the match to be played to a finish, although full marks must be given to Worcester who batted out the last few overs in murky light.

It was a low scoring game – Sussex 168, Worcester 154 – but it filled Lord's and the presentation of the Cup and medals was history in the making. Gillette had specially made an impressive platform which enabled the players to come up the steps on one side and receive their medals from the President of the MCC, and then go down the steps on the other side, and as Ted Dexter waved the Cup to his delighted supporters in the great tradition of Wembley, cheers rang out across Lord's. The Cup, incidentally, which Gillette had again specially designed, is of sterling silver and nine-carat gold and measures 14 inches from the top of the cover to the foot of the cup. It stands on a $3\frac{1}{2}$-inch rosewood plinth. On the foot of the cup, in nine-carat gold, are the crests of the seventeen first-class counties, to which the crests of all the minor counties competing have been added. The stem is surrounded by a stylized cluster of willow leaves in nine-carat gold, representing the traditional association between the willow tree and the sport of cricket. The MCC is represented by a modelled figure of Father Time, also in nine-carat gold, which surmounts the cup. It is based on the famous weather-vane at Lord's.

Norman Gifford, Worcester's spinner, was the first recipient of a 'Man of the Match' award in a final. In recent years Gillette have struck a tie for all their gold medal winners and every winner has received one, even Andrew Corran, of Nottinghamshire, who was tracked down somewhere in the outback of Australia. More recently still a tie for the adjudicators has been designed. The players' tie is dark blue with a single motif of the Gillette Cup in gold. The adjudicator's tie is similar, except that it has the letter 'A' underneath the Cup.

From this eminently satisfactory beginning the Gillette Cup event has never looked back. Gillette had signed a three-year agreement with an option to renew. The third three-year period was complete at the end of 1971. It has been renewed for 1972, 1973 and 1974. The option clause is still there.

Sussex not only were the first winners, but with Dexter's obvious liking for the competition and his astute cricketing brain, they had developed a technique for the game. Clearly, the pattern was diametrically opposed to that employed in the three-day game. Other counties began to realize this, too, and more important still, in counties where the attitude to the new competition had been barely lukewarm, the value of winning the cup, financially, was now fully appreciated. This was not a new toy. It was good cricket with great appeal to the county treasurers. So in 1964 sixteen counties were out after Sussex's blood. All failed. Dexter led his men of Sussex to their second triumph. It is interesting, not only that one county has shown such skill for this type of cricket, but so have individual players. Bob Barber of Warwickshire, David Green (Lancashire and Gloucestershire), Colin Milburn and Colin Cowdrey have each won a 'Man of the Match' award four times; how many, one wonders, would Milburn have won had his bitter tragedy not robbed him of his cricket, and the cricket world of him; his car crash deprived the game of one of its most rumbustious characters; this cavalier cricketer with the big heart and the big hit is never, lamentably, to be seen again.

In 1964 Sussex swept aside Durham at Hove by 200 runs, narrowly defeated Somerset at Taunton by 16 runs, disposed of Surrey by 90 runs in the Semi-Final at Hove where the gates were closed and many Surrey supporters made the journey from London in vain, and then made easy meat of Warwickshire in the Final by 8 wickets. There seemed to be no stopping them. On they went in 1965 by beating Worcester at Worcester by 58 runs. Then, at last, came their Waterloo at Lord's. The victors were Middlesex, and they did the job properly – the margin of victory was 90 runs. No longer were the Press asking if Sussex would keep the Cup as their property for all time if they won it for the third time in succession. This year there was bound to be a new winner. It was the end of triumph for Sussex, although twice since they have come back to Lord's to try for a third success; each time they have been foiled, first by Warwickshire (1968) and then by Lancashire (1970).

It was Yorkshire's year in 1965 in one of the most remarkable finals of them all. Torrential rain lashed Lord's for practically the whole of the Friday before the match and it was still raining well into the night. To the connoisseur it was the whole of Lom-

Lord's – the traditional home of cricket

At peace

At war: the macabre scene at Lord's in the February snow of 1970, where floodlights and barbed-wire were some of the measures taken to prevent the pitch being damaged by anti-apartheid demonstrators. At this point in time the tour by the South Africans that summer was definitely 'on'

Great umpires

Frank Chester

Syd Buller, OBE

bard Street to a China orange that no play would be possible. It just happened that one man was absolutely determined that there would be; the man was Billy Griffith. He felt that thousands of people had paid a lot of money to watch cricket on the Saturday, and they would not be able to attend on the Monday, particularly all those who were travelling down from Yorkshire. It was not so bad for the supporters of their opponents, Surrey, but many of those had other places where they were compelled to spend a Monday. Griffith enlisted the ground staff and the equipment from the Oval, which was brought across London as reinforcements for the over-worked Lord's staff, and the giant mopping-up operation began at dawn, or thereabouts. Lord's was transformed into a giant butcher's shop – there was more sawdust than grass to be seen. To all intents and purposes these were conditions totally unfit for a game of cricket. Clearly, the umpires would not have ordered a start had the matter been in their hands, and neither Captain wanted to play – they both felt there was too much at stake. But both Brian Close and Micky Stewart had a talk to the MCC Secretary and this distinguished triumvirate emerged from their deliberations with the surprising but happy news that play would begin at twelve o'clock.

The conditions which many of us felt were totally unfit for such a match produced the greatest individual innings ever seen in the competition. Boycott on that September day in 1965 has never been surpassed – and may never will. Stewart, faced with the dilemma of what to do when he won the toss, took the view that although his bowlers would have to contend with a wet ball the outfield would be palpably slow, and this influenced him to put Yorkshire in.

Obviously Boycott and Taylor thought very little of the conditions, and felt the need to get their bearings; proceedings were therefore somewhat laboured, and when Taylor was out with the score at 22, Close promoted himself in the batting order largely to be able to get the opportunity of having a few words with Boycott. The gist of this conversation has been a matter of speculation ever since. One ingenious lip-reader watching on television is alleged to have said that it was something to do with getting on

L

with it, or Close might run him out! Whatever those carefully chosen words were, they had a magnetic effect. Boycott shed all inhibitions with the nonchalance of tossing a banana skin over his shoulder, and turned on a performance which made the audience feel that his bat had somehow become a mighty sceptre or, indeed, a magic wand. He hit 146, and with Close in masterly form, too, scoring 79; the next wicket did not fall until the score had mounted to 214. Poor Surrey; it was virtually all over.

Boycott's innings, which lasted under three and a half hours, contained three sixes and fifteen fours. Yorkshire went buoyantly on to a total of 317 for 4 in 60 overs, and all on an arena which Ian Peebles described as being more suitable for receiving Bertram Mills' Circus than two teams of cricketers! There is food for thought here; that this match would never even have started had it been anything but a Cup Final, and yet it produced some cricket to savour for years. No other player has been able to produce such glittering entertainment on the great day as Boycott.

In 1966 Warwickshire took part in their second Final, an all-Midland affair, against Worcestershire. Warwickshire won a low-scoring match comfortably by five wickets; Worcestershire thus failed for the second time at the last hurdle. In 1967 Kent and Somerset brought to Lord's the most tremendous atmosphere of all the finals. Kent garlanded their balcony with hops; Somerset supporters, dressed in farmer's smocks, wielded pitch-forks and trundled barrels of cyder. This was a day when happiness and well-being seemed to radiate from every corner of Lord's. The sun shone, the cricket never reached great heights, but the pendulum of fortune swung to and fro and Kent won in the end by thirty-two runs.

The 1968 Final was a battle of the giants. Sussex were back to try to become the first county to land the Gillette Cup three times. Their opponents, Warwickshire, had won the cup once, and like Sussex, were appearing in their third Final. Round about half-past six, a distinguished member of the MCC's hierarchy who shall be nameless (but he has grey hair and bowled fast), said in the committee room that the match was all over and

Sussex had won! Practically every man woman and child on the ground at that moment would have agreed with him.

It just happened that there was one man who had altogether different ideas. He was the Warwickshire captain, Alan Smith. Sussex had made 214 for 7 in their allotted span of 60 overs. Warwickshire were 155 for 6, and there remained only 13 overs to be bowled with 60 runs wanted at very nearly 5 an over. Alan Smith knew that it was do or die; after him there was very little support for Amiss and it was now that he would have to risk his neck. He cut and carved with swashbuckling abandon. Amiss, on whose shoulders one had imagined the greater responsibility lay, was well content to stand and admire his Captain.

Warwickshire were home with three overs to spare. Cyril Washbrook, judging the 'Man of the Match' award, had been fluctuating at various times during the day between Parks, Stewart, Michael Buss and Amiss, but there were no more fluctuations now, and judging by the roar which greeted his announcement that Alan Smith was the 'Man of the Match' his decision was unanimously received. Warwickshire were now level with Sussex at two wins each, but they were not long to share this distinction between themselves. Yorkshire went back to Lord's in 1969 to win the Cup for the second time.

In 1969 the Gillette Cup did not stand alone as a sponsored competition. For a number of years Rothmans had shown considerable interest in an identification with cricket, and they had done a great deal in various ways. They had produced brochures, made films of Test matches, even sent the Chairman of the Cricket Writers Club to South Africa. Most of all they had run a cricket team known as the Cavaliers, who had played matches for beneficiaries on Sundays. These were televised and proved to be highly popular, but they ran into problems when County Championship matches were played on a Sunday (starting at 2pm in order to keep within the limits laid down by the Lord's Day Observance Society). The county players were therefore not available for Rothmans, but they kept going with players from overseas. The popularity which the Cavaliers had engendered, however, was sufficient to convince cricket's authorities that there was room for their own Sunday competition. It seemed a natural for Rothmans to sponsor. The cricket world at large was somewhat surprised when the sponsor turned out to be one of Rothmans great rivals in the tobacco industry – John Player and Sons. Some thought that Rothmans had been pretty harshly treated by the newly formed Promotion and Public Relations Committee at Lord's, whose function was to advise on money matters in sponsorship. Apparently it was a question of money pure and simple, not sentiment and appreciation of past contributions. Rothmans did not evaluate the new competition to the extent that Players did. For Players, this was an ideal vehicle to get their name on television in an indirect way, since the ban on cigarette advertising prevented the straightforward commercials, and one imagines that they are a good deal bigger and have much larger advertising and public relations budgets than Rothmans. One still feels sympathy for Rothmans, who have now moved out of the cricket scene to other fields of sponsorship. The international Cavaliers struggled hard to keep going, but the disappearance of television coverage killed any sponsor's interest.

Be all that as it may, the size of the sponsorship fee provided by John Player and Sons was said to be in the region of £60,000, and in addition, the following prize money was awarded to the players (the sponsorship fee was divided equally among the seventeen counties): to the winners of the League – £1,000. Runners-up – £500. Third place – £250. The winning team in every match – £50. Each time a batsman hit a six he received one share of £1,000. Each time a bowler took 4 wickets in an innings he received a share of £1,000. In addition to this, the BBC donated £250 for the fastest fifty in the competition.

The playing conditions for the competition were the same for first-class matches in the United Kingdom except as follows:

Duration

1   Matches will consist of one innings per side. Each innings is limited to 40 overs. (This was necessary because play on a Sunday could not begin until two o'clock).

2 If the team fielding first fails to bowl 40 overs by 4.10 pm the over in progress shall be completed. The innings of the team batting second shall be limited to the same number of overs.
3 If bad weather delays the start or suspends the length of either innings, the number of overs will be rearranged so that each side bats for the same number of overs.
4 Each team must bowl ten overs to ensure a result.

Bowling
1 No bowler may bowl more than eight overs.
2 Length of a bowler's run-up is limited to fifteen yards.

Result
1 The side with the higher aggregate will be the winners.
2 Suspension of play may prevent the team batting second from receiving its quota of overs. In this case, the match will be decided on the number of overs received by the side batting second. The winners will be the side achieving the higher score within the number of overs.
3 If scores are equal, the result is a tie.

Points
1 Winning team gets four points.
2 In the event of a tie each side gets two points.
3 In a no-result match, each side gets one point.
4 If, at the end of the season, two teams or more have an equal number of points, their position in the table will be decided by the higher run-rate per over.

In fairness to the organizers, the fact that play could not start until two o'clock, and was thus condensed into such a short space of time, meant inevitably that it must be a slogging match. Where rain interfered and the rules were amended as the game went on, it became a total travesty of cricket. To the connoisseur of the game, his reaction was similar to that of Arthur Sullivan. Sullivan's delight was composing an oratorio; the handsome rewards for his work came from composing the musical scores for comic opera. So it was to many of the players, especially as the Sunday matches were arranged while an ordinary three-day County

Championship match was in progress. It meant dashing off on Saturday night for a Sunday League match, and returning on Sunday night in readiness to continue the three-day game on the Monday. To the fast bowler the whole thing was a farce; his run was limited to fifteen yards, and most fast bowlers would rather have spent their Sundays on the golf course or in the garden. The spinners often could, as this type of cricket made little call on their talents.

A typical example of how farcical the situation could become on a rain-ruined afternoon, is a match between Surrey and Lancashire in the second year of the competition. Surrey, 106 for 8, beat Lancashire, 162–6. How can this happen? In the following complex way. Lancashire's innings, interrupted by rain, caused the game to be reduced to 34 overs. Then, when Surrey were batting, it rained again. This is what happened. Stewart consulted his *aide-memoire* about what Lancashire's rate had been, and efforts were made in the sixteenth over to make the seven runs required. But Simmons bowled a tight over conceding only three runs and, when the rain become heavy enough to send them off, Lancashire were still ahead. If the rain persisted for another fifty-five minutes, Lancashire had won. If it stopped, they were vulnerable, for between sixteen and twenty overs in their innings, they had struck a sticky patch. In fact, it did stop raining, reducing the match to twenty-five overs, which meant that Surrey at 51–2, needed another 56 in nine overs – and they got them. But what a way to run a cricket match! No wonder cricket becomes an ever deepening mystery to the uninitiated. In fact the most enlightened initiated would have struggled to follow this course of events.

But as one very famous cricketer (who shall be nameless!) once said: 'We are not in this game for fun.' The money was like manna from Heaven for counties and players alike, and this species of 'biff-bang' cricket did attract a new and sizeable audience. In fact the success of Lancashire enlisted the support of Manchester United supporters who had some free time in the summer and were happy to support a winning team, as long as it came from Lancashire, and as this one came from Old Trafford it was home from home!

Player's approach to this competition differed from that of Gillette. In view of the amount of money they had invested, Player's needed a return on it in terms of a hard sell, and yet, surprisingly, they made a tactical blunder in the first season by calling the competition 'The Player's League'; many people thought that the word referred to the players in the competition; the Company were swift to amend the title in the second year to 'The John Player League'.

So in 1969, the Sunday League was launched alongside the County Championship and the Gillette Cup. Sixteen matches were played by each county on a Sunday and the first winners were Lancashire, so their players collected £1,000 for their labours, plus the various individual slices of cake; Hampshire, as runner-up, collected £500, and Kent, in third place, received £250. Yet none of these sides did very much of importance in the Gillette Cup. Even including the Final, the great Gillette day of that summer was at Scarborough and Chesterfield, the battle-fields for the Semi-Finals. Both grounds were closed before the start, or very shortly afterwards; the procession of cars heading for the cricket ground brought the traffic in Scarborough to a virtual halt. The sun shone and Yorkshire and Derbyshire emerged triumphant, Derbyshire's win over Sussex ranking as one of the most sensational in the history of the competition. Derbyshire, having made a modest total of 136 shot Sussex out for 49, Peter Eyre playing the role of Lord High Executioner by taking 6 for 18. The Final in 1969 is not one to be remembered and treasured. From the very moment that Derbyshire's Captain put Yorkshire in, Derbyshire were never in the hunt. It was easy for Yorkshire. So for the first time, 1969 produced three Champions – Glamorgan, Yorkshire and Lancashire, but 1970 was quite a year – there were only two Champions – Lancashire scooped both the Gillette Cup and the John Player League. Their success brought a new dimension of support for cricket.

Lancashire's progress as they travelled the country in 1970

stimulated enormous enthusiasm. At one time it looked as if they might scoop the pool and win all three competitions. In the end Kent pipped them on the post for the Championship, but with all guns blazing Lancashire took the Cup and the Sunday League. As Sussex had won the Gillette Cup in the first two years of the competition, Lancashire had now done so with the John Player League.

What made Lancashire tick; was it chance? No, it certainly was not. They had the essential ingredients for success, Cedric Rhoades, a first-class Chairman, and a secretary, Jack Wood, who thought alike, breathed alike, and had the interest of the club and its players very much at heart. They had a splendid Captain in Jackie Bond, and the most essential necessity – a very fine team indeed, infused with a team spirit, which, lamentably, is lacking in places in cricket to-day. If you see Lancashire on the inside, and then see some other counties, you might be tempted to think that they were playing a different game. Perhaps, in some ways, they are! Lancashire had a tough nut to crack in the Gillette Final where they were up against the maestros, Sussex, but even if fortunes fluctuated a little, the pendulum never swung violently, and Lancashire were always in with a chance. But full marks to Sussex, playing in their fourth Cup Final in eight years; this is a great record which can never be taken away from them. Lancashire's 'Man of the Match' in this Final was Harry Pilling – who, when once asked if he was afraid of being run-out by the massive Clive Lloyd, replied that he was more afraid of being trampled on! I can see the little man now, sitting in the corner of the Lancashire dressing-room after the victory, clutching a pint in both hands whilst the rest of us downed champagne. That was not the stuff for him; he had been bred hard on good honest beer; he was as he was bred; no fancy façade for him, down to earth and the real salt of it. Lancashire have nurtured a lot like him over the years. I put him in the company of Ernest Tyldesley and Eddie Paynter and can pay him no higher compliment: all of them real 'pros', rich, earthy characters, the best that West Houghton Sunday School ever produced.

And so to 1971. The emphasis was very much on Lancashire.

Laid before them were the following possibilities: to win the County Championship for the ninth time (the last was in 1934); to win the Gillette Cup for the second time and so equal Sussex's record of winning it in successive years; and to win the John Player League for the third time and retain an unchallenged supremacy in this competition. It was a fascinating permutation.

For a time it looked as if Lancashire could win all three, but in the end they had to settle for the Gillette Cup. An amazing Semi-Final, at which the gates were closed at Old Trafford, saw David Hughes hit 24 in one over off John Mortimore of Gloucestershire, in semi-darkness, only a minute or two from nine o'clock. In the Final, Lancashire beat Kent – the best Gillette Final yet. Lancashire could then still win the Sunday League, but when they were beaten at Old Trafford by Glamorgan on 12 September, Worcester became the new John Player League Champions, and what a splendid effort by a Worcester side so bedevilled by injury for extensive periods, including the loss of their Captain, Norman Gifford, with a broken hand. Ron Headley, who led the side in Gifford's absence during the latter part of the competition, deserves full credit for mustering his depleted forces to such great purpose. Lancashire's tight grip on the Sunday League had been relaxed at last. Worcestershire, twice unsuccessful Gillette Cup Finalists, had now proved themselves masters in one-day cricket.

In the winter of 1971–2, one-day cricket and sponsorship moved into new fields with the announcement that Benson and Hedges were to sponsor a new one-day competition in 1972 operated on the principle of the World Soccer Cup. Great joy for the County treasurers; fear by the purists that three-day County Championship cricket, now further diminished, would have to fight desperately for its survival.

7 The South African Explosion

In May 1960 the publishers of *Playfair*, whose cricket annual has been famous since its inception in 1948, launched *Cricket Monthly*. Contributors to its first issue were The Rt Hon. Lord Birkett, Neville Cardus, John Arlott, Rex Alston, Ray Robinson, and that noted writer on cricket in the North, John Kay, who discussed the prospects in the Lancashire League for that summer of 1960. He wrote:

> Middleton give South Africa's leading non-European player his first chance to impress, and in Basil D'Oliveira consider they have secured a very good cricketer indeed. D'Oliveira's record at home is a remarkable one with centuries galore in good time and bowling performances bordering on the extraordinary. He comes to sample league cricket and take an MCC coaching course in his spare time.
>
> It is hard to 'get a line' on d'Oliveira's true worth. He has not had the opportunity of playing with or against the leading South African cricketers. But, playing for a Transvaal Invitation XI against another representative team that included Peter Walker, the Glamorgan all-rounder, and Peter Philpott of New South Wales, he hit an aggressive 48 and captured three cheap wickets. D'Oliveira captained the Transvaal side impressively and earned high praise for the manner in which he nursed his younger players.

In March 1971, John Kay appeared on television with Basil d'Oliveira, when d'Oliveira's eminence as a world figure was of sufficiently high standing for him to be the subject of a 'This is Your Life' programme. Kay told then of the utter bewilderment of this Cape coloured cricketer when he met him at the airport and travelled with him by train to the North for his first glimpse of England.

The water that has flowed under the bridge between 1960 and 1971 has given d'Oliveira world prominence and isolated

South Africa's white cricketers. Throughout this racial and political storm, d'Oliveira behaved impeccably and with great dignity; unwittingly he was the centre of it all; it was not his choice. One sentence in John Kay's article in 1960 went to the root of the trouble: 'He has not had the opportunity of playing with or against the leading South African cricketers.'

The crux of the issue was, that under South Africa's existing race laws, he never would, nor would any of his compatriots. This, not only to long-haired militants (as some indiscriminately chose to call all the protestors), but to sportsmen and fair-minded people all over the world, was repugnant. South Africa's politicians took the view that they made the laws in the best interests of the community, they were not understood by anyone outside South Africa, and it was no one else's business anyway. World reaction was that the strength of opinion against race discrimination in sport could best be shown by ceasing to play against South Africa's white teams. That, then, in essence is the d'Oliveira affair.

But in order to avoid giving the story a beginning, and an ending, but no middle, we should first take a look at d'Oliveira's cricket career, which took him from the shoddy makeshift wickets provided for the coloured cricketers in the Cape, to a Test player of world renown, of considerable skill, and with a temperament which was able to withstand not only tense moments on the field, but also moments off it which could have broken lesser men. In fact some of the pressures did affect him emotionally at times.

John Kay can take up the story again. He described d'Oliveira's first season at Middleton, in the 1961 *Playfair Cricket Annual*, as follows:

Middleton gambled on d'Oliveira making the grade and although conditions were new to him, the South African hit 930 runs for an average of 48, and claimed 71 wickets at eleven runs each – a remarkably fine performance for a man sampling English conditions for the first time. In addition, d'Oliveira proved himself a perfect sportsman in every respect, and with the season only a month old, Middleton secured his signature for a further two years and thus forestalled competition from other clubs. A natural stroke-player, d'Oliveira probably hit more sixes than any other League batsman, and although his medium-paced in-swingers were never devastating, they were ever dangerous. He backed up his splendid batting and bowling with some superb fielding near the wicket and set a perfect example for young cricketers to follow at the nets.

D'Oliveira came to Middleton at the height of the apartheid demonstrations against South Africa and received tremendous publicity. He conducted himself in the most gentlemanly manner possible and returned home in September with the good wishes and high esteem of all League cricket followers, who look forward to his return this summer with great anticipation of attractive cricket, from a modest and unassuming player, previously denied a chance to show his prowess outside his own coloured sphere in South Africa.'

These hopes were confirmed in 1961. D'Oliveira scored 1,073 runs at an average of 59·61 and took 31 wickets. He played for Middleton for two more seasons after this, by which time he had got his sights set on playing English county cricket. He joined Worcestershire in 1964, becoming eligbile for Championship matches in 1965; during his period of qualification he played for Kidderminster in the Birmingham League. D'Oliveira's performances in the 1966 season won him the full measure of a cricketer's acclaim – he was elected as one of *Wisden's* 'Five Cricketer's of the Year'. 1966 was the most memorable year of d'Oliveira's life. He became a British citizen; he played cricket for England, and he said himself: 'This is a fairy tale come true. Six years ago I was playing on mudheaps. Now I have played for England and met the Queen'.

His selection for England was an enormous thrill for a lot of people – his folk at home, John Kay, Tom Graveney, who, when on a Commonwealth tour with him had persuaded 'Dolly' that he was good enough to play county cricket, after Lancashire had turned him down. But perhaps it was John Arlott who derived the richest pleasure from all this, for it was Arlott who had first tried to get people in England interested in d'Oliveira; he had failed for a couple of years; but eventually, with the urgings of John Kay also (and history proved them to be right), right), Middleton offered him a contract for the 1960 season.

Life was good for d'Oliveira; he must have been well satisfied that all the faith which many people had placed in him had been overwhelmingly justified. On the distant horizon was the possibility of returning to South Africa as an England cricketer to play on all the grounds which he had never been able to sample as a Cape coloured. But would he be allowed to? Would the South African Government refuse to allow him to come? If they did, would MCC then cancel the tour? These thoughts were beginning to foment as cricket in England got under way in that summer of 1968 – a summer of disappointment because of the unprecedented amount of bad weather. The Test series against Australia became disjointed in the middle because of rain-ruined matches at Lord's and Edgbaston.

It seemed a summer of bitter disillusionment, too, for d'Oliveira; he lost his form and his place in the England side; for almost the first time this man of an ice-cool temperament was deeply worried by his loss of form. To return to South Africa as an England Test player was another crucial link in this golden chain of events; to fail to be chosen was letting down his many benefactors and admirers.

The Test matches against Australia came and went; Australia won the First at Old Trafford; the Second at Lord's was drawn with a tremendous psychological advantage with England; after scoring 351 for 7 declared they bowled Australia out on a rain-affected wicket for 78. The Third Test was drawn, so was the Fourth. There was no place for d'Oliveira, and when the team was chosen for the Fifth and Final Test at the Oval and d'Oliveira was still not there, the end of his South African dream seemed to have become a harsh reality. It was a bitter moment, but d'Oliveira could have no complaints; he knew full well that his form had not been convincing enough. He knew, too, if others didn't, that he would get a scrupulously fair deal from cricket's administration in this country.

There was no brief to the Selectors from higher authority that d'Oliveira should not be chosen, so that the tour to South Africa could go ahead unimpeded by controversy. This was proved beyond any shadow of doubt when Prideaux dropped out of the Oval Test match because of bronchitis. Cowdrey asked for d'Oliveira as the replacement. Some thought there were batsmen with better qualifications on current form than d'Oliveira; there were – but Cowdrey said that he wanted d'Oliveira's bowling to close up one end. Cowdrey, the Selectors, the MCC Committee, and the world at large, knew full well that if d'Oliveira was a success, then he must be in line for the South African tour, and if, after doing well, he was still not chosen for South Africa, then MCC would lay themselves open (even though this was untrue) to harsh criticism for deliberately not choosing him so that the tour could proceed unhampered.

Well, in the event, d'Oliveira did come off. He hit 158, and England won the match. The Selectors sat down that night to pick the team for South Africa. It was announced the next day – d'Oliveira was not included. Anticipating that a wind of anger would blow through the selection, D. J. Insole, the Chairman of the Selectors, explained that they regarded d'Oliveira from an overseas point of view as a batsman rather than as an all-rounder. Insole said: 'We put him beside the seven batsmen that we had, along with Colin Milburn, whom we also had to leave out, with regret.' If cricketers believed this – and most of them did, it was still incomprehensible to the non-cricketing fraternity.

Soon, however, there was a turn of events which was totally inexplicable to cricketer, non-cricketer, man, woman and child. Cartwright, one of the team's bowlers, withdrew because of a damaged shoulder. D'Oliveira, viewed, as the Chairman of the Selectors had himself said, wholly as a batsman, was now chosen to replace the injured bowler!

This made utter nonsense of Insole's first statement; it suggested that there was some dirty work going on somewhere. Cricket, surely, could not be so naïve as to think that the whole world, and especially South Africa, did not view their activities with suspicion. Mr Vorster, the South African Prime Minister, had not been put in a particularly good mood by the announcement that d'Oliveira was to report the tour for the *News of the World*. This was nothing new in cricket journalism for a newspaper to send a player who has just missed selection to report a tour. He would always be a name very much in the news. Both

Wardle and Close were sent abroad in similar circumstances. To the South Africans, however, this spelt intrigue with political undertones and anti-South African motives. When d'Oliveira was ultimately selected to replace Cartwright this was the last straw. Mr Vorster described d'Oliveira as a 'Political Cricket Ball', and announced that the England party as constituted was not welcome in South Africa. He said that South Africa was not prepared to receive a team which had been forced upon her by people with 'certain political aims'. Mr Vorster's speech in Bloemfontein broke the eighty-year-old links between English and South African cricket; it was a speech designed solely for internal political consumption. The *Daily Mail* described it as 'crude and boorish' words, with a harshness which can have won him little sympathy outside his own party.

All that remained now was for the MCC Committee to make the formal cancellation of the tour, and this they did on 24 September 1968. For MCC this was not just the end of a sad story; it was the beginning of another that was to drag on, and ultimately lead to the cancellation of another tour – South Africa to England 1970.

The MCC's handling of the d'Oliveira affair had produced sizeable groups of opposition. 'Why', it was asked, 'were South Africa not confronted directly with the problems months before? Why were they not asked six months previously: "If we pick d'Oliveira, will he be acceptable to you or not? If not, the tour is off." ' To make matters worse, news leaked out that Viscount Cobham, distinguished cricketer and administrator, though not then currently serving on any MCC Committees, had advised MCC of a conversation he had had with the South African Prime Minister who had made it perfectly clear that d'Oliveira would not be accepted, largely because of a risk of violence if white umpires gave him out. (This rather lame excuse was surely a red herring – there were many other more valid reasons.) But MCC, however, decided to disregard this information, and to rely instead on the counsel of Sir Alec Douglas-Home, who had apparently obtained a different impression from Mr Vorster.

Hindsight is a wonderful thing for solving problems, but it was a great pity that Lord Cobham's views were not given more serious attention, especially as a great body of opinion, well placed to judge, was absolutely certain that in no circumstances whatsoever would d'Oliveira be allowed into South Africa as a member of an England Test team. Mr Vorster is not concerned with sport; he is concerned with maintaining his apartheid policies as a politician. To have made an exception would be diametrically opposed to all these principles, and no politician worth his salt would have taken the risk, whatever the rest of the world might have thought.

The MCC were obliged to call a Special General Meeting requisitioned by twenty members, led by the Rev. David Sheppard, himself a Sussex and England cricketer, who were critical of the MCC's handling of this whole affair. The object of the Special General Meeting was to vote on the following:

1 That the members of the MCC regret their Committee's mishandling of affairs leading up to the selection of the team for the intended tour of South Africa in 1968-9
2 That no further tours to or from South Africa be undertaken until evidence can be given of actual progress by South Africa towards non-racial cricket
3 That a special committee be set up to examine such proposals as are submitted by the SACA towards non-racial cricket; the MCC to report on progress to the Annual General Meeting of the Club; and to the Governing Body for Cricket – the MCC Council.

The views of both sides were set out in an eight-page document sent to members prior to the meeting in the Assembly Hall, Church House, Dean's Yard, Westminster, on Thursday, 5 December 1968. In this document the MCC offered the following comments on the three resolutions:

Resolution 1
The Statement submitted by the twenty full members who have requisitioned the Special General Meeting suggests that we had put the Selectors into a position in which they could not do their job objectively. This we deny. The Selectors' brief was simply to choose the best available side. It is also suggested that we acted weakly and irresponsibly. We suggest that the history of the matter, which we have set out, constitutes a sufficient answer

Resolution 2
We adhere to the attitude which we have held throughout as set out in paragraphs 1, 2 and 3 at the beginning of our Statement. We suggest that the terms of this Resolution give the key to the true motives of the movers of these three Resolutions

Resolution 3
We suggest that the existing machinery of the Club and of the MCC Council will be quite adequate to deal with any such proposals as may be envisaged.

Members were invited to vote on these resolutions.

The voting on this most critical night in the MCC's history was as follows:

Resolution 1	For:	1,570	Against:	4,357
Resolution 2	For:	1,214	Against:	4,664
Resolution 3	For:	1,352	Against:	4,508

On the face of it, this was an overwhelming victory for the MCC and represented destruction of its opponents. On the other hand while the overall figures on this first motion were very substantial, those actually cast in the hall showed a much narrower majority, namely 386 to 314. The enormous difference was reflected in the postal vote, and it could be said after listening to the various points of view expounded at length, that this smaller majority was a fairer reflection of the merits of the case. This was not a rout for Sheppard's cause, but it showed that he did have quite substantial support. Nevertheless, loyal MCC members had responded in strength to support their Club when it was challenged in open court, as it were.

The basis of Sheppard's rational argument was that he agreed that both MCC and their players held many happy memories of matches with South Africa, but he felt that the country's politics were now interfering with its cricket to such a degree that it was really no longer possible to continue playing with them while the present state of affairs lasted. South Africa's National Elevens are not representative if they are selected only from the white minority. MCC are now not even permitted to play 'all coloured' sides, and many coloured South Africans are even denied the opportunity of watching the tourists. It is certainly not for any body to act as 'Inquisitor-General' of another country's politics. The fact that Spain and Russia have a form of government that does not readily appeal to us, does not stop us from playing football, for example, against them, because their politics are not entering their sport. Politics are interfering with sport in South Africa, and as such cannot be tolerated.

MCC's own line, which they pursued with undeniable sincerity and integrity, was that they felt that by continuing to play South Africa they may be helping to bridge the gap and bring inter-racial sport closer together. But there was no gap to be bridged between English and South African cricketers; they would go on playing against each other for eternity if allowed to, and South African cricketers, too, would play with and against any coloured community anywhere in the world. What MCC were trying hard to do was to bridge a gap between cricket and South African politics; they had about as much chance of succeeding as driving a car to the summit of Everest. Would President Nixon, for instance, substantially change his policies, in Vietnam, if he heard that America were playing North Vietnam at badminton? Of course not; neither would Vorster. Thus, MCC's desire was really an issue of nostalgia and bitter disappointment that an eighty-year-old chain of wonderful cricket between the two countries was in danger of being broken – as indeed, it was.

One altogether surprising aspect of the meeting was that Sir Alec Douglas-Home, on whose counsel so much of these arguments turned, was not present. It was said that he had a previously arranged political meeting to attend; this was perfectly true, but as it seemed that he was the principal witness for the defence in the case, one would have thought that the meeting would be arranged on a date when he was free, not only to attend, but also to speak. As a diplomat of very considerable experience in such matters his point of view could have had a great effect on the uncertain voters. Be that as it may, the matter was now closed. For MCC, however, worse trouble lay ahead. There was the cardinal issue of South Africa's tour to this country arranged for the summer of 1970.

Opposition all over the world to South Africa's apartheid policies in sport was beginning to snowball. Foolishly, some members of traditional establishments attributed the fomenting of feeling to pockets of long-haired militant students, who simply wanted something to demonstrate against. This was an insult to the conscience of hundreds and thousands of fair-minded people of all denominations who viewed the isolation from sporting contests of anyone purely on the basis of colour, as odious discrimination, and wanted to do something about it. It is time, too, that the term 'long-haired' was put in its right perspective. It is fashion now, just as 'short-back-and-sides' used to be; long hair does not make a man a hooligan, a thug, a communist, an atheist, or an anarchist. Without detracting one iota from their skill in their chosen profession, or their merit socially, we may have long-haired Prime Ministers, income tax inspectors, heavy-weight boxers, chiropodists or even psychologists. No, this resentment against South Africa's sporting divisions was more than a students' prank. It was reflecting sizeable national opinion.

Much of that opinion, as strongly as opposition to apartheid was felt, would not go so far as to take physical action. This, inevitably would be to contravene the laws of the land, but there was enough to form a 'Stop the Seventy Tour Committee', which planned precisely that. The first inkling of what was to happen was seen in the summer of 1969 when Wilfred Isaacs, a South African businessman, brought a cricket team of South Africans on a private tour of England. At their first match at Basildon, in Essex, a handful of demonstrators ran on to the field. The police, who were there in force, were able to deal with them, and that was that.

But it was a different matter at their next match in Oxford. A day or so before the match was due to start, the pitch was dug up; groundsmen, however, were able to repair it in time, but when a much larger gathering of demonstrators than had been seen at Basildon ran on to the field, play was held up for three-quarters of an hour or so, and then caused the abandonment of play for the day. This was a portent of things to come. It brought a sharp division of opinion across the country. The demonstrators took the view that, if they merely paraded outside the ground with placards, their silent protest would be more a cause of amusement than annoyance; on those terms it would probably achieve nothing, and positive action was the only alternative likely to produce results. Cricketers, and many other sections of the community, argued that to break the law must be an offence, whatever the provocation or reasons behind the motive, and that if twenty-two people are engaged legally and peacefully in playing a game of cricket they should be given maximum protection from anyone who physically interferes with their activities. This was the whole issue which divided the country, not apartheid itself. The country, as a whole, was bitterly opposed to depriving a sportsman of necessary opportunities for advancement on the basis of his skin.

One of the demonstrators who ran on to the field at Basildon was Peter Hain, who subsequently became Chairman of the 'Stop the Seventy Tour' Committee. During a long campaign, Hain was followed by television cameras recording his every move as his activities grew, snowball like, from small beginnings at Basildon to enormous proportions. There were times when his most violent opponents suggested that he should be deported back to his own country – South Africa. Hain, in fact, was born in Nairobi in Kenya and is, therefore, a British subject, although his parents were South Africans.

The 'Stop the Seventy Tour' organization was to have a full dress rehearsal provided by the South African rugby team – the world-famous Springboks, who were to be in England in the winter of 1969–70. Violence erupted on a number of occasions as massive police protection was provided at enormous cost. Because of this, the tour went through, but it posed a vital question. While it had been possible to protect thirty rugby players for an hour and a half, would it be possible, even with a vast armada of police to protect a cricket ground for a week or more since, with a Sunday included, a Test match lasts for six days.

The MCC and the seventeen counties were determined to try their best to do so, while on the other hand, every effort was made to persuade the MCC to change their minds in the light of the volume of opposition in this country at all levels of society. The MCC and the cricket world at large were adamant, and their reason for so being was perfectly logical. They believed that if they wanted to play a game of cricket it was a pretty poor country if they were not to be allowed to do so. They believed that it was their right to expect proper protection.

As the New Year, 1970, dawned, the issue of whether or not the cricket tour to England by the South Africans should take place had assumed world-wide importance. It was top priority news for press and television. The leader article in the February issue of *Cricket Monthly* suggested that to have a tour cancelled by forces outside cricket is reprehensible. There are, however, still two questions which need to be studied in precise detail. They are:

1 Is there likely to be damage caused to our cricket grounds by the militants?
2 Having sold Test match tickets in advance can the purchasers be guaranteed a day's play for their money? Test match tickets have always carried the phrase 'Play is not guaranteed'. This, however, is generally accepted to refer to the weather.

The leader went on to say:

Hope that something from South Africa might ease the problems for us have not materialized. Jack Cheetham's statement that the South African side would be chosen strictly on merit was a hollow one. There is no coloured South African (except d'Oliveira) anywhere near good enough, largely because of the lack of the necessary facilities to breed Test cricketers. Grants to coloured cricketers are admirable in their way. But what they really want is the chance to play with and against all cricketers. That is the only way they will improve their standards. The South African Prime Minister said in his New Year speech that his country would not be dictated to over its racial policies, and strongly indicated that he would not allow mult-racial sports teams to make overseas tours. He rejected a move by white South African sports administrators to circumvent the Government's apartheid sports policies.

Clearly, there were to be no concessions from South Africa. The Cricket Council were on their own. This monumental decision was theirs alone. MCC had a duty to cricket which they have administered with varying success over a very long period. It could be that if they felt that a great deal of damage could be done to cricket grounds, it might still be in cricket's overall interest to call off the tour. As cricketers, could they divorce themselves from growing world opinion? A major issue of principle was at stake.

The first positive move the Council made was to announce that the tour was definitely on, but that it had been cut from twenty-eight matches to twelve, and restricted to eight grounds to reduce the disruption by anti-apartheid demonstrators. In addition, artificial pitches would be installed to counter vandalism. Also, an eight-man delegation from MCC, including Mr G. O. Allen, Mr F. R. Brown and Mr S. C. Griffith, visited the Home Secretary, whose responsibility it would be to provide police protection for the tourists and the grounds. It was obvious, at this stage, that the Home Secretary was concerned with the many serious breaches of the peace which were almost certain to occur. What was his position in the matter? His job was the preservation of law and order. Could he justify the deployment of half his police force to ensure that some games of cricket would take place even if it was the right of those cricketers to expect protection? Would it be an incentive to criminals to indulge in increased activities, knowing that the Police's attentions were elsewhere?

The Cabinet was now heavily involved. It was their problem, too. The then Prime Minister, Harold Wilson, revealed his hand on television at the end of April by saying that he hoped that even at this late stage the Cricket Council would think again and call off the tour. David Sheppard announced the formation of his own campaign – the Fair Cricket Campaign, which was opposed to violence. The Cricket Council did not waver. Instead, barbed wire entanglements appeared on the grounds on which the South Africans would play. The traditionally English scene of county cricketers emerging from their winter's slumbers as the blossom appeared had a macabre backcloth. Cricket and barbed wire. Had the world gone mad? The artificial wickets were laid, top-level police conferences were called to plan what was virtually a military operation. It *was* a war, of sorts.

It was at this point that many cricketers and administrators felt that whatever the pros and cons of the issue, whatever moral issues were involved, whatever financial obligations were at stake, or however much they wanted to see what was virtually the best cricketing side in the world, the total disruption of the games, the atmosphere in which they would be played, the possible injury to players, and the almost certain damage to cricket grounds, would utterly outweigh all other considerations. Silently they shielded their hopes that somehow the tour would be called off, yet feeling, at the same time, that it was not they who wanted to call it off.

It hinged now entirely on the Government. South Africa would come, and our cricket administration would have them. Meanwhile, one development followed another. African and Asian countries were to boycott the Commonwealth Games in Edinburgh. Coloured cricketers in this country were instructed by their respective Boards of Control not to play against the South Africans. In addition, the Pakistan Government announced the cancellation of its Under-25 cricket tour. The Home Secretary once again besought the Cricket Council to call off the tour. The Cricket Council remained resolved not to do so. Following a further meeting at the Home Office Mr Callaghan, the Home Secretary, sent a letter to Mr M. J. C. Allom, President of the MCC and Chairman of the Cricket Council. He said:

> When you and Mr Griffith came to see me this morning, we discussed the statement issued on behalf of the Cricket Council on 19 May. You explained that the Council have come to their conclusion that the tour should go on after reassessing their own responsibilities, which were limited to the impact of the decision on cricket and cricketers, both in the United Kingdom and throughout the world, and on other sports and sportsmen. You emphasized, however, that although the Council were naturally concerned with various other matters of a public and political nature ... they feel that these matters fell outside their own responsibilities and that it was beyond their competence to judge what significance to attach to them ... The Government have come to the conclusion ... that on grounds of broad public policy they must request the Cricket Council to withdraw their invitation to the South African Cricket Association and I should be grateful if you would put this request before the Council.

The Cricket Council met the next day and were of the

unanimous opinion that they had no alternative but to accede to the request. The tour was off. *Cricket Monthly*, in its leader, wrote: 'The long, bitter, South African saga is over, temporarily at least. What the future is for South African cricket in the international arena is in the lap of the gods, or perhaps, rather more to the point, in the lap of Mr Vorster.'

One of the next most significant moves, however, did not come from Mr Vorster although it did come from South Africa. It showed that Mr Vorster's policies did not have the whole-hearted support of South Africa's sportsmen. In April 1971 white cricketers, playing in the last big match of the season – Transvaal *v* The Rest of South Africa – walked off the field at Cape Town's Newlands in protest against the South African Government's refusal to allow non-white players to be chosen for the Springbok team for Australia. The game began with Barry Richards and Brian Bath opening for Transvaal. Mike Procter sent down the first ball to Richards who hit it for a single. After taking the run, Richards, Bath, Procter and the rest of the players walked back to the pavilion. Then Mr Delport, Manager of the Rest, handed to an official of the South African Cricket Association a statement which read: 'We cricketers feel that the time has come for an expression of our views. We fully support the South African Cricket Association's application to invite non-whites to tour Australia, if they are good enough, and further subscribe to merit being the only criterion on the cricket field.' The players then returned to the field and the match continued.

This, perhaps, was the thinnest of cracks in a huge iceberg. With the limitation of their playing facilities there were no non-white players anywhere near good enough to be chosen. Mr Hassan Howa, President of the non-white Cricket Board could be well understood for his comment that he was opposed to two token non-whites' being in the team like dummies in a shop window. On the other hand, the demonstration was a step in the right direction. Think how small the Basildon affair was – and what it grew to ultimately!

This was followed quite swiftly by an announcement from Mr Vorster that three concessions were being made towards limited multi-racial sport in an apparent attempt to prevent South Africa's complete isolation in international sport. The move was announced in the South African Parliament after Mr Vorster had come under strong criticism from the opposition United party. The three new guide-lines in official policy were:

1 Top overseas visiting sides especially in rugby and cricket can play against non-white teams, but only in non-white areas before non-white spectators.
2 Non-white sportsmen will be allowed to compete with whites at tournaments which have an international ranking.
3 An International Sports Centre will be built where the different racial groups, whites, coloured, Indians and various Bantu tribes, can compete against each other.

Mr Vorster, however, made it clear that multi-racial sport generally would not be allowed. He said they are taking a firm stand against mixed sport at Club, Provincial and National level. Mr Vorster also said that the England rugby team to tour South Africa next year would play matches against a coloured (mixed race) side, and against Africans before non-white spectators. The other major change was to allow ranking non-white players to take part in matches of international status. Mr Vorster quoted the South African Open Tennis Championships, and said that it would be open to non-whites.

All this, once again, was the opening of a small crack. It was no more than that. Mr Vorster had made no reference to the ban on non-white players' touring with the cricketers to Australia and when questioned on whether he would agree to the MCC's insistence that they would send a touring team to South Africa only if it were accepted unconditionally by South Africa, Mr Vorster in his veiled reply said: 'We have to be very careful not to make any promise which we know cannot be carried out in practice.'

There are still far too many anomalies in the whole situation. Mr Hain commented: 'This only puts a glossy wrapping round racially-segregated sport. It simply accommodates apartheid when what we want and what non-white sportsmen in South Africa want is non-racial sport at all levels.'

Sir William Ramsay, President of the Rugby Union, whose contribution to world affairs through sport has been immeasurable, expressed surprise that no white spectators would be allowed to watch games against non-whites, as non-white spectators could watch white games from special enclosures. Alice would agree with Sir William that things were becoming 'curiouser and curiouser'.

History was to repeat itself on the other side of the world. A South African rugby tour to Australia convinced the authorities there, as it had done in England, that the problem of policing cricket matches in the face of powerful anti-apartheid demonstrations was too great to face. In September 1971 Australia was obliged to call off the Springbok tour scheduled to begin barely a month later. South African cricket was now totally isolated. It simply had no available opposition at a time when competition could easily have proved South Africa to be World Champions. Whose is the fault? Who is out of step – South Africa, or the rest of the world? The question answers itself!

The Seventeen First-Class Counties

Derbyshire
Formed 1870. *Colours* Chocolate, amber and pale blue. *Badge* Rose and crown. *County Championship* 1873-87, re-entered 1895. *County Champions* 1874, 1936

Essex
Formed 1864-5, *dissolved* 1866, *re-formed* in 1876 and 1886. *Colours* Blue, gold and red. *Badge* Three scimitars with word 'Essex' underneath. *Promoted to first-class status* 1894 (1895 in Championship)

Glamorgan
Formed 1888. *Colours* Blue and gold. *Badge* Gold daffodil. *Promoted to first-class status* 1921. *County Champions* 1948, 1969

Gloucestershire
Formed 1870. *Colours* Blue, gold, brown, sky blue, green and red. *Badge* Coat of arms of the City and County of Bristol. *County Champions* 1876, 1877. *Joint Champions* 1873, 1880

Hampshire
Formed 1863. *Colours* Blue, gold and white. *Badge* Tudor rose and crown. *Promoted to first-class status* 1895. *County Champions* 1961

Kent
Formed 1859, *re-formed* 1870. *Colours* Red and white. *Badge* White horse on a red background. *County Champions* 1906, 1909, 1910, 1913, 1970. *Gillette Cup winners* 1967

Lancashire
Formed 1864. *Colours* Red, green and blue. *Badge* Red rose. *County Champions* 1881, 1897, 1904, 1926, 1927, 1928, 1930, 1934. *Joint-Champions* 1875, 1879, 1882, 1889, 1950. *John Player Sunday League Champions* 1969, 1970. *Gillette Cup winners* 1970, 1971

Leicestershire
Formed 1873, *re-formed* 1879. *Colours* Scarlet and dark green. *Badge* Running fox (gold) on green background. *Promoted to first-class status* 1894 (1895 in Championship)

Middlesex
Formed 1864. *Colours* Blue. *Badge* Three seaxes. *County Champions* 1878, 1903, 1920, 1921, 1947. *Joint-Champions* 1949

Northamptonshire
Formed 1820, *re-organized* 1878. *Colours* Maroon. *Badge* Tudor rose. *Promoted to first-class status* 1905

Nottinghamshire
Formed 1841, *re-organized* 1866. *Colours* Green and gold. *Badge* County badge of Nottinghamshire. *County Champions* 1883, 1884, 1885, 1886, 1907, 1929. *Joint-Champions* 1873, 1875, 1879, 1880, 1882, 1889

Somerset
Formed 1875, *re-organized* 1885. *Colours* Black, white and maroon. *Badge* Wessex wyvern. *Promoted to first-class status* 1891

Surrey
Formed 1845. *Colours* Chocolate. *Badge* Prince of Wales's feathers. *County Champions* 1887, 1888, 1890, 1891, 1892, 1894, 1895, 1899, 1914, 1952, 1953, 1954, 1955, 1956, 1957, 1958, 1971. *Joint-Champions* 1889, 1950.

Sussex
Formed 1836, *re-formed* 1839 and 1857. *Colours* Dark blue, light blue and gold. *Badge* County arms of six martlets (in shape of inverted pyramid). *Joint-Champions* 1875. *Gillette Cup winners* 1963, 1964.

Warwickshire
Formed 1863, *re-formed* 1882 and 1884. *Colours* Blue, yellow and white. *Badge* Bear and ragged staff. *County Champions* 1911, 1951. *Promoted to first-class status* 1894 (1895 in Championship). *Gillette Cup winners* 1966, 1968

Worcestershire
Formed 1865. *Colours* Dark green and black. *Badge* Shield, argent bearing fess between three pears sable. *Promoted to first-class status* 1899. *County Champions* 1964, 1965. *John Player Sunday League Champions* 1971

Yorkshire
Formed 1863, *re-organized* 1891. *Colours* Oxford blue, Cambridge blue and gold. *Badge* White rose. *County Champions* 1893, 1896, 1898, 1900, 1901, 1902, 1905, 1908, 1912, 1919, 1922, 1923, 1924, 1925, 1931, 1932, 1933, 1935, 1937, 1938, 1939, 1946, 1959, 1960, 1962, 1963, 1966, 1967, 1968. *Joint-Champions* 1949. *Gillette Cup winners* 1965, 1969

County Champions from 1873

1873	{Glos / Notts}	1900	Yorks	1936	Derby
		1901	Yorks	1937	Yorks
1874	Glos	1902	Yorks	1938	Yorks
1875	Notts	1903	Middx	1939	Yorks
1876	Glos	1904	Lancs	1946	Yorks
1877	Glos	1905	Yorks	1947	Middx
1878	undecided	1906	Kent	1948	Glam
1879	{Notts / Lancs}	1907	Notts	1949	{Middx / Yorks}
		1908	Yorks		
1880	Notts	1909	Kent	1950	{Lancs / Surrey}
1881	Lancs	1910	Kent		
1882	Notts	1911	Warwk	1951	Warwk
	Lancs	1912	Yorks	1952	Surrey
1883	Notts	1913	Kent	1953	Surrey
1884	Notts	1914	Surrey	1954	Surrey
1885	Notts	1919	Yorks	1955	Surrey
1886	Notts	1920	Middx	1956	Surrey
1887	Surrey	1921	Middx	1957	Surrey
1888	Surrey	1922	Yorks	1958	Surrey
1889	{Surrey / Lancs / Notts}	1923	Yorks	1959	Yorks
		1924	Yorks	1960	Yorks
		1925	Yorks	1961	Hants
1890	Surrey	1926	Lancs	1962	Yorks
1891	Surrey	1927	Lancs	1963	Yorks
1892	Surrey	1928	Lancs	1964	Worcs
1893	Yorks	1929	Notts	1965	Worcs
1894	Surrey	1930	Lancs	1966	Yorks
1895	Surrey	1931	Yorks	1967	Yorks
1896	Yorks	1932	Yorks	1968	Yorks
1897	Lancs	1933	Yorks	1969	Glam
1898	Yorks	1934	Lancs	1970	Kent
1899	Surrey	1935	Yorks	1971	Surrey

The winners from 1873–86 are given, in the main, on the basis of fewest matches lost. MCC became responsible for awarding the Championship in 1895

Gillette Cup winners

1963	Sussex	1968	Warwk
1964	Sussex	1969	Yorks
1965	Yorks	1970	Lancs
1966	Warwk	1971	Lancs
1967	Kent		

John Player Sunday League

1969	Lancs	1971	Worcs
1970	Lancs		

England's Test Record

AUSTRALIA

Season	Visiting Captains	Won E	Won A	D	Total
1876–7	J. Lillywhite (E)	1	1	0	2
1878–9	Lord Harris (E)	0	1	0	1
1880	W. L. Murdoch (A)	1	0	0	1
1881–2	A. Shaw (E)	0	2	2	4
1882	W. L. Murdoch (A)	0	1	0	1
1882–3	Hon. Ivo Bligh (E)	2	2	0	4
1884	W. L. Murdoch (A)	1	0	2	3
1884–5	A. Shrewsbury (E)	3	2	0	5
1886	H. J. H. Scott (A)	3	0	0	3
1886–7	A. Shrewsbury (E)	2	0	0	2
1887–8	W. W. Read (E)	1	0	0	1
1888	P. S. McDonnell (A)	2	1	0	3
1890	W. L. Murdoch (A)	2	0	0	2
1891–2	W. G. Grace (E)	1	2	0	3
1893	J. McC. Blackham (A)	1	0	2	3
1894–5	A. E. Stoddart (E)	3	2	0	5
1896	G. H. S. Trott (A)	2	1	0	3
1897–8	A. E. Stoddart (E)	1	4	0	5
1899	J. Darling (A)	0	1	4	5
1901–2	A. C. MacLaren (E)	1	4	0	5
1902	J. Darling (A)	1	2	2	5

AUSTRALIA (cont.)

Season	Visiting Captains	Won E	A	D	Total
1903–4	P. F. Warner (E)	3	2	0	5
1905	J. Darling (A)	2	0	3	5
1907–8	A. O. Jones (E)	1	4	0	5
1909	M. A. Noble (A)	1	2	2	5
1911–12	J. W. H. T. Douglas (E)†	4	1	0	5
1912	S. E. Gregory (A)	1	0	2	3
1920–1	J. W. H. T. Douglas (E)	0	5	0	5
1921	W. W. Armstrong (A)	0	3	2	5
1924–5	A. E. R. Gilligan (E)	1	4	0	5
1926	H. L. Collins (A)	1	0	4	5
1928–9	A. P. F. Chapman (E)	4	1	0	5
1930	W. M. Woodfull (A)	1	2	2	5
1932–3	D. R. Jardine (E)	4	1	0	5
1934	W. M. Woodfull (A)	1	2	2	5
1936–7	G. O. Allen (E)	2	3	0	5
1938*	D. G. Bradman (A)	1	1	2	4
1946–7	W. R. Hammond (E)	0	3	2	5
1948	D. G. Bradman (A)	0	4	1	5
1950–1	F. R. Brown (E)	1	4	0	5
1953	A. L. Hassett (A)	1	0	4	5
1954–5	L. Hutton (E)	3	1	1	5
1956	I. W. Johnson (A)	2	1	2	5
1958–9	P. B. H. May (E)	0	4	1	5
1961	R. Benaud (A)	1	2	2	5
1962–3	E. R. Dexter (E)	1	1	3	5
1964	R. B. Simpson (A)	0	1	4	5
1965–6	M. J. K. Smith (E)	1	1	3	5
1968	W. M. Lawry (A)	1	1	3	5
1970–1*	R. Illingworth (E)	2	0	4	6
	IN AUSTRALIA	42	55	16	113
	IN ENGLAND	26	25	45	96
	TOTALS	68	80	61	209

*Matches at Manchester 1890 and 1938, and Melbourne 1971, abandoned.

†In place of P. F. Warner, who was taken ill after the first match of the tour at Adelaide.

SOUTH AFRICA

Season	Visiting Captains	Won E	Won SA	D	Total
1888–9	C. Aubrey Smith (E)	2	0	0	2
1891–2	W. W. Read (E)	1	0	0	1
1895–6	Lord Hawke (E)	3	0	0	3
1898–9	Lord Hawke (E)	2	0	0	2
1905–6	P. F. Warner (E)	1	4	0	5
1907	P. W. Sherwell (SA)	1	0	2	3
1909–10	H. D. G. Leveson-Gower (E)	2	3	0	5
1912	F. Mitchell (SA)	3	0	0	3
1913–14	J. W. H. T. Douglas (E)	4	0	1	5
1922–3	F. T. Mann (E)	2	1	2	5
1924	H. W. Taylor (SA)	3	0	2	5
1927–8	R. T. Stanyforth (E)	2	2	1	5
1929	H. G. Deane (SA)	2	0	3	5
1930–1	A. P. F. Chapman (E)	0	1	4	5
1935	H. F. Wade (SA)	0	1	4	5
1938–9	W. R. Hammond (E)	1	0	4	5
1947	A. Melville (SA)	3	0	2	5
1948–9	F. G. Mann (E)	2	0	3	5
1951	A. D. Nourse (SA)	3	1	1	5
1955	J. E. Cheetham (SA)	3	2	0	5
1956–7	P. B. H. May (E)	2	2	1	5
1960	D. J. McGlew (SA)	3	0	2	5
1964–5	M. J. K. Smith (E)	1	0	4	5
1965	P. L. Van der Merwe (SA)	0	1	2	3
	IN SOUTH AFRICA	25	13	20	58
	IN ENGLAND	21	5	18	44
	TOTALS	46	18	38	102

WEST INDIES

Season	Visiting Captains	Won E	WI	D	Total
1928	R. K. Nunes (WI)	3	0	0	3
1929–30	Hon. F. Calthorpe (E)	1	1	2	4
1933	G. C. Grant (WI)	2	0	1	3
1934–5	R. E. S. Wyatt (E)	1	2	1	4
1939	R. S. Grant (WI)	1	0	2	3
1947–8	G. O. Allen (E)	0	2	2	4
1950	J. D. Goddard (WI)	1	3	0	4
1953–4	L. Hutton (E)	2	2	1	5
1957	J. D. Goddard (WI)	3	0	2	5
1959–60	P. B. H. May (E)	1	0	4	5
1963	F. M. Worrell (WI)	1	3	1	5
1966	G. S. Sobers (WI)	1	3	1	5
1967–8	M. C. Cowdrey (E)	1	0	4	5
1969	G. S. Sobers (WI)	2	0	1	3
	IN WEST INDIES	6	7	14	27
	IN ENGLAND	14	9	8	31
	TOTALS	20	16	22	58

NEW ZEALAND

Season	Visiting Captains	Won E	NZ	D	Total
1929–30	A. H. H. Gilligan (E)	1	0	3	4
1931	T. C. Lowry (NZ)	1	0	2	3
1932–3	D. R. Jardine (E)	0	0	2	2
1937	M. L. Page (NZ)	1	0	2	3
1946–7	W. R. Hammond (E)	0	0	1	1
1949	W. A. Hadlee (NZ)	0	0	4	4
1950–1	F. R. Brown (E)	1	0	1	2
1954–5	L. Hutton (E)	2	0	0	2
1958	J. R. Reid (NZ)	4	0	1	5
1958–9	P. B. H. May (E)	1	0	1	2
1962–3	E. R. Dexter (E)	3	0	0	3
1965	J. R. Reid (NZ)	3	0	0	3
1965–6	M. J. K. Smith (E)	0	0	3	3
1969	G. T. Dowling (NZ)	2	0	1	3
1970–1	R. Illingworth (E)	1	0	1	2
	IN NEW ZEALAND	9	0	12	21
	IN ENGLAND	11	0	10	21
	TOTALS	20	0	22	42

INDIA

Season	Visiting Captains	Won E	Ind	D	Total
1932	C. K. Nayudu (I)	1	0	0	1
1933–4	D. R. Jardine (E)	2	0	1	3
1936	Maharaj Kumar of Vizianagram (I)	2	0	1	3
1946	Nawab of Pataudi (I)	1	0	2	3
1951–2	N. D. Howard (E)	1	1	3	5
1952	V. S. Hazare (I)	3	0	1	4
1959	D. K. Gaekwad (I)	5	0	0	5
1961–2	E. R. Dexter (E)	0	2	3	5
1963–4	M. J. K. Smith (E)	0	0	5	5
1967	Nawab of Pataudi (I)	3	0	0	3
1971	A. L. Wadekar (I)	0	1	2	3
	IN ENGLAND	15	1	6	22
	IN INDIA	3	3	12	18
	TOTALS	18	4	18	40

PAKISTAN

Season	Visiting Captains	Won E	P	D	Total
1954	A. H. Kardar (P)	1	1	2	4
1961–2	E. R. Dexter (E)	1	0	2	3
1962	Javed Burki (P)	4	0	1	5
1967	Hanif Mohammad (P)	2	0	1	3
1969	M. C. Cowdrey (E)	0	0	3	3
1971	Intikhab Alam (P)	1	0	2	3
	IN ENGLAND	8	1	6	15
	IN PAKISTAN	1	0	5	6
	TOTALS	9	1	11	21

Index of Players

Abel, R., 28, 29, 31, 36, 93
Abid Ali, S., 116
Adcock, N. A. T., 100
Alimuddin, 119, 121
Allen, G. O., 46, 83, 106, 107, 135, 140, 174
Alletson, E. B., 85, 86
Allom, M. J. C., 112, 175
Altham, H. S., 63
Alward, James, 11
Amarnath, L., 116, 117
Amar, Singh, 115
Ames, L. E. G., 82, 83, 96, 97, 137
Amiss, D. L., 155
Appleyard, R., 89, 113
Armstrong, W. W., 81, 86
Asif Iqbal, 70, 122
Astill, E., 103

Bacher, A., 101
Bailey, T. E., 89, 108
Balaskas, X. C., 95
Bannerman, C., 72, 80
Barber, R. W., 91, 152
Barber, W., 52, 53
Bardsley, W., 81
Barling, T. H., 37
Barlow, E. J., 100, 101
Barlow, R. G., 32
Barnes, S., 87
Barnes, S. F., 79, 80
Barnett, C. J., 83, 113, 150
Barrington, K. F., 57, 90, 91, 100, 109, 114, 119, 121, 122
Beauclerk, Lord Frederick, 15
Beaumont, J., 31
Bedi, B. S., 115, 116
Bedser, A. V., 9, 24, 36, 57, 85, 87, 89, 98, 99, 106, 117, 123, 150
Bedser, E. A., 57
Beldham (Silver Billy), 10
Benaud, R., 87, 88, 90
Bennett, G., 21
Binks, J. G., 63
Blackham, J. M., 73, 83, 127
Bland, K. C., 100, 101
Blythe, C., 40, 41
Bolus, J. B., 63, 149

Bond, J. D., 160
Booth, M. W., 37
Bosanquet, B. J. 102
Bowes, W. E., 50, 51, 52, 53, 59
Boycott, G., 66, 68, 71, 90, 91, 92, 153, 154
Bradman, Sir D. G., 51, 78, 81, 82, 83, 84, 85, 87, 92, 114, 120, 123, 124, 128, 129-33, 134, 136
Briggs, J., 93
Brown, F. R., 88, 147, 174
Brown, J. T., 37
Brown, S. M., 60
Brown, W. A., 84
Burge, P. J., 90
Burke, J. W., 88
Burki, J., 121
Burnet, J. R., 62
Burton, D. C. F., 44
Buss, A., 68
Buss, M. A., 155
Butcher, B., 110

Caesar, Julius, 19
Caffyn, W., 19, 20, 21
Calthorpe, Hon. F. S. G., 102, 104, 106
Cameron, H. B., 95, 96
Carr, A. W., 49, 136
Cartwright, T. W., 167
Challenor, G., 102, 103, 104
Chandrasekhar, B. S., 115, 116
Chapman, A. P. F., 81, 82, 94, 104
Cheetham, J. E., 99, 100
Clark, T. H., 57, 58
Clarke, William, 17, 18
Clay, J. C., 41, 42, 60, 61
Close, D. B., 63, 65, 66, 68, 147, 153, 154, 167
Cobden, F. C., 24
Cobham, Viscount, 167, 168
Compton, D. C. S., 54, 60, 84, 85, 87, 89, 98, 99, 106, 117, 120, 121
Coldwell, L. 67
Connolly, A. 91
Constable, B., 57
Constantine, Lord, 101, 102, 103, 104, 105, 106

Index of Players

Copson, W. H., 53
Cowdrey, M. C., 70, 88, 90, 91, 92, 103, 109, 110, 111, 114, 121, 122, 152, 165, 166
Cowie, J. A., 113
Cowper, R. M., 91
Crawford, J. N., 36

Darling, Joe, 78, 79
Day, A. P., 40
Darnley, 8th Earl (Hon. Ivo Bligh), 74, 75
Davidson, A. K., 90
Davies, Emrys, 61
Dempster, C. S., 112
Denton, D., 37
Denness, M. H., 70
Dexter, E. R., 90, 109, 113, 114, 118, 119, 121, 149, 150, 151, 152
D'Oliveira, B. L., 67, 91, 115, 162–78
Dollery, H. E., 61, 62
Donnelly, M. P., 111, 112
Douglas, J. W. H. T., 79, 80, 81, 90
Duckworth, G., 47, 82
Duleepsinhji, K. S., 113, 115
Durston, J., 44

Eagar, E. D. R., 63
Eckersley, P., 49
Edrich, J. H., 67, 91, 92, 114
Edrich, W. J., 54, 60, 84, 85, 87, 89, 97, 98, 106, 128
Edwards, M. J., 71
Endean, W. R., 100
Engineer, F. M., 115, 116
Evans, T. G., 85, 87, 89, 118, 121
Eyre, T. J. P., 159

Farnes, K., 84, 97, 105
Faulkner, G. A., 94, 95
Fazal Mahmood, 119, 120, 121
Felix, 16
Fender, P. G. H., 37, 49, 85, 86
Fingleton, J. H., 83, 84
Fishlock, L. B., 57, 85
Flavell, J. A., 67, 150
Fleetwood-Smith, L. O'B., 87
Fletcher, D. G. W., 57
Foster, F. R., 80
Freeman, A. P., 82, 95, 104
Fry, C. B., 36, 47, 78

Gardner, F. C., 61
Gavaskar, S., 116
Geary, G., 82, 150
Gibb, P. A., 85, 96, 97, 98
Gibbs, L. R., 110
Gifford, N., 67, 151, 161
Gilligan, A. E. R., 81, 95, 102

Gilligan, A. H. H., 102
Gladwin, C., 98, 99
Gleeson, J. W., 123
Goddard, J. D., 107, 108
Goddard, T. L., 100
Gomez, G. E., 108
Gover, A. R., 37
Grace, G. F., 74
Grace, E. M., 74
Grace, W. G. Dr., 16, 23, 28, 32, 48, 72, 74, 75, 76, 77, 78, 79, 83, 93, 123–9, 130
Grant, R. S., 106
Graveney, T. W., 66, 67, 89, 109, 110, 117, 120, 121, 129, 150, 164
Greenwood, F. E., 43, 51
Gregory, J. M., 80, 86
Gregory, R. J., 37
Griffin, G., 100
Griffith, C. C., 110
Griffith, H. C., 104, 105
Griffith, S. C., 107, 153, 174
Griffiths, G. 21
Grimmett, C. V., 82, 83, 87, 131
Gunn, G., 36, 49, 79, 80, 105

Hadlee, W. A., 112
Hafeez, A. (Now A. H. Kadar), 119
Haig, N. E., 44, 46, 105
Haigh, S., 37, 39
Hall, W. W., 101, 109, 110
Hallam, M. R., 148
Halliday, T. M., 48
Hallows, C., 47, 48, 104, 128
Hammond, W. R., 33, 48, 81, 82, 83, 84, 85, 87, 95, 96, 97, 98, 103, 104, 113, 116, 123, 128, 137
Hampshire, J. H., 65, 68
Hanif Mohammad, 119, 120, 121
Hardinge, H. W. T., 40
Hardstaff, J., 84, 85, 117, 150
Harris, David, 9, 16
Harris, Lord, 73, 128
Harris, C. B., 49
Harvey, R. N., 87, 88, 112
Hassett, A. L., 84, 85, 87, 88, 89, 123
Hawke, 7th Lord, 34, 54, 78, 93, 102
Hayward, T., 36, 79, 128
Hazare, V. S., 115, 117
Headley, G. A., 66, 101, 105, 106
Headley, R. G. A., 67
Hearne, J. T., 79
Hearne, J. W., 44, 46, 80
Heine, P., 100
Hendren, E. H., 44, 46, 82, 105
Hill, Clem, 78, 81
Hillyer, W. R., 16
Hirst, G. H., 34, 37, 39, 71, 79
Hitchcock, R., 61
Hoad, E. L. G., 104

Index of Players

Hobbs, Sir J. B., 14, 37, 51, 79, 80, 82, 87, 103, 104, 123
Holford, D., 110
Hollies, W. E., 61, 132
Holmes, P., 14, 44, 45, 46, 50, 52, 103
Hopwood, C., 49, 53
Hornby, A. N., 32
Hughes, D. P., 161
Humphreys, E., 40
Hunte, C. C., 110
Hutton, Sir Leonard, 52, 54, 59, 80, 84, 85, 87, 88, 89, 92, 97, 98, 99, 103, 106, 108, 113, 117, 118, 121
Hutchings, K. L., 40

Iddon, J., 48, 49, 53
Ikin, J. T., 85
Illingworth, R., 63, 65, 66, 68, 69, 88, 91, 92, 111, 115
Imtiaz Ahmed, 119
Ingleby-Mackenzie, A. C. D., 63, 64
Insole, D. J., 166
Intikhab Alam, 71, 121

Jackman, R. D., 71
Jackson, Rt. Hon. F. S., 34, 37, 77
Jackson, L., 67
Jardine, D. R., 37, 82, 91, 104, 116, 134, 135, 136, 137, 139
Jessop, G. L., 85, 86
Johnson, I. W., 88, 90
Johnston, W. A., 87
Jones, Alan, 69
Jones, W. E., 61
Jupp, H., 73, 104

Kanhai, R. B., 109
Keeton, W. W., 49
Kenyon, D., 66, 67
Key, K. J., 31
Khan, Jahanghir, 69
Khan, Majid, 69
Khan, Mohammad, 119
Kilner, R., 45, 46, 103
Knott, A. P. E., 70, 91, 92, 115

Langridge, James, 85
Laker, J. C., 29, 36, 57, 87, 88, 89, 90, 100, 103, 108, 113, 117, 125
Larwood, H., 49, 82, 83, 95, 104, 130, 134, 135, 136, 137, 138, 139, 140, 141
Lawry, W., 90, 91, 92
Lee, H. W., 44
Lever, P., 122
Leveson-Gower, Sir H. D. G., 95
Lewis, A. R., 69
Leyland, M., 45, 46, 52, 82, 83, 84, 95, 137, 138
Lillywhite, James, 19, 73

Lillywhite, John, 19, 22
Lillywhite, William, 16, 17, 19
Lindsay, J. D., 101
Lindwall, R. R., 29, 87, 88, 89
Livingstone, D. A., 64
Lloyd, C. H., 111, 160
Loader, P. J., 37, 57, 121
Lock, G. A. R., 29, 36, 55, 57, 58, 88, 89, 100, 103, 113
Lockwood, W. H., 28, 32, 34, 36
Lohmann, G. A., 27, 31, 32, 33
Long, A., 67, 71
Lord, Thomas, 12
Lowry, T. C., 112
Luckhurst, B. W., 70, 92
Lupton, A. W., 46
Lyon, B. H., 43

Macartney, C. G., 80, 81
Mackay, K. D., 88
Macaulay, G. G., 45, 46, 50, 52
Maclaren, A. C., 78, 90
Mahmood Hussain, 119
Mailey, A. A., 86, 87
Makepeace, H., 47
Mankad, Vinoo, 115, 117, 118
Mann, F. G., 98
Mann, F. T., 44, 46
Maqsood Ahmed, 119
Marner, P., 148
Marshall, R. E., 64, 101, 108
Martindale, E. A., 105
Mason, J. R., 40
May, P. B. H., 57, 58, 88, 89, 90, 100, 103, 109, 113, 117, 118, 121
McCabe, S. J., 82, 136
McCool, C., 85, 87
McDonald, E. A., 47, 48, 49, 86
McGlew, D. J., 100
McIntyre, A. J., 57
McKenzie, G. D., 90, 91
McLean, R. A., 100
Mead, C. P., 80, 82
Meckiff, A., 90
Melville, A., 97, 98
Mercer, J., 48
Merchant, V. M., 115, 117
Midwinter, W. E., 73, 75
Milburn, C., 91, 110, 150, 152, 166
Miller, K. R., 29, 85, 86, 87, 88, 89
Mitchell, A., 52
Mitchell, B., 95, 96, 97
Mitchell, T. B., 53
Morkel, D. P., 95
Morris, A. R., 87
Mortlock, W., 21
Mudie, W., 21
Muncer, L. B., 61
Murrell, H. R., 44
Murdoch, W. L., 74, 81

Index of Players

Mushtaq Ali, 115, 117
Mushtaq Mohammad, 121
Mynn, A., 16

Nash, M. A., 69
Nayudu, Col. C. K., 115, 116
Nissar, Mahommad, 115
Noble, M. A., 78, 79, 81
Nourse, A. D., 94, 95
Nourse, A. D. Jnr., 95, 96, 97, 98, 99
Nunes, K. R., 102, 103, 104
Nurse, S. M., 110
Nyren, R., 9, 12

Oldfield, W. A., 83, 134, 135, 137
Oldroyd, E., 45, 46
O'Neill, N. C., 90
Ord, J. S., 61
O'Reilly, W. J., 82, 83
Oscroft, W., 23
Owen-Smith, H. G. O., 95

Padgett, D. E. V., 62, 63, 68
Palairet, L. C. H., 39, 108, 139
Parfitt, P. H., 114, 121
Parker, J. F., 57
Parkhouse, W. G. A., 61
Parkin, C. H., 46, 47
Parks, J. M., 90, 109, 155
Parr, G., 18, 20, 112
Pataudi, Nawab of, 115
Pataudi, Nawab of (Son), 115, 116, 119
Paynter, E., 49, 53, 84, 96, 97, 113, 137, 140, 160
Peebles, I. A. R., 154
Pegler, S., 95
Perks, R. T. D., 52, 97
Pilch, Fuller, 14, 16
Pilling, H., 160
Pocock, P. I., 71
Pollard, R., 85
Pollock, P. M., 100, 101
Pollock, R. G., 100, 101
Ponsford, W. H., 82
Pooley, E., 29, 73
Pope, A., 53
Prideaux, R. M., 165
Pritchard, T. L., 61
Procter, M. J., 176
Pullar, G., 119, 121

Rae, A. F., 108
Ramadhin, S., 101, 103, 107, 108
Ranjitsinhji, K. S., 33, 77, 79, 81, 113, 115, 125
Read, M., 28, 29, 31
Read, W., 28, 29, 31, 32, 93
Reid, J. R., 112, 114
Rhodes, H. J., 55

Rhodes, W., 37, 39, 44, 45, 46, 71, 79, 80, 105
Richards, B. A., 176
Richardson, A. W., 53
Richardson, D. W., 67
Richardson, P. E., 150
Richardson, T., 28, 33, 34, 36, 79, 123
Roach, C. A., 104, 105
Robertson, J. D., 60, 107, 150
Robins, R. W. V., 60
Robinson, Ellis, 59
Roller, W. E., 31
Roope, G. R. J., 71
Root, F., 103
Rowan, E. A. B., 96, 97, 99

Sainsbury, P. J., 64
Sandham, A., 37, 105
Schwarz, R. O., 94, 95
Sellers, A. B., 51, 54, 58, 59, 62
Sewell, T., 21, 23
Seymour, J., 40
Shackleton, D., 64
Sharpe, P. J., 65, 66, 68
Shaw, A., 30, 58, 72, 73, 74, 76, 125
Shepherd, D. J., 69
Sheppard, D. S., 121, 168, 169, 174
Shrewsbury, A., 29, 30, 31, 76
Shujauddin, 119
Shuter, J., 27, 31, 32
Simpson, R. B., 88, 90, 91
Simpson, R. T., 117, 120, 121
Sims, J. M., 54, 60
Small, John, 9
Smith, A. C., 155
Smith, D., 53
Smith, E. J., 80
Smith, J., 105
Smith, M. J. K., 88, 90, 100, 114, 119, 121
Smith, T. P. B., 85
Snow, J. A., 68, 91, 92, 111
Sobers, G. S., 101, 103, 109, 110, 111
Spofforth, F. R., 72, 73, 74, 127
Spooner, R., 79
Staples, S. J., 49, 82
Statham, J. B., 29, 67, 89, 100, 109, 113, 118, 121, 125
Stephenson, H. H., 20, 21
Stevens, E. ('Lumpy'), 9
Stevens, G. T. S., 44, 46
Stewart, M. J., 57, 70, 71, 121, 153
Stoddart, A. E., 77, 78
Stollmeyer, J. B., 101, 108
Storey, S. J., 71
Stott, W. B., 62
Strudwick, H., 33, 80, 123
Subba Row, R., 90, 109
Surridge, W. S., 56, 58
Sutcliffe, B., 112, 113

Index of Players

Sutcliffe, H., 44, 45, 46, 50, 51, 52, 53, 54, 82, 103, 104, 113, 137, 150

Tallon, D., 87
Tate, M. W., 82, 95, 104
Tayfield, H. J., 100
Taylor, H. W., 95
Toshack, E. R. H., 87
Townsend, L. F., 53, 105
Trott, A., 85, 86
Trueman, F. S., 29, 63, 65, 66, 67, 68, 89, 100, 108, 109, 110, 114, 117, 118
Trumper, V. T., 80, 81
Tunnicliffe, J., 34, 37, 65
Turnbull, M. J., 41, 42, 60, 84
Tyldesley, E., 47, 48, 49, 53, 82, 104, 160
Tyldesley, J. T., 79
Tyldesley, R., 46, 49
Tyson, F. H., 89, 91, 113, 121

Umrigar, P. R., 117, 119
Underwood, D. L., 68, 70, 91, 115

Valentine, A. L., 101, 107, 108
Valentine, B. H., 96, 97
Van Der Merwe, P. L., 94, 100, 101
Venkataraghaven, S., 115, 116
Verity, H., 50, 51, 52, 53, 54, 59, 84, 96, 137
Viljeon, K. G., 97
Vizianagram, Maharajah of, 116
Voce, W., 49, 83, 85, 105, 135
Vogler, A. E. E., 95

Waddington, A., 45, 46
Wade, H. F., 94, 96
Wadekar, A. L., 116
Wainwright, W., 34
Waite, J. H. B., 100
Walcott, C. L., 101, 103, 108
Walker, P. J., 69

Walker, T., 9, 14
Ward, William, 13, 14, 15
Wardle, J. H., 62, 69, 89, 121, 167
Warner, Sir Pelham, 44, 79, 80, 93, 94, 102, 138
Washbrook, C., 53, 85, 87, 89, 98, 99, 103, 113, 150, 155
Watkins, A. J., 117
Watson, F., 47, 48, 49, 53, 103
Wazir Mohammad, 119
Weekes, E. D., 101, 102, 103, 107, 108
Wenman, E. G., 16
Wheatley, O. S., 69
White, J. C., 82, 95
White, T. ('Shock'), 9, 10
Whysall, W. W., 49
Wilder, E., 20
Willes, John, 14, 15
Willis, R. G. D., 71
Willsher, E., 20, 22, 125
Wilson, D. 65, 68
Wilson, J. V., 63, 65
Winslow, P. L., 100
Wisden, John, 18
Wood, A., 84
Wood, H., 31, 93
Woodfull, W. M., 82, 134
Wooller, W., 60
Woolley, F. E., 40, 79, 80, 82, 87, 95, 112, 148, 150
Worrell, Sir Frank, 101, 103, 107, 108, 109, 110, 111
Worthington, T. S., 53, 116
Wright, D. V. P., 85, 87, 97, 106
Wyatt, R. E. S., 105, 137

Yardley, N. W. D., 54, 85, 106
Yarnold, H., 67
Young, J. A., 60
Younis Ahmed, 71

Zahir Abbas, 122